Roman Catholic Worship

James F. White

Roman Catholic Worship

Trent to Today

Foreword
by
Nathan D. Mitchell

Second Edition

A PUEBLO BOOK

Liturgical Press Collegeville, Minnesota

www.litpress.org

A Pueblo Book published by the Liturgical Press.

Design by Frank Kacmarcik, Obl.S.B.

Library of Congress Cataloging-in-Publication Data

White, James F.
    Roman Catholic worship : Trent to today / James F. White ; foreword by
Nathan D. Mitchell.—2nd ed.
        p. cm.
    Includes bibliographical references and indexes.
    ISBN 0-8146-6194-7 (alk. paper)
    1. Catholic Church—Liturgy—History.   2. Catholic Church—History—
Modern period, 1500–   I. Title.

BX1970 .W47   2003
264'.02'00903—dc21

                                                        2002040625

For
CLAIRE DUGGAN WHITE
as a sign of
my love for her

Contents

Foreword

Although modern historians often write about "the Tridentine Mass" or "Trent's reform of Catholic worship," readers of James F. White's classic study *Roman Catholic Worship*, first published in 1995, know that the bishops meeting at that Council's frantic final session in December 1563 did not actually enact so much as a single liturgical reform! Instead, in a momentous decision, they turned reform of "the missal and breviary" over to the pope. The so-called "Tridentine liturgy" is thus a collection of rites reformed *after* Trent under papal auspices. Moreover, the pope himself did not personally prepare the new editions of breviary (1568) and missal (1570). Instead, that work was entrusted, for the first time in history, to a panel of scholarly experts who—as Pius V tells us in his bull *Quo primum*—followed five basic principles: (1) That *a single rite* for Mass and Office should be used throughout the Latin Church; (2) that *qualified scholars* should determine the antiquity and probity of the new books' contents; (3) that the rites should be restored according to the "pristine norm of the Fathers" *(ad pristinam Patrum normam)*; (4) that from now on, this "norm" will be *regulated strictly by the pope* through *editiones typicae* that he promulgates; and (5) that *nothing can be added or subtracted from the text without the pope's approval.*

Thus, the first truly "modern" liturgical reforms (using scholarly criteria for evaluating sources and their content) were launched not in the twentieth century but in the sixteenth—by both Protestant reformers and papal commissions formed after Trent! On this point, critics of the Missal of Paul VI (1970) are often mistaken. They accuse Vatican II's *periti* of applying "modern" (i.e., scholarly, secular, humanist) principles to the reform of liturgical books; but in fact the first council to embrace "modernist reform principles" was Trent! White's book shows us, systematically, how Trent's vision of renewed corporate worship—launched during the crisis of the sixteenth century—became the fuel that energized the Catholic Reformation through several succeeding eras (Baroque, Enlightenment, Romantic). Given this historical context, Vatican II merely reflects the logical culmination of a larger, longer process that began four hundred years earlier, among both Catholics and Protestants.

Strictly speaking, therefore, neither Trent nor Vatican II "reformed" Roman Catholic worship. Instead, each called for the creation of papally appointed commissions to carry out that task. The history of Vatican II's reform has been chronicled exhaustively by Annibale Bugnini, a *peritus* who worked on the Consilium for the Implementation of the Constitution on the Liturgy (1964–1969), and later became secretary of the Congregation for Divine Worship (1969–1975). For those who blanch at the prospect of tackling the nearly one thousand pages of Bugnini's magisterial book, *The Reform of the Liturgy, 1948–1975* (Collegeville: The Liturgical Press, 1990), White's *Roman Catholic Worship* provides a clear, succinct, and user-friendly guide to the official documents that have determined our ritual forms and formulas since the sixteenth century, as well as the major events, places, and persons (including artists and architects) that have shaped pastoral practice within local communities. Moreover, because he not only knows what the sources say but understands how rituals actually work in the daily lives of people of faith, Professor White proves himself a reliable, congenial companion for anyone seeking to explore the complex, sometimes contested terrain of Catholic worship over the past 450 years.

As we approach the fortieth anniversary of *Sacrosanctum concilium*, readers will be especially intrigued by Professor White's assessment of the future of Roman Catholic worship, especially in light of recent developments on both sides of the Atlantic. As he notes at the beginning of chapter 7 ("The Journey Beyond the Second Vatican Council"), most of the conciliar reforms have "continued to thrive and grow"; still, "bit by bit some of [them have been] . . . challenged or even reversed." It is this "zigzag process" of renewal to which White calls our attention in the final portions of his work, where readers will find trenchant analyses of documents such as *Built of Living Stones; Varietates legitimae* (on the Roman liturgy and inculturation, 1994); and *Liturgiam authenticam* (on translating liturgical texts, 2001).

White understands, of course, that the future of Roman Catholic worship lies beyond mere public documentation and ritual detail. Powerful cultural and theological forces are also at work—e.g., the crisis brought about by declining numbers of clergy and charges of sexual misconduct by priests; the ongoing debate about women's participation in church leadership and decision-making; controversy about traditional doctrines (e.g., the meaning of real presence, transubstantiation, eucharistic sacrifice). Despite all this, we can, I believe, share White's optimistic conclusion: "[T]he same restless Spirit that has continued through two millennia to give Christians new ways to express that which is 'too deep for words' . . . will not leave us speechless but will go on interceding for us throughout all time."

Nathan D. Mitchell
University of Notre Dame
4 November 2002, Feast of St. Charles Borromeo

Preface

A great deal has happened in Roman Catholic worship since the Second Vatican Council promulgated the Constitution on the Sacred Liturgy on December 4, 1963. But the myth persists that very little happened in the four centuries between the end of the Council of Trent on December 4, 1563, and Vatican II.

This book was written to explore just what did occur in those four hundred years before Vatican II and how the stage was set for all the changes that have come about since the council. It may be true that liturgical texts were frozen during those intervening centuries (although there are some qualifications even of this assertion), but to assume that liturgical texts are the whole of liturgy is very questionable. Our central historical thesis is that the worship life of Roman Catholicism was in constant transition during this entire period despite the intransigence of liturgical texts.

Our intention is to produce a "catholic" view of liturgical history. In this sense, there are no "bad" periods in liturgical history, only those now unfashionable or out of favor. For at all times and all places the Holy Spirit helps us pray (Rom 8:26). If we can testify to this belief, our central theological thesis will have been demonstrated.

We shall also look at the cultural shifts of society in Europe and North America and the global impacts of these developments. All of social life affects liturgy. Worship, after all, is part and parcel of the rest of life; we do not check our personhood at the church door. Much has been written in recent years about the importance of "full, conscious, and active participation" in worship. But we shall also have to look at some of the factors affecting passive and unconscious participation: the way sacred space is organized as church architecture, the visual accompaniments of worship, and how the sound behaves during worship. These rarely rise to the level of conscious articulation. One does not stop to say, "What is this space doing to me?" But the experience of church architecture is always an important ingredient in worship. Thus the sacramental principle of the outward and visual being a representation of the inward and spiritual is a constant reality. We shape our churches, art, and music and they ever after shape us. It is no accident that I have chosen to use church architecture as a paradigm for each historical period in this study.

We shall also want to examine more than just what happens at Sunday morning Mass. The rhythms of daily, weekly, yearly, and life-long cycles both reflect us and shape us constantly. For the marginal Christian, the pastoral offices of becoming a Christian (Christian initiation), marrying as a Christian, and dying in a Christian community may be the sole contacts with the Christian community. For those on the furthest margins of Christianity, baptisms, weddings, and funerals may be their only contact with the Church. Hence for those people—and they are numbered in the millions—these are the Church's most important services. For other millions, a similar function pertains to the greatest festivals, especially Christmas or Easter, or maybe St. Patrick's Day or the Feast of Guadalupe, according to one's ethnic origins. We shall try to suggest the variety of Roman Catholic worship for different participants.

In other words, we shall make an effort to write from the pew, not the altar. This is easier said than done, since it contradicts the method of most liturgical studies, which are far more concerned about the priest with his chalice than the parishioner with her rosary. Yet worship occurs wherever people come together in Christ's name, and we shall try to reflect the variety of persons and locales this involves.

Our premise is that one of the best ways to describe a subject such as Roman Catholic worship is to chronicle its history. Nineteenth-century scholarship established this conviction about the value of history as part of our way of thinking. Although history certainly gives only a partial glimpse of any subject, it helps us see something as fluid and flexible instead of static and rigid.

Part of the insufficiency of a historical approach is that it reflects as much of ourselves as it does of the subject at hand. We are intrigued by those elements of the past that have relevance to the present. Thus efforts to introduce the vernacular in the eighteenth century now seem most foresighted to us, even though fifty years ago they were still being condemned. Attempts to revive plainsong now seem like a good run down the wrong road, but two generations ago they could stir people.

So we must honestly admit that we write and rewrite history from our own perspectives. We ask the questions whose answers interest us; we seek out usable history. Let us be clear: this history is written from the perspectives of North America in the first decade of the third millennium of Christian worship. Those are the spectacles through which we shall be reading the history of the past four and a half centuries of Roman Catholic worship. Our pace will be fast, because there is so much to cover in a short space. If we are to meet our goals of being both balanced and comprehensive, we must also be brief. We shall not loiter long over any topic, no matter how interesting it may be. For those who want to know more, the footnotes and bibliography will indicate further reading.

We shall use the term "Roman Catholic worship" throughout in order to make it clear that we are not claiming to cover all forms of Catholic worship. There are a number of Eastern Rite Churches that can justly claim the term "Catholic." In the United States alone their faithful number about half a million. Many of the statements we shall make do not apply to them at all, so that to call everything we discuss "Catholic" would imply that these people are excluded from that communion. Although a trifle awkward, we shall stick to the term "Roman Catholic worship" except in those few instances when we refer to the worship of all those in communion with Rome. This minor inconvenience seems a small price to pay for linguistic justice.

It remains to acknowledge how much I learned in twenty years of teaching in the graduate program in Liturgical Studies at the University of Notre Dame. I learned much from my students, especially those who took my seminar on the subject of this book in the spring of 1992: Raphael Graves, James Lodwick, Mark Luttio, Anne McGuire, Mattheus Michels, Lester Ruth, and Mark Torgerson; and in the spring of 1994: Jane Burton, Joseph Dougherty, Walter Ray, LaVerne Thomas, Tobias Winright, and John Witvliet. I am also greatly indebted to the special assistance of Harold Dyck, Michael Moriarty, Johan van Parys, and John Witvliet. Fathers Regis Duffy and John Melloh read the entire manuscript and contributed countless improvements. Cheryl Reed and Sherry Reichold produced a clean manuscript from my messy copy.

The opportunity to produce a revised and updated edition is most fortunate. Not only have I profited from more research but there are eight more significant years of history to chronicle. The character of liturgical renewal has shifted in that short time. Thus my central thesis that Roman Catholic worship is constantly evolving is further demonstrated. I am grateful to Nathan Mitchell for his kindness in writing a foreword and to Father Edward Foley, Capuchin, for encouraging this revised edition. The comments of Fathers Michael Driscoll and John Melloh and Monsignor Frederick McManus have been most helpful. Once again, I depend with complete confidence on the secretarial abilities of Cheryl Reed and Nancy McMahon. And to my wife, Claire Duggan White, I gratefully dedicate this book as an outward and visible sign of my love for her.

James F. White
University of Notre Dame
July 1, 2002

Chapter One

The Legacy of the Council of Trent

The Council of Trent meandered off and on through eighteen years (1545–1563), concluding in a final spurt of activity on December 4, 1563. Exactly four hundred years to the day later (December 4, 1963), an avalanche of liturgical change began with the promulgation of the Constitution on the Sacred Liturgy. Trent had been essentially conservative, trying to fit broken pieces back together in a familiar form. The Second Vatican Council went in the other direction, shattering many time-worn patterns of Roman Catholic worship, yet at the same time trying to recover much of value from the totality of tradition.

In this chapter we shall trace the liturgical reforms of the last third of the sixteenth century, both those generated by the Council of Trent and those of other origins. The first generation of reformers were dead by then; Ignatius Loyola died in 1556, John Calvin in 1564. Trent had failed to reunite the Churches of the West, but it had rallied the forces of Catholicism. There are strange ironies in that so much that Trent did to conserve the past eventually led to radical changes in Roman Catholic worship, especially in the centralization of liturgical authority. Liturgically, Trent marks the beginning of a new era in worship just as much as it caps late medieval developments.

We shall begin by looking at changes in liturgical space as a paradigm of the period. Then distinctive events and significant persons of this period will be chronicled. Afterwards we shall see the effects of change on the rhythms of time and devotions, the Mass itself, the rhythms of the life cycle, church music, preaching, and public prayer. Items undergoing change will be more apt to catch our attention than stable matters.

FROM SHRINE TO THEATER

For the average worshiper, the most startling change in Roman Catholic worship in the last third of the sixteenth century must have been the gradual shift in the type of church building that was being built or reordered to shelter worship. From our perspective, we can see a whole new image of liturgical space overcoming existing concepts as new churches were built. One would not design the same type of building for Roman Catholic worship in 1600 as would have been considered quite satisfactory in 1500.

The late medieval church building in the West was essentially a shrine built to house the altar. The high altar was protected from space for the laity both by distance and by the roodscreen, a wooden partition between chancel and nave. The whole building was a series of discrete spaces segregated from each other according to function. Increasingly, chapels were screened off for various private Masses.

The nave looked at a distance to the high altar. The laity stood in the nave or sat down as pews were introduced in the fourteenth century. Between them and the high altar intervened a long chancel with stalls where the clergy in major and minor orders sang the daily Office. The roodscreen, through which the laity could glimpse the priest's back during Mass, clearly separated clergy from lay people. It is recorded that it was not uncommon for them to shout at the elevation, "Heave it higher, Sir priest!" Thus they were shielded by the roodscreen from the holy events transacted at the high altar and further removed by a chancel that might be half as long as the nave itself. Church law treated nave and chancel as two different buildings—church for lay people and chancel for clergy. Architecturally they were quite distinct spaces.

Within a hundred years this was not the type of building being built for Roman Catholic worship in Europe or in the new missions overseas. The new buildings for worship were conceived of as a single space in which most barriers between the people and the high altar had disappeared. There are clear analogies to the design and function of a theater in the new emphasis on both visibility and audibility. Instead of two almost separate buildings in which the laity watched from afar and heard little, if any, of the Mass, the church now appeared as a single, unified space. The high altar was dramatically visible, and the congregation could see everything, with only the priest's body intervening between altar and people. Roodscreens no longer were built in new buildings, and many were destroyed where they existed.

Ironically, Anglicans were more conservative and retained the two distinct spaces for another century, using the chancel for the Eucharist and the nave for daily prayers and the service of the Word.

Behind this radical shift in church architecture lay an important development in the Catholic Reformation: the advent of the Jesuits. Traditional religious orders had centered on the obligation of monastics to say and sing the daily Office together in the choir of the church. The medieval monastic hegemony of worship had passed this pattern on to parish clergy, and parish churches were also built with long chancels for saying the daily Office. But Ignatius Loyola, in founding the Jesuits, saw another goal—that of service anywhere in the Lord's vineyard—and hence he refused to enforce on his priests the choral obligation and the vow of stability that it necessitated. As the Jesuits were dispensed from having to say the daily Office together, the need for choir space in their church buildings disappeared.

The result was the emergence of a whole new concept of liturgical space. No building was as important to this development as the chief Jesuit church in Rome, Il Gesù. Built from 1568 to 1575, it was "the first monumental Roman church of a formal and liturgical style adopted as widely in Italy as was the Counter Reformation itself."[1] The Jesuits had no need of the choir space requisite in monastic churches and their parochial imitators. Instead, the high altar was situated in a rather shallow semicircular apse. There was no screen or other barrier from congregational space. Instead of being half concealed, the Mass became a spectacle for all to see. Furthermore, in the design of the church, preaching became a major factor. A vigorous debate ensued as to what kind of a ceiling was best for preaching acoustics: a stone vault or open wood trusses. At Il Gesù the stone vault won. A prominent pulpit stood high in the middle of the north wall of the nave. Acoustics had become an essential concern for architectural planning. The spoken word, not sung chant, was now the center of attention.

In liturgical arrangement Il Gesù is the prototype of Roman Catholic churches built almost without exception for the next four hundred years. The concepts of one unified liturgical space, an altar visible to all, and acoustics favorable to preaching were accepted for centuries

1. James S. Ackerman, "The Gesù in the Light of Contemporary Church Design," *Baroque Art: The Jesuit Contribution,* ed. Rudolf Wittower and Irma B. Jaffe (New York: Fordham University Press, 1972) 15.

despite a largely unsuccessful nineteenth-century effort to return to a medieval arrangement. Even then, neo-Gothic churches usually ended up with the same liturgical arrangement as that of Il Gesù. What made the new Jesuit floor plan even more significant was that the centralized bureaucracy of the order could make it mandatory whenever plans for new churches were sent to be reviewed in Rome. The explosion of Jesuit missions in all parts of the world in the sixteenth, seventeenth, and well into the eighteenth centuries made the new Jesuit plan the basis for thousands of new churches outside of Europe as well as within it.

A few matters of liturgical arrangements were worked out contemporaneously, but from another source. In 1577, Carlo Borromeo (1538–1584), archbishop of Milan, published a meticulously detailed work entitled *Instructions on the Architecture and Furnishings of Churches*. It gives great detail for every aspect of the building, including the iron peg for the priest to hang his biretta on. Not every item in the directive was followed, especially the decree that there be a wooden partition down the middle of the church to separate the men from the women. But several items that Borromeo prescribed became widespread throughout Europe and persisted until Vatican II.

Most important of all was the mandate that the tabernacle be placed on the main altar: "a provincial decree has made it obligatory to put the tabernacle of the most Holy Eucharist on the main altar."[2] Medieval reserved hosts had been kept in wall cupboards (aumbries), hanging images, often of doves (pyxes), or in freestanding towers (sacrament houses). Now a visual association was made between devotions to the consecrated Host and the liturgical experience of the Mass. What now seems spatial confusion of these two functions persisted until after Vatican II.

Almost as familiar was the advent of Communion rails, which had been prescribed at a provincial synod in Milan in 1576. These lasted to our time but are a sixteenth-century development. Medieval Christians did not need such conveniences to kneel to receive Communion.

Borromeo's influence was also experienced until recently in the "wooden furniture which serves to hear confessions in a convenient

2. Evelyn Carole Voelker, "Charles Borromeo's *Instructiones Fabricae et Supellectilis Ecclesiasticae, 1577*: A Translation with Commentary and Analysis" (Ph.D. diss., Syracuse University, 1977) 160.

and proper way, and which we call the confessional."[3] Several are mandated in his *Instructions* of 1577—at least two, "so that the men do not find themselves intermingled or crowded together with the women," a great hazard to true penitence. The design, dimensions, and locations, all of which prevailed until recently, are prescribed. Medieval confessions had frequently been heard at the roodscreen, but without the distinct space to ensure secrecy. Northern Italy added some lasting contributions to the design of church buildings.

The image of how a church appeared and worked changed profoundly in the last third of the sixteenth century. Only in recent years have some of the underlying principles been challenged; others are still operative.

LITURGICAL EVENTS AND PERSONS

This period saw some very significant developments in the history of Roman Catholic worship. Most important of all, of course, was the Council of Trent. Ironically, the basically conservative approach of Trent led to some radical changes in the way liturgy was managed. A major factor in this whole period was the possibilities that the new technology of printing were unleashing. The possibility of central control, whether in national government or in liturgical uniformity, was being realized for the first time. Furthermore, the reaching of missions into the Western hemisphere and Asia was stretching the imagination of Europeans as new peoples and cultures were encountered.

The conservatism of Trent was manifested in nailing down sacramental theology in terms almost identical to those stated under Eugenius IV in 1439 in his "Decree for the Armenians," itself based on Thomas Aquinas's thirteenth-century treatise "Of the Articles of Faith and Sacraments of the Church." Early on (1547) the Council had condemned anyone maintaining that "the sacraments of the New Law were not all instituted by Jesus Christ, our Lord; or, that they are more, or less, than seven."[4] The fathers of the Council did not define where Christ had instituted all of the seven because they themselves could not agree. But they did insist that all seven "contain the grace which they signify" and "confer that grace on those who do not place an obstacle thereunto."

3. Ibid., 297.
4. Philip Schaff, *The Creeds of Christendom* (Grand Rapids, Mich.: Baker Book House, n.d.) 2:119.

Over the ensuing years, dogmatic statements on all seven sacraments were made. We shall examine them individually. The fathers also approved (December 1563) "the legitimate use of images" but added the caution that "in the invocation of saints, the veneration of relics, and the sacred use of images, every superstition shall be removed, all filthy lucre be abolished; finally, all lasciviousness be avoided."[5]

One single phrase was to have crucial significance for the future of Roman Catholic worship. In the pell-mell rush of the Council's final two days, it was enacted that the new index of books recently compiled by the fathers could be "given over to the most holy Roman pontiff, that it may by his judgment and authority be completed and made public" and added that "the same it commands shall be done with regard to the catechism by the Fathers to whom it was assigned, and *likewise with regard to the missal and breviary.*"[6] Only two of the liturgical books are mentioned—those for the daily Office and the Mass, not those for episcopal or pastoral use.

This momentous phrase bore fruit in rather short time with the publication of the Roman Breviary in 1568 and the Roman Missal in 1570. They were preceded by a new Index in 1564 and the Roman Catechism in 1566, both based on work done at the Council. Several things are significant in this new development. Rome was accorded unprecedented liturgical control. Medieval Europe had seen a wide range of liturgical books in dioceses and religious orders. The bishop or the general of an order had been the liturgical authority, not the Roman Curia. Except for an effort in the eleventh century by Gregory VII to suppress the Mozarabic rite in Spain, an effort only partially successful, Rome had practiced liturgical laissez-faire.

Liturgical standardization was a new concept, radical in its implications but made possible by the technology of the first mass-produced product, the printed book. Lutheranism, by contrast, remained conservative, simply continuing a variety of regional uses. In order to preserve the past, Trent initiated a radical change by consigning liturgical revision to Rome. It initiated what some see today as the chief problem of Roman Catholic liturgy, namely, the apparent inability or disinclination to adapt to local cultures and circumstances.

5. Ibid., 203.

6. H. J. Schroeder, *The Canons and Decrees of the Council of Trent* (Rockford, Ill.: Tan Books, 1978) 255. Italics added.

The details of the processes of revising the Breviary and Missal are unknown; minutes of the commissions have not survived. The products clearly indicate that essentially the Roman ways of doing things prevailed, for the final results bear close resemblance to existing Roman service books.

Reform of liturgical books was not unprecedented in Rome. Pope Clement VII had entrusted a Spanish cardinal, Francisco de Quiñones, with a revision of the Breviary, which Quiñones published in 1535, perhaps influenced by Martin Bucer's Strasbourg Psalter of 1525. Quiñones restored a weekly recital of the Psalter and the reading of most of the Bible in the course of a year instead of the fragments of Scripture then in use. It was intended for private recitation, so such choral elements as antiphons and responses were eliminated, producing a much simpler Office in which psalms and Scripture predominated. A subsequent modified edition of 1536 proved extremely popular but was considered still too radical by many and was briefly forbidden by Paul IV in 1558.

A less radical solution appeared in the new Breviary promulgated in 1568 under Pius V. A commission appointed by Pius IV and presided over by Cardinal Guglielmo Sirleto had corrected some of the problems of the Breviary, especially the congestion of saints' days, which interfered with orderly recital of the Psalter. Nevertheless, saints' days continued to accumulate over ensuing centuries to clog the steady flow of the Psalter. Since the sanctoral Office was shorter than the ferial (daily) Office, it tended to be more popular. Local practices that could not prove at least two centuries of continuous use were condemned.

Two years later Sirleto's commission produced The Roman Missal as Revised by Decree of the Holy Council of Trent and Published by Order of Pope Pius V. It was promulgated by Pius V in July 1570 with the bull *Quo primum*. The bull cites research in the Vatican Library based on ancient and accurate writings. The new Missal was meant to replace all uses less than two hundred years old. This is the so-called Tridentine Missal, which remained in effect exactly four hundred years, although with minor emendations by Clement VIII and Urban VIII. Essentially a conservative revision, it pruned back the saints' days largely to those Rome had commemorated in the first millennium and excised all but four of the rich medieval assortment of sequences (hymns sung before the gospel).

Although Trent never mandated the revision of other liturgical books, the process continued. A major improvement was the revision of the calendar in 1582 under Pope Gregory XIII. In that year the calendar skipped from October 4 to October 15, catching up with the time lag that had plagued the ancient Julian calendar in use since before the time of Christ. Over the years the slight inaccuracy in calculating the length of the year had added ten days. The English-speaking world did not follow suit until 1752, provoking Voltaire's jibe that Protestants would rather defy the sun than follow the pope!

Under the same Pope, the Roman Martyrology was revised and published in 1584. Taking as its basis the medieval Martyrology compiled by Usuard in the ninth century, ten scholars, including Cardinal Cesare Baronius, a noted historian, labored on it. Baronius published corrected revisions in 1586 and 1589. Meant to be read in religious communities at the daily Office of Prime, its perennial problem has been that of achieving historical accuracy rather than promoting edifying but spurious legends. It was the most frequently revised liturgical book in recent centuries as subsequent research and fresh canonizations necessitated new editions.

In 1596 the Roman Pontifical, the book of bishops' services, appeared. It is essentially the thirteenth-century Pontifical of William Durandus, bishop of Mende in France, as filtered through a 1485 printed edition done by A. Patrizi Piccolomini, the bishop of Chiusi. The new Pontifical was made universally mandatory under Clement VIII, with all other Pontificals being suppressed. Under the same Pope there appeared in 1600 a new type of book, although with medieval precedents. This was the *Caeremoniale Episcoporum,* or Ceremonial of Bishops. It consists of rubrics dealing with the liturgical duties of, and the honors due, a bishop.

Nearly half a century of liturgical revision was brought to an end with the publication of the Roman Ritual in 1614. With a long history as the pastor's handbook or manual, this book dealt with the priest's pastoral offices other than Mass and the daily Office. It included sacraments, blessings, and processions. In general, it followed contemporary Roman use, but great local latitude continued to be observed, especially with marriage and funeral rites and a wide variety of blessings. Much of the Roman Ritual was based on work by the Dominican Alberto Castellani, who published a book for priests in 1523, and on a subsequent ritual (1601) undertaken by Cardinal Giulio Antonio Santori. Pope Paul V urged bishops and priests to use the new Ritual, but he did not mandate it. As a result, "outside of Italy, the integral Roman Ritual was received hardly anywhere before the middle of the nineteenth century, and down to Vatican II many dioceses had their local appendixes to it."[7]

Two decades after the new Roman books began to appear, a momentous innovation came about as part of the general organization of the Roman Curia under Sixtus V. Fifteen Congregations were originally organized in 1588, each headed by a cardinal. Not until Pius X in 1908 was the Curia completely reorganized. Among the original Congregations was the Congregation of Sacred Rites. Specifically, the original functions of the Congregation of Sacred Rites may be summarized in eight categories:

1. Vigilance for the observance of sacred rites.

2. Restoration and reformation of ceremonies.

3. Reform and correction of the liturgical books.

4. Regulation of the Offices of patron saints.

5. Canonization of saints.

6. Celebration of feast days.

7. Reception of princes and other visitors to the city of Rome.

8. Solution of controversies over precedence and other liturgical matters.[8]

The work of the Congregation fell basically into two areas: liturgy and the processes of beatification and canonization.

The Congregation of Sacred Rites saw its work as establishing and maintaining uniformity in worship in the West and to this end from time to time published particular decrees dealing with individuals or localities and general decrees dealing universally in the West. The archives have long shelves of collections of questions sent in to be resolved from all over the world. The more important of these prior to 1927 were collected in the *Decreta Authentica*. So efficient was the Congregation that it shaped Roman Catholic worship in every part of the world. More often than not, doubts were resolved by mandating what was current practice in Rome itself. So it became a very effective way

7. P. Jounel, "The Pontifical and the Ritual," in *The Sacraments*, Vol. 3 of *The Church at Prayer* (Collegeville, Minn.: The Liturgical Press, 1988) 8.

8. Frederick R. McManus, *The Congregation of Sacred Rites* (Washington: Catholic University of America Press, 1954) 27.

of interpreting the rubrics of the new liturgical books, themselves Roman in origin, in a very Roman fashion. In modern terms, the whole world was to be inculturated into the Roman ways of doing the liturgy.

Theodor Klauser speaks of this era as that of "rigid unification in the liturgy and rubricism"[9] and provides several amazing instances, such as allowing only the current Roman form of the chasuble. It was a period in which liturgy was subject to a basically juridical and legalistic mentality. The values of history and cultural diversity were submerged in favor of administrative efficiency and uniformity.

It may be noticed that the figures shaping liturgy in this period, especially Cardinals Carlo Borromeo, Guglielmo Sirleto, Giulio Antonio Santori, the architects of Il Gesù, and a series of popes were all from the Italian peninsula. There is a certain irony in the fact that just as Christianity was embarking on a global quest, so much of liturgical character was funneled through a single part of western Europe. The liturgical agenda of the period was the Romanization of the liturgy, and it was only natural that Italian ways appealed to Italians.

RHYTHMS OF TIME AND DEVOTIONS

The Council of Trent had no particular reason to deal with questions of the calendar and devotions, yet it set in motion changes in these aspects of the liturgy. These took most concrete form in the reforms made in the calendars of the Breviary of 1568 and the Missal of 1570. Preceding centuries had shown a steady accumulation of saints' days in the calendar, a process that accelerated as new religious orders and new devotions clamored for a place in the sun. By the late sixteenth century most dates in the calendar had been claimed, some several times over.

Theodor Klauser traced the results of the reforms of the Breviary and Missal and found that nearly half of the year was purged of saints' days altogether, especially in the Lenten season. In addition, 85 percent of the days claimed for saints belonged to those of the first four centuries, half of the saints were martyrs, and 18 percent were popes. He concluded that the revisers' purpose "was fundamentally to return to the ancient calendar of the city of Rome; and that they also intended to enrich this calendar sparingly with a few more recent

9. Theodor Klauser, *A Short History of the Western Liturgy,* 2nd ed. (Oxford: Oxford University Press, 1979) 117–152.

groups of feasts (those of the founders of religious orders, the doctors of the thirteenth century, and those venerated in the declining years of the Middle Ages as helpers in times of adversity.)"[10] The result was to make the calendar even more specifically Roman at the same time the books were being prepared for worldwide use.

Such a purging of many observances did not set an abiding precedent. The accumulation of saints' observances continued to mushroom as each century reaped its harvest of holy men and women. And so the twentieth-century reforms have had to repeat the same process of pruning back the overgrown foliage of saints dear to various orders or regions.

Ordinary people were more affected by a series of devotional occasions which had been incubating during the late Middle Ages and which now burst forth full of new life. One common factor seems to have been a certain theatrical flare in which the emphasis is on a visual focus. In many ways these were a forceful response to the concepts of the Protestant reformers, who tended to disparage too much attention to outward display.

The feast of Corpus Christi had thirteenth-century origins and led in the late Middle Ages to processions with the Blessed Sacrament so that people assembled outside the church building could see and be blessed by the consecrated Host. They thus testified to their faith in the Eucharist. The sight of the sacred Host was meant to have a saving effect on the beholders. This belief led to impressive processions through the streets on the feast of Corpus Christi, with the Host displayed in a monstrance. Several factors led to these developments. There were reactions to various medieval groups that denied the Real Presence; the distancing of participation in the Eucharist had left a vacuum, and positive emphases on the great feast the Lord gives in the Real Presence demanded devotional responses.

The same factors led in the late Middle Ages to display of the consecrated bread on the altar in the form of Exposition of the Most Holy Sacrament. By the end of the fifteenth century it was common in northern Germany to leave the Host on the altar even during celebration of the Mass. From there it was a short step to evening services of Benediction. Various devotions such as forms of Perpetual Adoration or Forty Hours' Devotion radiated from this cult of the eucharistic presence of the Lord. The Forty Hours' Devotion apparently originated

10. Ibid., 126.

in sixteenth-century Italy, based on the belief that Christ's body lay in the tomb for forty hours. It began and ended with a solemn high Mass and a procession. During the intervening hours the Host was exposed, and the faithful prayed before it in turns. Various religious orders kept up the practice of Perpetual Adoration.

The common feature of these emerging devotions was their dramatic, even theatrical, nature, with emphasis on the "saving gaze." These devotions had been developing ever since the twelfth century with the advent of the elevation of the bread (and eventually of the chalice).[11] At the same time, a decline of frequent Communion had occurred, so that contact with the saving Flesh was through the eyes rather than the mouth. And this contact with Christ came to the forefront in the decades following the Council of Trent.

For better or for worse, it was probably accentuated by the Protestant reformers, who sought, with uneven degrees of success, to return the people to frequent (that is, weekly) Communion. In a sense they were the real conservatives, probably too much so to be very successful. For Roman Catholics, "ocular communion" (through the eyes) could become a frequent, even daily, experience. The new devotions supported the practice of visual Communion.

THE MASS

Nevertheless, Trent hoped to encourage more frequent Communion, although only through the species of bread. The thirteenth session, meeting in 1551, urged that the faithful "be able frequently *(frequenter suscipere possint)* to receive that supersubstantial bread." Yet the late medieval practice of infrequent Communion surfaced in Trent's canon that the faithful of both sexes, after having attained the age of reason, are obliged "to communicate every year, at least at Easter." Frequent Communion for the majority of the laity had to wait until the twentieth century. Medieval injunctions dating back to the thirteenth century were reinforced by the mandate that anyone conscious of mortal sin had to receive sacramental confession first. Trent also maintained that little children "are not by any necessity obliged to the sacramental Communion," although it was noted that they did receive Communion in the early Church.

Trent is most conservative on the Eucharist, concerned to maintain existing practices even when acknowledging them to be contrary to

11. Édouard Dumoutet, *Le désir de voir l'hostie* (Paris: Beauchesne, 1926) 50.

ancient practice. This is most clear with regard to Communion under both species. Notwithstanding that several popes, under pressure from the emperor, would have conceded the chalice to the laity and that there was precedent in the Compactata of Prague of 1433, Trent refused to admit its advisability. Even though the laity had received the chalice up through the thirteenth century, the Council proclaimed that "communion under either species is sufficient for them [the laity] unto salvation." This was maintained on the basis of the power of the Church to change the dispensation of the sacraments "according to the difference of circumstances, times, and places" (July 1562), a remarkable statement of contingency. The Council reserved for a later time discussion that both species could "be conceded under certain conditions," but this never got resolved.

Early on, in October 1551, the Council reaffirmed the practice of reserving the Sacrament. Other existing practices were affirmed too. The sanctity of the old Roman Canon was maintained as "pure from every error" (September 1562). The ceremonies of the Mass were commended, including saying the Canon in a low voice. Although the Communion of the faithful was advocated at every Mass where they were present, private Masses in which the priest alone communicates were approved (September 1562). Mixture of water with the wine was mandated. And "it has not seemed expedient to the Fathers, that it [the Mass] should be everywhere celebrated in the vulgar tongue." Nevertheless, priests were urged to expound to the people "some mystery" of the Mass on each Sunday and festival.

No less steadfast was the doctrine of the Mass. The doctrine of the Real Presence was affirmed, and the conversion of the bread and wine into body and blood "the Catholic Church most aptly [aptissime] calls Transubstantiation" (October 1551). Furthermore, "the whole Christ is contained under every part of each species" (concomitance). In the reserved Hosts, the true body of the Lord remains.

Likewise, the concepts of the Mass as a sacrifice were staunchly maintained. The twenty-second session, meeting in 1562, asserted that "this sacrifice [the Mass] is truly propitiatory, and that by means thereof this is effected, that we obtain mercy, and find grace in seasonable aid." The fruits of the bloody sacrifice of the cross were received in a new, unbloody fashion and were effective for the Christian dead as well as the living. It did not suffice to speak of it simply as "a sacrifice of praise and of thanksgiving" or as "a bare commemoration of the sacrifice consummated on the cross." Nor did it derogate from the sacrifice of the cross to call the Mass a sacrifice. Obviously, many of these statements were directed against such Protestant theologians as Martin Luther and Thomas Cranmer. The Council had decided in its early days that it "would delimitate the Catholic doctrine of the sacraments from the Protestant by means of canons anathematizing specific propositions that stated the contents of Protestant teaching, even if they were not formally found in their writings, and thereby reject them as contrary to the Catholic faith."[12]

To infer that Trent merely ratified the past with regard to the Eucharist would not be wholly accurate. The Council made clear its opposition to "avarice, irreverence, and superstition." Priests were not to profit from "importunate and unbecoming demands" for saying Mass. Magical treatments of the consecrated bread were to be resisted. Unseemly behavior by "wandering or unknown" priests, the presence of "notoriously wicked" persons, and indecent church music were forbidden. Celebrations at improper hours or unauthorized "rites or ceremonies" were not to be allowed.[13] And anything that would distract the faithful from reverent attention on these holy mysteries was forbidden.

Even more positive was the attempt to revise the Missal. As we have seen, this bore fruit in 1570 with the publication under Pius V of the Roman Missal. His bull *Quo primum* made this Missal mandatory universally for the Roman Rite except for churches that could prove use of over two hundred years, that is, prior to 1370. Numerous dioceses could have made this claim; only a few chose to do so (Lyons, Braga). Even more important were the detailed General Rubrics in the Missal and the list of defects that might occur in such celebrations. In effect, the Roman ways of doing things prevailed almost as absolutely as the Roman words for saying Mass. The effect was the attempt, not always successful, at universal standardization of the Mass based on a Roman model. This revolutionary development prevailed for over four hundred years. In a world that welcomes cultural diversity today, this may seem an anomaly.

We have already seen how new concepts of liturgical space adopted a theatrical form in which the altar was dramatically visible. The

<hr />

12. Hubert Jedin, *A History of the Council of Trent* (St. Louis: B. Herder Book Company, 1961) 2:381.

13. Schroeder, *The Canons*, 151. Also, Reinold Theisen, *Mass Liturgy and the Council of Trent* (Collegeville, Minn.: St. John's University Press, 1965) 110–113.

emerging devotions focusing on visual participation both reflected the architectural changes and reinforced them. Increasingly, the altar tended to become a throne on which Christ could repose in the Host in the monstrance. Thus we have a divided devotional attention to Christ's presence in the monstrance while his liturgical presence is in the Mass celebrated at the same altar.

At the same time, the norm for Mass remained the low Mass celebrated by a single priest and server without the benefit of musicians. A sermon might or might not be preached at a Mass celebrated with a congregation, even though various canons mandated such a homily. At the same time, that the visual setting for Mass and the eucharistic devotions surrounding it were evolving, the words and actions of the Mass were permanently fixed.

As a result, there was little connection between what the priest did at the altar and the congregation standing or sitting in the nave. As an English Catholic bishop, Stephen Gardiner, remarked in 1547: "The people in the church [nave] took small heed what the priest and the clerks did in the chancel, but only to stand up at the Gospel and kneel at the Sacring [bell], or else every man was occupied himself severally [individually] in several prayers. . . . And therefore it was never meant that the people should indeed hear the Matins or the Mass, but be present there and pray themselves in silence."[14] It is not surprising that visual participation had such an attraction for the laity in this period; they had few other possibilities.

RHYTHMS OF THE LIFE CYCLE
The Council of Trent represents the end of a long disintegration of the unity of Christian initiation in the West. The trajectory from the late medieval period through the sixteenth century was a dissolution of initiation into three separate occasions: baptism, first Communion, and confirmation. Except for the Anabaptists, baptism was not a serious point of contention between Catholics and Protestants. Some, such as the Church of England, ratified the same dissolution of initiation symbolized by Trent. For Eastern Catholic and Orthodox Churches, these problems never arose, since they allowed priests to complete initiation on a single occasion.

14. *The Letters of Stephen Gardiner*, ed. James A. Muller (New York: Macmillan Co., 1933) 355. Spelling modernized.

Until the twelfth century in the West, children were normally communicated at baptism by placing on their lips the priest's little finger dipped in the consecrated wine. This practice had long disappeared in the West because of scrupulosity about allowing anyone other than priests to partake from the chalice. Trent notes that the memory of the previous practice of more than a thousand years had not entirely disappeared and admits the "most holy Fathers had a probable cause for what they did in respect of their times" but anathematizes anyone now claiming that "communion of the Eucharist is necessary for little children" (July 1562). The Fourth Lateran Council in 1215 had further complicated matters by mandating confession before receiving first Communion. Nevertheless, sporadic instances of infant Communion survived until the sixteenth century.

The connection between baptism and confirmation had been largely shattered already. In early centuries children and adults tended to be baptized and confirmed at Easter or Pentecost unless in imminent danger of death. By the thirteenth century, children were generally baptized within eight days of birth because of the fear of their dying unbaptized and hence losing the possibility of salvation. Obviously, bishops were not available on such short notice, and confirmation was delayed until a bishop was available. The possibility of presbyterial confirmation was tried at various places in the West (Gaul, Spain, and Ireland) but failed to survive. So bishops came to be the only ministers of confirmation in the West. But previously "for over a thousand years the Church in the West had been pleased to give confirmation to children of any age at their initiation, as the Eastern Church does to this day."[15]

Despite occasional exceptions, by the sixteenth century confirmation was delayed at least until the age of seven. Quite likely the majority of people in the late Middle Ages never came close enough to a bishop to be confirmed but regarded it as a pious "extra," not necessary for their salvation. The Council defended confirmation as more than a catechical exercise (as Bucer and Calvin had argued) but was vague about what it gives other than to say that the ordinary minister was the bishop. The Catechism of Trent (1566) effectively put an end to confirmation of young children with the words "until children shall have attained the use of reason, its [confirmation] administration is

15. J.D.C. Fisher, *Christian Initiation: Baptism in the Medieval West* (London: S.P.C.K., 1965) 139.

inexpedient. If it does not seem well to defer (confirmation) to the age of twelve, it is most proper to postpone this Sacrament at least to that of seven years."[16]

Other than simply ratifying the dissolution of the unitive rite of initiation, Trent had little to contribute on initiation except to defend the baptism of infants and, ironically, baptism by heretics with the proper form and intention (March 1547). In practice, baptism of infants by immersion had been gradually disappearing in the West, although most medieval fonts were constructed large enough to facilitate dipping the infant. "By the time the Reformation began, even if the ritual books allowed for, or even prescribed, immersion, sprinkling was in practice almost universal. Immersion was practiced only in very conservative circles. . . . immersion was still fairly common in Germany,"[17] and it was clearly Luther's preference. One can trace the abandonment of immersion of infants by chronicling the size of the fonts, which, before recent reforms, rarely could accommodate immersion of a twenty-inch infant. Sacramental minimalism, as far as sign value is concerned, had become standard practice.

Very late in the Council, matrimony was defended as a sacrament, polygamy was prohibited, and the degrees of affinity from Leviticus prohibiting marriage were affirmed (November 1563). The fathers, themselves all celibate, affirmed that it is "better and more blessed to remain in virginity, or in celibacy, than to be united in matrimony." Most remarkable is the decree for reform of matrimony, *Tametsi*, approved in the closing days of the Council. Marriage had always been a "hot potato" both in sacramental theology and canon law. *Tametsi* provided for the publishing of banns in hopes of forbidding clandestine marriages, e.g., Romeo and Juliet. Normally the parish priest was to preside, with two or three witnesses present. However, in an uncharacteristic display of impartiality, the Council declared: "If any provinces have in this matter other laudable customs and ceremonies in addition to the aforesaid, the holy council wishes earnestly that they may be by all means retained."[18] These words sound more like Vatican II, and indeed are quoted in the Constitution on the Sacred Liturgy.

---

16. *Catechism of the Council of Trent for Parish Priests* (New York: Joseph F. Wagner, 1934) 208.

17. Hughes Oliphant Old, *The Shaping of the Reformed Baptismal Rite in the Sixteenth Century* (Grand Rapids, Mich.: Eerdmans, 1992) 265–266.

18. Schroeder, *The Canons*, 185.

This cultural diversity seems to have been widely honored in ensuing centuries. Concubinage is to be punished, marriage is to be contracted freely, and marriages cannot be contracted during Advent, Christmastide, Lent, or Easter Week, but at all other times "with becoming modesty and propriety." The Roman Missal of 1570 provided Propers for a nuptial Mass, with a blessing of the couple just before the conclusion of the Lord's Prayer. The holy women of the Old Testament are mentioned, and prayers ask that the couple may see their children's children until the third or fourth generation. The rite ends by warning the couple to remain chaste.

Although marriage was discussed at the end of the Council, "the Sacrament of Extreme Unction" *(Sacramentum Extremae Unctionis)* had been discussed a dozen years earlier (November 1551). The medieval development is clear; far from being a sacrament of healing the body, this is treated as almost incidental ("at times obtains bodily health"). The emphasis is on cleansing the soul before death, and it is called "the sacrament of the departing *(exeuntium)*." Bishops or priests alone are the proper ministers of the sacrament. The Council justifies its teaching largely by appealing to the fifth chapter of the Epistle of James. Unction is clearly seen as a prelude to death rather than a sacrament of healing. The Roman Missal of 1570 provided Propers for Masses for all the deceased faithful, for the day of death or the funeral, and for anniversaries of death. An abundance of Proper prayers appear for daily Masses celebrated for the dead.

In the case of penance, the fathers of the Council were equally concerned to maintain late medieval practices of penance as private, repeated, and intended for everyone. All this contrasts with the early practice of a public, once-in-a-lifetime process intended only for unusually notorious sinners. The familiar form "I absolve you," the acts of contrition, confession, and satisfaction, along with the insistence on a priest (or in reserved cases a bishop) as the only minister, are simply reiterated (November 1551). Mortal sins must be confessed in number and species at least once a year, preferably in Lent in preparation for the mandatory Easter Communion. The theological statement is fulsome, although some of the historical facts are now questionable.

Penance or confession began to be moved from the body of the church or the steps of the chancel to confessional booths in the late sixteenth century to prevent any possible scandal. If anything, this heightened the sense of penance as chiefly a judicial process, with the priest concealed from sight and touch. Penance had become and remained a completely private process isolated from the rest of the church. It was, however, necessary for salvation for those who had reached the age of reason and who had committed serious sin. Most, if not all, went to confession before receiving Communion, which they did at least once a year at Easter. Hence confession came to be seen as a kind of Lenten discipline.

CHURCH MUSIC

Music is mentioned several times in the decrees of Trent, especially in one rather negative sentence: "They shall also banish from the churches all such music which, whether by the organ or in the singing, contains things that are lascivious or impure."[19] Two main views had surfaced in the Council's deliberations: "Some wished to have a total suppression of music in the services of the Church, but others, and happily these were the greater number, wished to have a reform of music, so that any improper, impure, or lascivious aspects should be removed."[20] It is hard to imagine bishops siding with Zwingli on church music, but the abuses must have been abundant.

A serious problem was the conflict between musical austerity and elaborateness. The best composers often wrote secular music for the court that tended to reward glittering virtuosity. Frequently they carried the same styles and the melodies from love songs and even a famous battle song, "The Armed Man," into their church work. Complaints coming before the twenty-second session of the Council in 1562 revolved around irreverence on the part of the singers, the music submerging or almost ignoring the text, secular melodies, and musical instruments not considered appropriate for church use. One bishop, Cardinal Otto Truchsess of Augsburg, employed a minor composer, Jacobus de Kerle, to compose exemplary music for worship during the Council. His restrained style shorn of embellishments received the Council's approval.[21]

Still, there were negative developments. The elimination of most of the medieval sequences from the Mass in 1570 cut down on the possibilities for musical expression. Ignatius Loyola took a dim view of much music and forbade it among his novices. At the same time,

19. Ibid., 151.

20. Robert F. Hayburn, *Papal Legislation on Sacred Music* (Collegeville, Minn.: The Liturgical Press, 1979) 29.

21. Erik Routley, *The Church and Music* (London: Duckworth, 1950) 129.

a brilliant period of musical creativity was already in progress. The old monopoly of chant in unison had been replaced by polyphonic singing, in which many parts were sung at the same time, sometimes even six or seven. This was a highly complex and professional level of music that ruled out congregational participation.

Such gifted composers as Giovanni Gabrieli in Venice, Orlando di Lassus in Rome, Tomas Luis de Victoria in Madrid, and Giovanni Pierluigi da Palestrina in Rome all wrote church music. Palestrina was able to compose with sufficient restraint so that counterpoint did not interfere with the audibility of the text. His *Missa Papae Marcelli,* probably written in 1555, became the official ideal for music that was musically sophisticated to a high degree yet did not submerge the text of the Mass. This represents a compromise between liturgical austerity and musical elaborateness. It is clearly highly professional music written for six parts. Congregational song was left largely to Protestants.

PREACHING

Preaching of the Word of God was a main point in the Protestant Reformation, and it soon became a central factor among Roman Catholics. Very early on, in 1546, the Council enacted a strong statement on the necessity of preaching. Calling "preaching of the Gospel . . . the chief duty of the bishops," it mandated that all prelates "are bound personally . . . to preach the holy Gospel of Jesus Christ." Priests who had the cure of souls were required to preach "at least on Sundays and solemn festivals."[22] Severe penalties were prescribed for those who neglected such responsibilities. If a parish priest was not able to preach, someone else had to be employed to do so.

At the same time, considerable caution was exercised to ensure that the "life, morals, and knowledge" of the preachers were appropriate. Extra caution applied to members of religious orders, who had to have the permission not only of their superiors but also of the bishop to preach in churches not belonging to their order.

The Council returned again to these themes late in its sessions, mandating in 1563 that there should be preaching in parish churches "at least on all Sundays and solemn festival days, but during the season of fasts, of Lent and of the Advent of the Lord, daily, or at least on three days of the week."[23]

22. Schroeder, *The Canons,* 26.
23. Ibid., 195.

Preaching was a major occupation for the members of the new religious orders of the century: Capuchins, Oratorians, Theatines, and above all, the Jesuits. The Oratorians, for example, held daily services in the evening with a sermon; Capuchins were noted for their enthusiastic preaching. Much of the preaching was dedicated to reviving the lukewarm, but it became an important part of missionary work among unbelievers. As the vision of a worldwide Church gradually became a reality, preaching became a main factor in winning converts around the globe.

The Jesuits made most dramatic use of preaching. Their churches were designed so that the acoustics reinforced the hearing of the Word, and their members were schooled in sacred rhetoric so as to produce a most convincing case for the gospel. Questions of moral behavior became especially important topics, and controversies over doctrinal matters often invaded the pulpit.

PUBLIC PRAYER

The daily Office was going through a profound period of change in the sixteenth century. Although obligatory for all religious and clergy in major orders, its form was changing drastically. The advent of mendicant orders in the thirteenth century and the simultaneous growth of universities, attended largely by clergy, had disrupted the concept of stable communities of religious and clergy singing the Office together daily in choir. The necessities of mission and study were gradually changing it from a public Office to a private one. Eventually even parish clergy who were not excused because of mission or study took to reading the Office privately rather than in community. (Most medieval parish churches had sufficient clergy in major and minor orders to make communal recitation a possibility.) The twenty-first session of Trent (1562) hinted at the "divine offices" as still being public and accessible to the people. But Robert Taft remarks that "by this time the early and medieval notion of the public office in common as the only one normative for all had died under the pressure of new forms of spirituality and apostolic and religious life."[24]

A major force in all this was the new order of Jesuits, but other new religious orders also abolished the obligation to do the Office in choir and accelerated the move to the Breviary as a private prayerbook.

24. Robert F. Taft, *The Liturgy of the Hours in East and West* (Collegeville, Minn.: The Liturgical Press, 1986) 301.

Ignatius was motivated by the need to render apostolic service to people. Joseph E. Weiss writes of this transformation: "Jesuits would not glorify God through the regular obligation to choir but by the regular obligation to labor strenuously in the world for the sake of neighbor. The work (opus) of medieval religious life was choir. Ignatius changed the work (opus) to service."[25]

Accordingly, the Formula of 1540 (the year of the Jesuit Society's formal recognition) stated: "Since all the members should be priests, they should be obliged to recite the Divine Office according to the ordinary rite of the Church, but privately and not in common or in choir."[26] This did not abolish the possibility of choral recitation in common, but it did prevent it from becoming an obstacle to service.

The official Roman Breviary published under Pius V in 1568 regained the choral elements Quiñones had eliminated but kept some of his reforms. The sanctoral cycle, which had come to dominate the Office (and Mass), was cut back to more reasonable proportions. Almost half of the days of the year (157) were left free of special commemorations. The Offices were abbreviated and made easier to follow.

With the exception of dioceses and orders that could prove the existence of their practices for over two hundred years, the new Roman Breviary was made obligatory universally. It was above all Roman. "It would have gained from a revision which took account of the usage of other Churches. For all the liturgies which were on their way to disappearance had riches hidden away."[27] The basic pattern that remained had shaped and reflected the life of monastic communities and was convenient to their lifestyle. In various ways, the medieval hegemony of monastic worship continued through the Breviary long after monasticism ceased to be a dominant force in Western Christianity.

In terms of the life of laity, the daily Office meant very little except for oblates and members of third orders. Some lay people attended Sunday Vespers, but when most parish clergy ceased to sing the Office together on a daily basis, there was little public worship except for that of the sacraments.

25. "Jesuits and the Liturgy of the Hours" (Ph.D. diss., University of Notre Dame, 1992) 138.
26. Cited ibid., 132.
27. Pierre Salmon, *The Breviary Through the Centuries* (Collegeville, Minn.: The Liturgical Press, 1962) 98.

Roman Catholic worship underwent major transformations in the late sixteenth century. Paradoxically, many of these came about from the determination to preserve continuity with medieval practices. But the ensuing liturgical standardization and uniformity were a far cry from the pluralism and local initiative prevalent in the medieval West. It was a time of major transition and set up the conditions for Roman Catholic worship for the next four centuries. Only in the late twentieth century were many of the decisions and developments of the era of Trent called into question and sometimes reversed.

Chapter Two

The Baroque Age

The baroque age produced a remarkably consistent unity of Roman Catholic worship, spirituality, and art. All these reflected the growing confidence of the Catholic Reformation that had begun in the sixteenth century. The baroque age achieved a synthesis, unequaled ever since, of the visual and musical arts and the devotional and liturgical spirit of the times.

The term "baroque" originally referred to a rough pearl, and that image provides a good description of the exuberance, the brilliance, the ornateness, sometimes the grotesqueness or the whimsy of the art of the seventeenth and early eighteenth centuries. Obviously, baroque art is not neatly encapsulated in the seventeenth century; in the visual arts it can be traced back to Michelangelo (1475–1564) and in music reached its peak in Bach (1685–1750). In this chapter we shall concentrate on the liturgical developments of the seventeenth century, when the arts and liturgy so neatly reflected each other.

In terms of worship, the baroque age was a major transformation. Joseph Jungmann notes: "The contrast between the baroque spirit and that of the traditional liturgy was so great that they were vastly different worlds. The new life-spirit which would wrap earth and heaven in one whirling tempest—how different from the quiet dignity of the old Roman orations."[1] Yet this new world of the baroque shaped most of the attitudes and practices of Roman Catholic worship right up to the Second Vatican Council. Whatever the qualities of these practices, they

---

1. Joseph A. Jungmann, *The Mass of the Roman Rite* (New York: Benziger Brothers, 1950) 1:142.

proved enduring, and Roman Catholic traditionalists would like to revive them even today.

Another feature of this period was the beginning of serious liturgical scholarship. We have already seen the concern to make the readings of the saints' legends better accord with history. Many of the crucial decisions Roman Catholics and Protestants previously had to make about worship had been based on a very limited knowledge of what worship in the early Churches had actually been like. Such scholars as Jean Mabillon and Giuseppe Tommasi began to fill in gaps in knowledge by slow and patient scholarship. The consequences were not immediate, but the advances in liturgical scholarship over ensuing centuries led to profound changes after Vatican II.

THE THEATER BECOMES A
HEAVENLY THRONE ROOM

The most conspicuous, and perhaps the most accurate, manifestation of Roman Catholic worship during the seventeenth century was the great outburst of energy expressed in the visual arts, particularly architecture. Enormous emphasis was placed on outward and visible splendor in contrast to the inwardness that had increasingly preoccupied late medieval piety. The baroque age was a whole new world in which public exhibitionism dominated rather than private piety that disdained outward expression.

Church architecture provided the most dynamic expression of this new piety. In essence, the move to the theatrical model that we have seen in the sixteenth century progressed to making the church building God's audience chamber. The altar became Christ's throne, from which God Incarnate reigned in solemn majesty. This became increasingly apparent as the altar was transformed from only a place for saying Mass to being in addition a repository for the tabernacle and also a throne for exposition of the Blessed Sacrament. Its function had trebled from that of the medieval altar, but the simple tabletop had been diminished by the subsequent additions. The Body of Christ in the viewed Sacrament came to be the supreme relic, surpassing all other cults of the relics of saints. Everything in the building beckoned one's attention to the glory and majesty of Christ present in the consecrated Host.

It seemed only natural that Christ's earthly presence on the altar should be celebrated in the most sumptuous manner possible, and baroque architecture was the ideal medium for this. Today we refer to this as "triumphalism," with a certain disdain; in the seventeenth century the term, had it existed, would have been an accolade. Everything in both piety and architecture focused on the splendor, the power, the majesty, the glory of God reigning in heaven but also present in that segment of earthly space enclosed by the church building. The church building was indeed a heavenly throne room set on earth.

Baroque architecture specialized in contrast and movement, finding every device to heighten the visual effect. The flat surfaces and subdued ornamentation of high Renaissance architecture gave way to twisted columns, volutes, swags, and a whole array of details to entice the eye. Every device was used to create effects: contrasts of light and shadow, vivid color, contorted planes, and much energetic movement. Nothing was placid, restrained, or simple. The total effect was dazzling exuberance, vitality, and sumptuousness, all calculated to produce a moving effect. The church building was indeed a vision of heaven built upon earth.

Rome became the prime mover in this artistic crusade. Under Sixtus V (1585–1589) much of Rome was redesigned, which often involved destroying ancient remnants. A series of brilliant architects pushed the possibilities of baroque art to its climax. Certainly the most distinguished of these was Gianlorenzo Bernini (1598–1680), who became the quintessential form-maker for this period. He is best known for interior and exterior ornamentation at St. Peter's Basilica, including the baldachino over the high altar, with its twisted columns and rich ornamentation. Trained as a sculptor, Bernini accomplished a "dramatic breakdown of the traditional boundaries between painting, sculpture and architecture to produce an overwhelming theatrical illusion."[2] In the Church of St. Andrea al Quirinale, he developed an oval plan, with the altar recessed on one of the long sides. All details lead the eye toward the high altar. In the Cornaro Chapel in St. Maria della Vittoria, light becomes a part of the building materials in creating an illusion to frame his statue of St. Teresa in ecstasy.

Bernini's manipulation of surface and light was carried even further by his contemporary Francesco Borromini (1599–1667), under whose hands even a cupola became a writhing upward spiral at St. Ivo. In St. Agnese, he and a variety of painters and sculptors produced a great monument of high baroque in which the contrasts of light and

2. P. and C. Cannon-Brookes, *Baroque Churches* (London: Paul Hamlyn, 1969) 14.

shadow and the dissolution of flat surfaces created a façade and interior of dazzling excitement.

The focal point of all these churches was the high altar, now no longer reticently half concealed behind a roodscreen. And on the altar perched a tabernacle, often grown to several feet in height in contrast to medieval pyxes the size of a dove. A conspicuous place was provided for a monstrance for exposition of the sacred Host.

Increasingly, the baroque period was fascinated by centrally planned churches that were essentially one-room spaces. The sharp distinction of sanctuary and nave was muted in favor of making all things at the altar clearly visible throughout the church. Christ reigned enthroned in the monstrance or tabernacle and beheld adoring subjects on all sides. The most famous of the centrally planned churches, St. Maria della Salute in Venice, was designed by Baldassare Longhena (1598–1682) to commemorate the ending of a plague. It was designed as an octagon, with the high altar immediately adjacent to congregational space, so that the high altar grasped one's attention on entering until one reached the center, and only then could one glimpse the six side altars.

The seventeenth century was the great century of church building in mission countries around the globe. And the baroque churches of the Italian peninsula provided the model for a new global architecture. In Spain, baroque often was fused with Moorish detail. Since friars and Jesuits from Spain predominated among the missionaries in the Western hemisphere, most of the mission churches were an architecture of nostalgia, replicating in more modest ways churches recently built in Spain. New Mexico provided an exception in that the Native American pueblos had a sophisticated architecture that missionaries were willing to adopt and adapt. Yet even there baroque concepts of space abounded, and baroque devices appeared, such as the clerestory windows facing the altar to bathe it in light.

So pervasive did baroque become that it represented, until relatively recently, the popular image of how Roman Catholic churches should look and function. In the battle of styles of the nineteenth and early twentieth centuries, baroque usually won, as a drive around the inner suburbs of any North American city demonstrates. And even when Romanesque, Gothic, or Renaissance did prevail, the baroque concepts of unified space usually determined the floor plan. All these buildings were designed as Christ's throne room on earth and adorned with corresponding magnificence.

As we have seen, the era of creating new liturgical books came to an end with the Roman Ritual of 1614. By that time a variety of minor emendations had already appeared in the books only recently published. Clement VIII brought out new editions of the Breviary (1602) and the Missal (1604), making historical corrections in the readings and adding saints' days, some of which had been only recently eliminated. Urban VIII made revisions in the Breviary in 1632, especially in the Latin hymns. A new edition of the Martyrology appeared in 1630, of the Missal in 1634, and of the Pontifical in 1644. These popes were not deterred by the "perpetual, strong, order" given in establishing the sixteenth-century editions by their predecessors. The *Caeremoniale Episcoporum* was tampered with more often: by Innocent X in 1650, Benedict XIII in 1727, Benedict XIV in 1752, and Leo XIII in 1902. Most of the changes were minor; major changes in all these books had to wait until late in the twentieth century. Not only were texts mostly immutable, they were also largely untranslatable. Alexander VII threatened in 1661 to excommunicate anyone translating the Missal, although attempts were made in France.

The work of enforcing these liturgical books and the rubrics for carrying out the services devolved upon the Congregation of Sacred Rites. The innovation of being constituted a body to pass judgment on the propriety of worship practices around the world did not inhibit the Congregation from exercising its powers with diligence. At the same time, it processed a never-ending parade of beatifications and canonizations.

One liturgical issue proved a continuing concern for other Roman Congregations, particularly the Sacred Congregation of Propaganda and the Holy Office, and also for a number of popes. This was the so-called Chinese Rites Controversy, which epitomized the encounter of European Christian culture with other world cultures. Two issues predominated: filial piety, expressed in respect for the ancestral dead, and the cult of Confucius. Both were basic to Chinese culture in the late Ming dynasty, when the first missionaries arrived. "The spirit of filial piety thus pervaded Chinese society; but more than this, it went beyond the boundaries of this world, beyond the death of one's parents, and it reached into the shadows of the ancestors."[3] The close

---

3. George Minamiki, *The Chinese Rites Controversy from Its Beginning to Modern Times* (Chicago: Loyola University Press, 1985) 5. Also Mark D. Luttio,

association of the living and dead was reinforced by the family altar in the home. It was the responsibility of each generation to revere and respect the wishes of the departed as if they were still among the living. Failure to observe these ceremonies was seen as an affront to public propriety.

The cult of Confucius was inextricably involved with imperial government and with scholarship. Ceremonies involved reverent gestures such as the kowtow and the offering of incense, money, food, and wine at family shrines. The question for Westerners was whether these rites and ceremonies were purely civil and cultural or whether they were religious and hence idolatrous. In other words, were ancestral and Confucian rites compatible with Christianity?

The early Jesuit missionaries, including Matteo Ricci, who came to Pekin in 1601, were of the opinion that "since they do not recognize any divinity in these dead ones, nor do they ask or hope for anything from them, all this stands outside of idolatry, and also one can say there is probably no superstition."[4] And he concluded that Confucianism "is really only an academy set up for the good governance of the republic."[5] Accordingly, the Jesuits inclined to a lenient approach to such practices as endemic to the culture and not explicitly idolatrous. Converts could still continue in the mainstream of Chinese society. The Jesuits were convinced that "Christianity was not meant to totally supplant another culture, but rather to be implanted into the matrix of that culture. Anything that was patently superstitious . . . [was] to be removed; but the rest could be tolerated."[6]

The Jesuits had the Chinese mission to themselves for fifty years, but in the 1630s Dominican and Franciscan missionaries arrived. Juan Baptista Morales, O.P., disagreed violently with the Jesuit methods of evangelization and submitted seventeen propositions to the Holy Office in Rome. It is significant that he described the Chinese practices in specifically religious terms, not as cultural artifacts. It is not surprising, then, that the Holy Office approved, Propaganda issued, and Innocent X sanctioned a decree in 1645 that forbade Christians to participate in most of the rites for the dead and the cult of Confucius.

"The Chinese Rites Controversy (1603–1742): A Diachronic and Synchronic Approach," *Worship* 68 (1994) 290–313.

4. Minamiki, *Chinese Rites Controversy*, 18.
5. Ibid., 20.
6. Ibid., 22–23.

Now ensued a century of controversy in which both lenient and rigid positions were affirmed in Rome and in China according to who had the advantages of information, power, and extraordinary circumstances.[7] Several Chinese emperors were even involved in the struggle. Finally, after much controversy, in 1742 Benedict XIV decreed in the bull *Ex quo singulari* that concessions to ancestor rites and the Confucian cult were not permissible for Christians, and all missionaries were required to take an oath repudiating the Chinese rites. Not until 1939 was the oath rescinded. The evangelization of China suffered a severe, if not fatal, blow in the process. These controversies exacerbated the Chinese apprehension that Christianity was basically a foreign and imperialistic intervention.

Another problem was in Europe itself. The Roman Ritual of 1614 was not imposed with the same firmness as the other liturgical books, especially the Roman Pontifical. Various diocesan rituals continued to function. In what would become Germany, the Ritual of Constance paved the way for the Roman Ritual, but in Spain the latter did not prevail until the nineteenth century and in France not unanimously until 1853.[8] France, in particular, showed a liturgical independence that accelerated during the seventeenth and eighteenth centuries and affected the Breviary and Missal as well as the Ritual. In a sense, this was a liturgical reflection of Gallicanism, the position of the independence of French Catholicism that affirmed the liberties of the French Church against papal interference and control. In the following century the Enlightenment also contributed new goals, especially historical accuracy. The decrees of Trent were not promulgated in France, and liturgical conformity hardly followed.

During the course of the seventeenth and eighteenth centuries, a series of diocesan service books appeared in France, collectively known as Neo-Gallican liturgies. These are not based on the Gallican rites of a thousand years earlier but are named after their French origins. Quite frequently the rubrics and instructions were published in French. The first of this genre was the Ritual of Alet, published for that diocese in 1667. Although condemned by Clement IX, twenty-nine

7. J. S. Cummins, *A Question of Rites: Friar Domingo Navarrete and the Jesuits in China* (Aldershot, Hants, Eng.: Scolar Press, 1993; Brookfield, Vt.: Ashgate Publishing, 1993) 144–168.

8. Cyrille Vogel, *Medieval Liturgy: An Introduction to the Sources* (Washington: Pastoral Press, 1986) 265.

French bishops commended it. A decade later the archdiocese of Reims published its own ritual. In 1678 the archbishop of Vienne, Henri de Villars, issued a new Breviary with sweeping changes, especially in replacing traditional antiphons and responsories with ones drawn from Scripture. Next, Paris published a Breviary in 1680 and a Missal in 1684, with emphasis on scriptural sources and a lessening of the cult of the saints. Even monastics, although not obliged to follow the Roman books, continued liturgical revision. The Breviary of Cluny appeared in 1686 and caused some controversy in its preference for Scripture over traditional responses and its decrease in feasts of the Virgin and the saints, especially Peter and the popes. In all these attempts, greater concern with historical fact prompted revision of the legends in the Breviary, and growing fastidiousness about Latin poetry caused revision in the Latin hymns. This trickle of books in the seventeenth century increased in the eighteenth.

Despite their demise in the nineteenth century, these Neo-Gallican rites contained some excellent items, some of which were reclaimed for the universal Church after Vatican II. They have been shown not to deserve the aspersions cast on them in the nineteenth century by Prosper Guéranger.[9] And they kept alive the ancient tradition of variety in regional and local usages while retaining some genuinely ancient practices. Such diversity now seems to be an enrichment of the Churches, not a diminishing of unity. The attempts at use of the vernacular, even in limited form in the rituals, appeal to moderns.[10] But these lights were extinguished in the nineteenth century, not to be rekindled for more than a century.

Part of the controversy of the Neo-Gallican rites involved their connection with a major spiritual movement in France and the Netherlands during the seventeenth and eighteenth centuries known as Jansenism. The movement takes its name from Cornelius Jansen (1585–1638), bishop of Ypres at his death. Jansen was remembered for his book *Augustinus*, published two years after his death. He argued that people could obey the commandments of God only by special grace and that grace was irresistible. The theological gravamen of the

9. Michael Kwatera, "Marian Feasts in the Roman, Troyes, and Paris Missals and Breviaries and the Critique of Dom Prosper Guéranger" (Ph.D. diss., University of Notre Dame, 1993).

10. F. Ellen Weaver, "The Neo-Gallican Liturgies Revisited," *Studia Liturgica* 16 (1986/1987) 54–72.

movement ran contrary to the prevailing Scholastic theology with its high estimate of human ability.

The consequences of Jansenist theology were a rigorous morality and faithful adherence to Church discipline. The adherents were numerous and included the Convent of Port-Royal near Paris, the Abbé de Saint-Cyran, Blaise Pascal, Antoine Arnauld, and Pasquier Quesnel. Jansenism had many adherents among bishops and religious (especially the Oratorians) in France and the Netherlands but was vigorously opposed by the Jesuits and a series of popes. Innocent X in 1653 condemned five propositions said to be held by Jansen, the factuality of which Jansenists refused to concede, although many submitted temporarily in 1668. Clement XI condemned 101 Jansenist propositions in the bull *Unigenitus* in 1713, leading a number of bishops and the Sorbonne (the Appellants) to appeal against the decree to a future council.

Two aspects of Jansenism affect worship primarily: the frequency of Communion and controversies over the confessional. Antoine Arnauld (1612–1694) published *De la fréquente communion* in 1643, arguing that thorough preparation was necessary before receiving Communion. The book produced a tempest.[11] Opponents interpreted it as discouraging frequent Communion; proponents saw it as restoring ecclesiastical discipline and encouraging more knowledgable participation in the Mass. Arnauld was not trying to discourage frequent Communion, but it had that effect on some of his followers. His sister, the abbess of Port-Royal, Mere Angélique, abstained for long periods out of concern over her own dispositions.

The moral rigorism that characterized Jansenism was a continuing source of controversy. Blaise Pascal and others attacked the Jesuit-inspired use of probabilism in confession. By this system, a precept of liberty could be counseled in hearing confessions if any precedent for allowing a course of action could be found historically, even though the preponderance of evidence was contrary. The Jesuits were largely identified with probabilism, and controversies continued throughout the seventeenth and eighteenth centuries. Since control of the confessional was a great source of power, especially among confessors of the elite, the debates between Jansenist severity and what often seemed to be Jesuit laxity led to constant conflict.

11. Louis Cognet, *Le Jansénisme* (Paris: Presses Universitaires de France, 1964) 44.

The seventeenth century saw the full development of some festivals and devotions and the abeyance of others. As indicated, the visual aspects of eucharistic devotion came into highest prominence. Benediction of the Blessed Sacrament increasingly became a very popular devotion. Elaborate musical performances could be accommodated at it, some items of the vernacular could appear in prayers, and preaching could stir up devotion. But above all, the Savior could be seen reigning in the midst of God's people. The Host was the relic par excellence and was for the baroque period what the relics of saints had often been in the medieval period—the immanent presence of the holy.

Exposition of the Blessed Sacrament often occurred even during Mass. Forty Hours devotions and Perpetual Adoration were observed by various communities. Eye contact was the chief form of participation, especially in the absence of frequent Communion. Corpus Christi processions were spectacular, particularly in Spain and Spanish colonies.

Something similar to the preeminence of the Host as relic occurred with regard to devotions to the saints. In this case, Marian devotions tended to crowd out the cults of individual saints and increasingly paralleled commemorations of the Lord. This parallelism is shown most clearly in what came to be the most significant devotional developments of the century, the cult of the Sacred Heart of Jesus and its parallel in the Immaculate Heart of Mary.

Here is seen the baroque imagination in high gear. The love of Christ was represented in visual fashion by images of the Sacred Heart, and exercises were provided to respond to this love in a highly affective and dramatic fashion. The roots go back to medieval devotions, especially to the wounds of Christ. But in this case, two seventeenth-century French religious gave abiding forms to both devotions and liturgies revolving around the Sacred Heart of Jesus.

St. John Eudes (1601–1680) was a priest of the Oratory of Jesus until he founded the Congregation of Jesus and Mary (1643). In his writings, Eudes sought to give theological foundations to devotions to the Sacred Heart and eventually to provide liturgical texts for the public commemoration of it. It is clear that for him devotions to Mary are closely related to those honoring her Son. The Sacred Heart is seen as a furnace of love for his Eternal Father, for his Most Holy Mother, for the Church, for each one of us, and for us in the Blessed

Sacrament.[12] His prose is highly dramatic in depicting the sufferings of Christ on our behalf and focusing on the Heart of Jesus as burning with love for us: "The most loving Heart of our benign Saviour is a burning furnace of most pure love for us; a furnace of purifying love."[13] In 1668 Eudes composed Propers for an Office and Mass of the Sacred Heart. He also composed various other prayers and rosaries for the Hearts of Jesus and Mary. The collect of the Mass prays "that our hearts, being consumed in unity among themselves and with the Heart of Jesus, we may perform all our works in His humility and charity."[14]

The other leader was a Visitation sister, St. Margaret Mary Alacoque (1647–1690), one of the few women who can be given credit for helping to shape liturgical history. At her convent in Paray-le-Monial, she had several revelations of the Sacred Heart in visions from December 1673 to June 1675. Her first vision occurred while she was praying before the Blessed Sacrament and seeing the Lord place her heart inside his as in a blazing furnace. In the second vision

"Christ then spoke of His love for people and of the ingratitude and coldness which He received in return, and He ordered the Saint to make reparation by receiving Holy Communion on the first Friday of each month and on each Thursday night to spend the hour from eleven to midnight prostrate on the ground in prayer, sharing in the sadness which our Lord suffered in the Garden of Olives."[15]

To those who received Communion on the first Fridays of nine consecutive months, a holy death was promised. The final vision asked that the Friday after the octave of Corpus Christi be set aside as a special feast in honor of the Sacred Heart and as a "solemn act of reparation for the indignities I have received in the Blessed Sacrament while exposed on the altars of the world."[16]

---

12. St. John Eudes, *The Sacred Heart of Jesus,* trans. Richard Flower (New York: P. J. Kenedy & Sons, 1946), chapter titles.

13. Ibid., "Eighth Meditation," 133.

14. Ibid., 139.

15. J. O'Connell, *The Nine First Fridays* (London: Burns Oates & Washbourne, 1949) 6.

16. Timothy T. O'Donnell, *Heart of the Redeemer* (Manassas, Va.: Trinity Communications, 1989) 135.

The subsequent publication of St. Margaret Mary's visions was briefly put on the Index but eventually released long after her death. In 1765 the Polish bishops petitioned for a feast of the Sacred Heart, and Clement XIII approved a Mass and Office for the feast on the Friday after the octave of Corpus Christi. Pius IX made it a universal feast in 1856.

The characteristics of this devotion came to be the annual feast day and attendance at first Friday Masses, Communion on that occasion as an act of reparation, and a Thursday evening Holy Hour in memory of the agony in the Garden of Gethsemane. For the devout, the devotion brought more frequent Communion. It highlighted the sufferings of Jesus during his passion but also added reparation for his sufferings in unrequited love for the outrages at the hands of both nonbelievers and indifferent Catholics. It was a highly personal act in which the individual tried to compensate for the outrages of others toward the suffering love of the Savior. One sensed the suffering of Christ from injuries to his love both in the past and in the present. This involved a psychological act of trying to concentrate on the feelings of Christ in one's own imagination. And thus it was an intensely personal and individual form of devotion expressed in vivid and emotional forms.

The seventeenth century also saw the spread of a three-hour Good Friday devotion (Tre Ore). It originated in Peru in 1687 after an earthquake and consisted of meditations on the seven last words from the cross, interspersed with hymns and prayers. The three hours, usually observed from noon to three o'clock, commemorated Christ's time on the cross.

THE MASS

Frequency of Communion was the most contentious issue during this period, as Jansenists were blamed for discouraging frequent Communion. In their favor, it must be said that Jansenists were more concerned about reverent and informed attendance at Mass and that their high moral standards discouraged Communion except after serious self-examination. Arnauld went out of his way to defend his doctrinal orthodoxy in an attack on Calvinists, *La Perpétuité de la foi catholique touchant l'Eucharistie.*

At the same time, it must be realized that frequent Communion was a rarity even where Jansenism was unknown. Robert Cabié asserts of this period: "Abstention from Communion was so much a part of local mores that those who wished to communicate would do so after the crowd had gone, lest they appear to be 'flaunting themselves.' In time, the practice arose of celebrating a 'communion Mass' for such people at an early hour."[17] It may seem an anomaly today, but well up into the twentieth century Communion was not normally given to the people at what is assumed to be the appropriate moment, after the Communion of the priest, but before, after, or from a side altar at any point during the Mass. It was almost a private devotion divorced from any real sense of common action of the community.

In most parishes there was one high Mass on Sundays, sung by priest and choir, with little participation and not much comprehension by the laity of the action of the liturgy. Private devotions occupied them while the priest proceeded to celebrate at the altar on their behalf. Translations of the Mass were forbidden under pain of excommunication. It was regarded as a daring act even to recite the Canon in Latin so as to be audible by the congregation. The general rubrics labeled the Canon "secreto."

Conscientious pastors did preach on the meaning of the Mass, and various writers produced "Exercises for Holy Mass," that is, pious reflections for use during Mass, some even being paraphrases of the Mass texts in the vernacular.[18] But for the most part, the laity were left with the rosary and their own prayers to occupy themselves until they could glimpse the Body of Christ at the elevation.

That is not to say there was nothing to see. The ceremonial was splendid and enacted with a full panoply of visual display. Most conspicuous were the vestments of the priest. The chasuble, once full and naturally flowing, became a stiff, formal sandwich known as a "fiddleback." This baroque chasuble had shed its functions as a garment and had become an ecclesiastical billboard, a symbol covered with other symbols of the season or occasion and shaping the actions of the priest. Often finely embroidered and covered with expensive materials, it was a clear sign of triumphalism and about as remote from simple and natural vesture as one could get.

But this was the age of the triumph of the outward and visible and a reversal of the inwardness of much late medieval piety. Reticence and subtlety were lost in a court ceremonial that proclaimed the power and majesty of God and addressed the Ruler of the universe through

17. *The Eucharist*, vol. 2 of *The Church at Prayer*, ed. A. G. Martimort (Collegeville, Minn.: The Liturgical Press, 1986) 178.
18. Ibid., 181.

forms appropriate to the sovereign of an earthly kingdom. Baroque art and architecture were the perfect reflection of this approach to the divine.

In England, where the practice of Roman Catholicism was regarded as treason, a quite different situation prevailed. Various penal laws forced the Roman Catholic Mass underground. Priests risked their lives to bring the sacraments to their flocks worshiping in secret conventicles. Here simplicity and secrecy prevailed of necessity. The Colony of Maryland provided a brief exception. Colonists arrived in 1634, and the first Mass was celebrated by three Jesuits on Annunciation Day. Despite a very early Toleration Act passed by the Assembly in 1649, persecution eventually ensued in Maryland as elsewhere in most English colonies.

RHYTHMS OF THE LIFE CYCLE

The Roman Ritual of 1614 only slowly replaced existing books. New diocesan rituals continued to appear, especially in France late in the seventeenth century. Local customs held sway in many rites, especially those of marriage and burial.

The biggest change in initiation rites was the sudden resurgence of adult baptism as missions expanded beyond Europe. Ever since the conversion of the Scandinavian countries by the end of the twelfth century, infant baptism had been the normal practice throughout Europe, with a growing urgency to get the infants to the font as soon after birth as possible. Now suddenly hordes of converts of every age were being baptized on the mission frontiers. The instructions in the Roman Ritual provided that "adults being baptized ought first, according to Apostolic rule, to be diligently instructed in the Christian faith and holy morals." The candidates renounced Satan and all his works and pomps before professing Trinitarian faith. For most unbelievers, idolatry was repudiated; Muslims, Jews, and heretics abjured their previous adherence. Extensive exorcisms then preceded the actual baptism.

The rubrics provided that if a bishop were present, he administered confirmation. This was the exception rather than the rule in many mission fields, and priests were sometimes given the power to administer confirmation despite the canon of Trent restricting confirmation ordinarily to the bishop alone. Likewise, the rubrics indicated that in cases of "baptizing multitudes as in India and the new world," portions of the prescribed rites might be omitted.

Even though baptism of infants by immersion had virtually disappeared, the Ritual of 1614 still contains the rubric "where however it is the custom of baptizing by immersion, the priest takes the infant, and being careful not to hurt it, he carefully dips it, and with a triune immersion baptizes." Most seventeenth-century fonts would not have allowed room for infant immersion, to say nothing of adults. After an area was Christianized, infant baptism soon after birth became the norm because of fear that a child dying unbaptized would not be saved.

Marriage rites remained the most flexible. All that is required in the Ritual of 1614 is amazingly simple: the espousal vows, the joining of hands and pronouncing them married, the blessing and giving of a ring, and a prayer. Normally it would occur in the context of a nuptial Mass with benediction of the couple. The banns were provided for in advance, and the prohibition against weddings in sacred seasons were reiterated. The instructions advised that "weddings ought to be restrained and dignified," probably a good indication that many were not.

Local customs survived in various areas. Rites of betrothal were frequently appended to the beginning of the marriage rite. The use of a canopy, the giving of precious coins, two rings, the legitimization of previously born children, and even prayers against impotence appeared in various Neo-Gallican rites.[19] The ritual for the diocese of Coutances, France, included abundant exhortations and provision for blessing the nuptial chamber "for the overcoming of all obscene and indecent spirits and the fire of intemperate passion."[20]

Rites for the dying and funeral rites were provided in abundance in the 1614 Ritual. Instructions were found for visiting the dying, and rites appear for the commendation of the soul, at the moment of death, the funeral rites (other than the Masses in the Missal), and the Office of the Dead. In addition, there were forms for giving Viaticum and an apostolic benediction at the moment of death. These rites dwelt forcefully on the consequences of sin and the threat of earthly sinfulness to heavenly blissfulness. The dangers of hell and the punishments of purgatory seemed as important preoccupations as the joy of heaven. A medieval prayer, which has since disappeared from the

19. Kenneth W. Stevenson, *To Join Together: The Rite of Marriage* (New York: Pueblo Publishing Company, 1987) 102–103.

20. Mark Searle and Kenneth W. Stevenson, *Documents of the Marriage Liturgy* (Collegeville, Minn.: The Liturgical Press, 1992) 189–209.

funeral rite, set the tone: "Do not enter into judgement with your servant, Lord, before whom no one shall be justified, unless through you remission of all sins be granted."

The chief image of God in the 1614 rite seems to be that of judge. Of course, being entirely in Latin, it had little consolation to offer to mourners except the knowledge that everything was being properly done for the benefit of the deceased. Local customs continued, such as casting soil upon the coffin or tolling church bells. In France, the Neo-Gallican rituals "contained thorough pastoral directives pertaining both to funerary care and theology and to new liturgical rites. . . . [The Ritual of Alet shows] a concern for a biblical emphasis and a reserve about unchristian pomp."[21]

Rites of reconciliation—or the sacrament of penance, to give it the name of that aspect of the sacrament that predominated in the seventeenth century—occupy few pages in the 1614 Ritual, chiefly a prayer and the form of absolution. Absolutions of the excommunicated, both living and dead, are also included. But abundant controversy filled many pages of debates over the advice the priest was to give in the confession. Casuistry was the discipline of moral theology devoted to resolving particularly perplexing cases. Several competing systems evolved: probabilism, probabiliorism, and equiprobabilism. These revolved around questions of the extent or even existence of laws governing specific acts and how much the conscience of the sinner was bound by them.

The Ritual of 1614 gives detailed instructions as to how confession is to be made. A place for confession is to be located in the church, with a screen between the penitent and the priest. The priest may question the penitent if he or she does not confess the number and species and circumstances of sins. The priest is then to suggest appropriate satisfaction, including charitable acts, fasting, and may, in some cases, recommend that the penitent go to confession and receive Communion monthly or on solemn days. The 1614 rite had lost virtually all communal sense. "It is quick, efficient, and almost aliturgical. . . . Almost every element of praise and prayer is absent . . . the liturgy was effectively reduced to confession and absolution."[22]

21. Richard Rutherford and Tony Barr, *The Death of a Christian: The Order of Christian Funerals* (Collegeville, Minn.: The Liturgical Press, 1990) 106.

22. James Dallen, *The Reconciling Community: The Rite of Penance* (New York: Pueblo Publishing Company, 1986) 178–179.

Nevertheless, the sacrament of confession became important in revitalizing church life, and frequent confession was achieved more often than frequent Communion. Thus was "established as a staple of Catholic piety frequent regular confession not only of mortal sins but also of venial."[23] The Jansenists sought return to the public and severe penance of the early Church, and Arnauld denied that private confession had even existed at that time. But even more conventional leaders tended to make "confession more basic and frequent than communion."

What today is called "anointing of the sick" was still known as "extreme unction." In the Roman Ritual of 1614, the rite is accompanied by the seven penitential psalms, the litany of the saints, and forms for the visitation and care of the sick. In all these, emphasis is on the forgiveness of sin. The note of fear seems much stronger than that of hope. The paschal tone of the modern rites is noticeably absent. Since the rites were in Latin, the content of consolation must have been largely the thought that grace was conferred.

Nevertheless, there is some evidence that unction was not restricted solely to those in danger of death but that the possibility of physical healing was sometimes taken seriously. But in popular mentality unction was associated with last rites and was seen as a preparation for death more than as restoration to health. The healing intended was spiritual, not bodily. The rite's modern restoration as a sacrament of physical healing belies centuries of association with death rather than life.

CHURCH MUSIC

The history of church music during this period seems to be a series of inconsistencies: musical brilliance coupled with liturgical irrelevance, congregational song detached from the Mass, operatic skills isolated from the liturgy, and secular style in sacred context. Much of the musical literature of this period seems admirable in every way except liturgically.

On the one hand, the conservative views of Trent were reflected in attempts in Rome to print a corrected standard version of the chants in the Gradual, and in 1614 and 1615 the Medicean Gradual was published. This had been largely "corrected" according to the ideals of Palestrina. What was not realized until several centuries later was just how much these editions departed from traditional chant. Palestrina and his assistants "were experts in polyphony, [but] they knew little about the

23. Ibid., 181.

ancient melodies of the Church. Thus their ignorance of the Gregorian tradition resulted in the perpetration of a chant which was disfigured and not in accordance with the ancient melodies of the Church."[24]

Others were less concerned about safeguarding the past as innovation abounded. The first opera was written about 1600, and a new musical style soon developed in which solo voices, especially in extended arias and recitatives, became a high musical art. But opera was also far removed from the communal nature of church music by its display of individual voices. Operatic music cultivated the skill of individuals often employing very emotional forms. Above all, opera demanded professionals. One religious consequence was the development of a new musical form, the oratorio, which dealt with biblical texts and stories in much the same way that opera dealt with secular tales. Oratorios, however, functioned more as sacred concerts than as liturgical pieces.

Giovanni Gabrieli and Claudio Monteverdi, both working at St. Mark's Basilica in Venice, wrote works using two or more choirs. Monteverdi's Vespers, for example, employed choirs, solo voices, and musical instruments. Frequently it was the courts of princes that encouraged these new developments in both secular and church music and set styles for parish churches to emulate. More and more, church music was dominated by lay singers rather than by clergy. Splendor in church music came to be relished as much as splendor in architecture and vestments in cathedrals and court chapels. The disadvantage of this was that many new compositions had little to do with the liturgy itself. Many composers forgot that music "was meant to subserve the liturgical action. As a result of this, the music often fitted very poorly into the liturgical setting . . . the liturgy was not only submerged under this ever-growing art but actually suppressed."[25]

Attempts were made to redress the balance. Alexander VII in 1657 decreed that church musicians were to take an oath to conform to certain standards. These included that nothing be sung "except those compositions which have words which are prescribed in the Breviary and Missal." As to tunes, "music which imitates dance music and profane rather than ecclesiastical melody must be excluded, and must be banished from the churches."[26]

24. Robert F. Hayburn, *Papal Legislation on Sacred Music* (Collegeville, Minn.: The Liturgical Press, 1979) 64–65.

25. Joseph A. Jungmann, *The Mass of the Roman Rite*, 1:149.

26. Hayburn, *Papal Legislation*, 77.

A tradition of congregational singing in the vernacular had been present in Germany even before the Reformation, although only loosely connected with the Mass. The Cantual of Mainz of 1605 provided a method whereby German hymns could be inserted into the Latin Mass. All this was part of the ongoing problem of giving the laity something to do during Mass, especially the illiterate, who could not make use of devotional prayer books. But such efforts at a singing congregation were sporadic and local.

The choir of trained musicians, clergy and laymen, had come to be musical specialists. It is significant that in baroque churches the musicians were no longer in the chancel but in a balcony at the furthermost remove from the liturgy at the high altar. This location in spatial terms was often emblematic of functional shifts. The organ increasingly played a major role in reinforcing singing or substituting for various parts. Other instruments, both string and wind, could make the music yet more glorious. It was all part of the baroque imagination in adorning the throne room of God with sound just as it had with splendid visual decoration.

PREACHING

As with the music, much of the preaching in the baroque era was also aliturgical, having little or no connection with the Mass of the day. In similar fashion to the move of the choir loft away from the altar, the pulpit had begun a similar journey, often ending up halfway down the side of the nave. In the absence of fixed seating in many churches, this was probably an ideal spot to gather an audience, but it also symbolized dissociation from the action at the altar. Usually the sermon had little connection with the epistle or gospel read at the Mass; it was an entity unto itself. Preaching, when it occurred, often happened outside the Mass altogether. Historians have not been kind to the preaching of this age. In many parishes the Sunday sermons that Trent had envisioned never materialized except in Advent and Lent, and then they usually dealt with fasting. Brilioth speaks of Roman Catholic preaching of the late baroque era as "a period of decline which reaches its lowest point in the seventeenth century."[27]

A major exception was the French Church, which distinguished itself with a series of princes of the pulpit worthy of the age of the Sun

27. Yngve Brilioth, *A Brief History of Preaching* (Philadelphia: Fortress Press, 1965) 143.

King, Louis XIV (1643–1715). All the devices of classical rhetoric were harnessed to make preaching a scintillating display of rhetorical techniques. The most famous luminary of the pulpit was Jacques Bossuet (1627–1704), bishop of Meaux. He was gifted with a winsome personality, a fine voice, and a brilliant mind. His sermons attracted rapt audiences, particularly in court circles. Some of his best-known sermons were funeral orations for members of the nobility. His sermons frequently dealt with doctrine; occasionally he treated controversial subjects. His commanding presence helped make his views most persuasive. He played an important role in 1682 in persuading the French clergy to accept the Four Gallican Articles, which asserted the ancient liberties of the French Church. His contemporary Louis de Bourdalove, S.J., preached effectively on morality, using a rational rather than emotional approach.

A later generation produced Jean-Baptiste Massillon (1663–1742), bishop of Clermont. Again, much of his preaching occurred at court, including the funeral oration of Louis the Great, which began with the words "God alone is great." His preaching was particularly noted for his stress on moral seriousness. François Fénelon (1651–1715), the archbishop of Cambrai, was long engaged in conflict with Bishop Bossuet on theological issues and mysticism. Fénelon was known for his eloquent sermons as well as his writings on spiritual matters.

A major factor working toward improving the general level of preaching was the advent of new diocesan seminaries, which Trent had mandated for every diocese. Not only did these raise the educational level of diocesan clergy, but most gave instruction in preaching. Preaching often became a point of conflict in areas where Catholics and other Christians were mixed and was often directed to making converts.

Some religious orders made preaching their special mission, including the older orders (Franciscans and Dominicans), and particularly the Jesuits among the new orders. In the missions overseas, preaching became an important means of making new converts. In Europe battles between Jansenists and Jesuits were often conducted from the pulpit.

PUBLIC PRAYER

By the seventeenth century the Breviary was recited in private by most clergy except for those living in religious houses of the older orders, where the Office was still sung in choir. This is all the more remarkable, since the Breviary of Pius V kept choral elements of antiphons and responsories, the deletion of which under Quiñones had caused such a stir.

The two revisions of the Roman Breviary made in the seventeenth century were partly a factor of growing historical knowledge that questioned some of the more imaginative legends of the saints. Developing historical scholarship was evident in the revision of 1602, largely the work of Cardinal Cesare Baronius (1538–1607). Another force was a growing fascination with the literary quality of Latin poetry. Just as seventeenth-century Romans were inclined to add missing limbs to classical statues, so under Urban VIII, a poet himself, the poetry of the Latin hymns of the Breviary was amended in a 1632 edition. This led to wholesale tampering with the poetry of the hymns, nearly a thousand emendations, to bring them into conformity with the supposedly superior qualities of classical Latin verse. These two revisions basically ended revision of the Roman Breviary until the twentieth century except for occasional additions of feasts and their Propers. The new feasts of saints only served to increase the dominance of the sanctoral cycle over the temporal and further interfered with the orderly recitation of the Psalter.

The Neo-Gallican reformers had a different agenda, namely, to make rites biblical and intelligible, not to fastidious Latin stylists but to ordinary priests and lay folks. The first major attempt with the Breviary was the Breviary of Vienne, published in 1678. Many traditional antiphons and responsories disappeared, to be replaced by portions drawn from Scripture. Two years later the Breviary of Harly was published in Paris. The revisers were motivated by a concern that as much of the Office as possible should be drawn from Scripture. They emphasized dominical feasts rather than those of the Virgin and the saints. The monks at Cluny went even further in reforming the monastic Breviary in their edition of 1686. Here again, many ancient elements were replaced by scriptural passages. Legends were suppressed and saints' days were reduced or diminished. A diocesan Breviary in Orléans in 1693 followed a similar pattern.

The instructions and rubrics often appeared in French. Scripture gained the preeminence in these efforts, as Quiñones and Cranmer had advocated a century and a half earlier. Scruples about historical accuracy more and more impinged on the colorful and imaginative accounts of the deeds of the saints. One can detect a not too subtle Gallicanism in downgrading the festivals of St. Peter and the popes.

Frequently the Jansenists took the lead in revisions. "In the circle of liturgists, in fact, it is difficult to find one at this period who has no connection whatsoever with the Port-Royal group."[28] The ferment of the time knew no strict boundaries.

For the laity, even these reforms were largely meaningless, since the Breviary remained a book for clergy and religious. Various prayer manuals were available for devout lay people, but largely for individual and private use. In England, prayer manuals were kept in print from the sixteenth until the nineteenth century. Many of these made such items as the Little Office of the Blessed Virgin Mary, the Office of the Dead, and the penitential psalms available in the vernacular. That they went through so many editions shows that devout individuals found them useful for private devotions in every age. They often contained calendars and sanctoral material for individual use. Since they were meant for lay use, they were not subject to the regulations of the official books published in Rome.[29]

One is struck by how well all parts of the baroque age cohere. The splendor of the architecture, music, preaching, vestments, and everything else all go together and are unmistakably of this period. We may wince at some of the extravagances, at the failure to glimpse that less is more, at the lack of any subtlety. Louis Bouyer, in his classic work of 1955, *Liturgical Piety*, vigorously assails the whole period. He speaks of "the purely pagan character of Baroque religion when it is examined in its essence . . . sacred means untouchable, something to be preserved intact at any price, and something which cannot be kept intact without the complete renunciation of all attempts to make the practice of it intelligent and living."[30] There is a certain amount of overkill in this passage. One cannot help but admire the passion behind the baroque. If it was not always discerning, at least it never lacked enthusiasm. It found new ways of praising God in terms of the culture of its time.

28. F. Ellen Weaver, "The Neo-Gallican Liturgies Revisited," 61.

29. Patrick L. Malloy, "A Manual of Prayer (1583-1850): A Study of Recusant Devotions" (Ph.D. diss., University of Notre Dame, 1991).

30. (Notre Dame: University of Notre Dame Press, 1955) 52.

Chapter Three

The Enlightenment

Liturgical scholars have tended to make a long detour around the eighteenth century as if all of it was hostile territory for worship. They were right—it was hostile. It was hostile in many ways to much that is central in Christian worship, but there were seeds planted in the eighteenth century, even if trampled on at the time, that have grown and blossomed into many twentieth-century liturgical reforms.

The Enlightenment of the eighteenth century was one of the greatest intellectual and religious crises of Western civilization. It affected every aspect of social life. For example, the Enlightenment brought changes in Protestant worship at least as drastic as the shifts from medieval worship had been in the sixteenth century. And Roman Catholic worship was greatly affected, even in reacting to the Enlightenment. That is true because the Enlightenment set up the terms and conditions of modern social life, especially in the political sphere. The Declaration of Independence is an Enlightenment document par excellence.

The Enlightenment's questioning of authority of any kind made "religious authority" in particular seem an oxymoron. Only the rational individual, freed from "self-incurred tutelage," possessed religious authority. Immanuel Kant claimed the motto of the Enlightenment was "Have courage to use your own reason!" Authority in religion as elsewhere was vested in the autonomous individual. Reason was to be the guide in all things, and the age of the Enlightenment is often called the "Age of Reason." All things, past and present, were to be examined in the cold light of reason and rejected if not found reasonable.

This naturally led to tremendous erosion in religious matters. The Enlightenment was not necessarily atheistic; it simply made God emeritus. Creation was God's marvelous work but, now completed, the Creator had vanished from any interaction with creation and humans. One could believe in God but not invoke God with any expectation of divine intervention. The result was a desacralized universe in which it was difficult to see power or meaning or grace behind anything physical. Physical objects were only what outward appearance indicated and no more.

This meant that sacramental worship was rigorously questioned along with anything else that seemed miraculous, mysterious, or supernatural. If water was only a chemical compound, it was hard for many to believe that it could also be a saving bath. Sacraments seemed little more than visual aids rather than efficacious instruments. The sacraments do revitalize human memory, but the Enlightenment denied that there was any agency other than the human involved in sacramental worship.

The one item the Enlightenment did relish in Christianity was its function as a moral agency. Enlightenment thinkers could applaud the sacraments when seen as reinforcing morality but denied that they were efficacious means of grace. Christian teaching about responsibility to one's neighbor and the fear of the afterlife were congenial topics for the Enlightenment. Hence there was the temptation to reduce Christianity to a system of morality with ceremonial accoutrements.

Obviously, much of Roman Catholic worship was threatened by this whole era. The excesses of the French Revolution showed just how much antagonism there was between the spirit of the age and traditional worship. It is not strange that much of Roman Catholicism reacted to these developments in a most defensive fashion. That fortress mentality of a Church besieged by a hostile world persisted until Pope John XXIII threw open the windows in the 1960s.

We shall be dealing in this chapter with the eighteenth century and the first third of the nineteenth. The Enlightenment arrived early in some parts of Europe and late in others. And in some countries it was much more violently opposed to religion than in others; in France it echoed Voltaire's violent dictum "Destroy the infamous thing!" that is, the Church. In England, John Locke's irenic treatise *The Reasonableness of Christianity* (1695) gave hope that reason and faith could live together more or less comfortably.

THE THRONE ROOM BECOMES YET MORE ORNATE
Church architecture does not give as unambiguous a sign of change in this instance as in the previous two centuries. That in itself is signifi-

cant, because it suggests a parting of ways between worship and culture, exactly what was happening in many parts of Europe. With few exceptions, church buildings were not the great monuments of this period. Most of these exceptions were in Germanic lands, where the Enlightenment was slower in its arrival. The same century also saw massive destruction of churches in France, where the Enlightenment was most vehement.

The artistic style most distinctive for eighteenth-century churches is known as "rococo." Continuing the marine metaphors of baroque (rough pearl), the word derives from the form of a seashell. Rococo was the final development of baroque, carried to its utmost fancifulness. In church architecture rococo was the final playing out of the baroque imagination. Rococo was replaced in the late eighteenth century by a cold, archaeological Greek classicism, devoid of passion.

The rococo churches of the eighteenth century, especially in France and Germanic lands, were essentially the throne room of God made yet more ornate. This was done by pushing surfaces to their ultimate distortions in convoluted and swirling forms. Bright colors and an abundance of gilt contrasted with shadows and recesses. Plaster gave the possibility of molding forms, so that what was visible may have had little to do with the actual structure. "The decoration spreads over the surfaces of the building until a total dissolution of structure takes place resulting in an insubstantial, almost fairy-tale effect."[1] A severe classicism came to dominate architecture in France in the late eighteenth century and eventually spread eastward into Germanic lands. It was a stern reaction to rococo's excesses.

While giving glory to the setting of the liturgy, rococo was highly subjective and individualistic and directed to summoning the emotions. Thus the liturgy tended to be buried in a devotional milieu. One's attention was led hither and yon, to gesticulating saints, to incursions of heavenly hosts, all informative but extraneous to the gathering of the people of God here on earth. It is not surprising that many of the greatest monuments of rococo art were pilgrimage churches and that several focused on relics of saints.

In the Church of the Fourteen Saints (*Vierzehnheiligen*) in central Germany, the shrine of the saints appears in the center and dominates

---

1. P. and C. Cannon-Brookes, *Baroque Churches* (London: Paul Hamlyn, 1969) 151–152.

the entire church. The high altar is of secondary importance, although certainly exuberant enough. The shrine itself is pure fantasy, combining plaster images of saints, a state coach, and hints of Bernini's baldachino in St. Peter's Basilica. Balthasar Neumann began work on it in 1743, to be superseded a decade later by Jacob Michael Kuchel, who was responsible for the shrine, altar, and pulpit.

Contemporary with this was the pilgrimage church, *Die Wies*, in Bavaria, built to commemorate a miraculous statue of the Flagellated Savior. Dominikus Zimmermann was the architect. He conceived the magnificent pulpit as evoking the wind of the Holy Spirit at Pentecost, fixed in gilded and painted plaster. Everything was done throughout the church to make the supernatural visible. Sculpture and murals combined to unleash the divine in visible form. This last phase of baroque could go no further, and the future lay in a reversion to the rational dignity of buildings inspired by ancient Greek buildings rather than the fanciful rhapsodies of eighteenth-century architects, sculptors, and painters.

The chief survivor today of rococo is lace, which was added to decorate already ornate vestments and altar cloths. Lace seems out of place in sparsely decorated modern churches but still survives in many instances.

The advent of the French Revolution (1789) brought on a short but highly destructive time of iconoclasm and destruction of churches in France. Particularly vulnerable were the churches of monastic orders. The great twelfth-century abbey church of Cluny, considered the greatest church ever built, was destroyed along with many other churches. Churches were profaned with pagan images placed on the altars.

Fortunately, churches continued to proliferate in the New World and wherever missionaries ventured. This was the period of the mission churches of the Franciscans and Jesuits in Texas, Arizona, and California. Rococo hardly reached these buildings in the wilderness, but many features of Spanish village churches reappear. Ironically, in missions—of all places—details from Moorish architecture sometimes appeared, as at Carmel, California, and San Antonio, Texas. These churches were not indigenous buildings as are the missions of New Mexico, but they reflect an architecture of nostalgia in which memories of Old Mexico and Spain were kept alive in adobe, stone, and wood. Christianity was advancing in the New World even as it was being battered in France and much of Enlightenment Europe.

The age of official revision of the Roman liturgical books was now history. That did not prevent some adjustments in the *Caeremoniale Episcoporum* by Benedict XIII in 1727, and Benedict XIV revised several liturgical books in the 1740s and 1750s.

If new official books no longer flowed from Rome, that did not change the situation in France, where Neo-Gallican liturgies were a growth industry, building upon and expanding the work done in the seventeenth century. The influence of Jansenists or their sympathizers, the Appellants (who appealed over the pope for a general council to resolve the controversy over Jansenism), is apparent in many liturgical books. Another important factor in these disputes was the development of liturgical scholarship. Repeated efforts were made to justify liturgical changes by appealing to the practices of the early Church as these were being rediscovered by historians. The preference for scriptural passages over traditional texts was common. And a clear disposition to prefer the reasonable to the miraculous became paramount in the legends of the saints. All these strains contributed to the production of new Breviaries, Rituals, and Missals in eighteenth-century France.

The result was that by 1789 in France, "out of 130 bishoprics, 80 had turned their backs on the Roman liturgy and had recourse once more to the pre-Tridentine national traditions."[2] Much that was in these new books was ancient, much was new. The Jansenists had long fought to make the Bible available in French and to encourage all believers to read it. They even had the audacity to encourage women to read. Such bold ideas were condemned firmly in the constitution *Unigenitus* of Clement XI in 1713, especially the propositions that "the reading of the Holy Scriptures is for all persons" or that "the knowledge of religious mysteries ought . . . to be communicated to women by reading holy books."[3]

A series of diocesan Breviaries appeared in France in the eighteenth century. Major additions from Scripture, both Old and New Testaments, were woven into their fabric.[4] Fresh selections from the sermons of the

2. Theodor Klauser, *A Short History of the Western Liturgy*, 2nd ed. (Oxford: Oxford University Press, 1979) 119.

3. Translated by F. Ellen Weaver, "Scripture and Liturgy for the Laity: The Jansenist Case for Translation," *Worship* 59 (November, 1985) 520–521.

4. F. Ellen Weaver, "The Neo-Gallican Liturgies Revisited," *Studia Liturgica* 16 (1986–87) 62–64.

ancient Fathers often appeared or were rearranged from traditional locations. New hymns were composed to fit the cycles of the year. The saints' legends were purged of anything dubious. In general, saints' days were often curtailed or eliminated in Lent, and feasts of the Virgin were fewer in number, as were those of St. Peter and the popes.

Diocesan Missals also flourished. Gaston Fontaine claims that at least eighty-two were produced in France between 1680 and 1845.[5] These included those of Troyes (1736), Poitiers (1767), Chartres (1783), Sens (1785), and Paris (1738). Lyons, which had been the guardian of genuinely ancient liturgies in its Breviary and Missal, scrapped both in the eighteenth century for new versions. The Missal of Paris, published by the authority of Archbishop Charles de Vintemille, became the model for more than half the dioceses of France. Both Jansenist and Gallican tendencies surfaced in these new Missals. In some cases ancient local usages were carefully maintained; in others entirely new prayers were produced. Many of the ancient sequences that the 1570 Roman Missal had eliminated were retained and new ones composed. The Missal of Meaux made an effort to have the Canon read in an audible voice. In some Missals a theme for the day, often inspired by the gospel, shaped the other Propers, often with a moralistic tone.

The Rituals continued to be a natural focus for local adaptations, especially in weddings and funerals. Here the attempt to be edifying was even more paramount. The Coutances Ritual of 1744 has twenty-two pages of instructions.[6] In some cases the desire to perpetuate local customs reflected an intensely conservative instinct; in another sense it was part of the liberal Gallicanism that sought to emphasize local versus papal control.

An unexpected new factor emerged in the French Revolution with the Civil Constitution of the Clergy (1790), which gave the government the power to realign the dioceses on the basis of the civil departments rather than the traditional diocesan boundaries. It also provided for the election of clergy on a parochial basis. The result meant liturgical chaos; in some dioceses as many as six different sets of liturgical books were now in use side by side. The Gallican liturgical principle of diocesan usages itself was shattered by the new realignments. The

5. "Présentation des missels diocésans Français du 17ᵉ au 19ᵉ siècle," *La Maison-Dieu* 141 (1980) 97–166.
6. John K. Brooks-Leonard, "Another Look at Neo-Gallican Reform," *Ephemerides Liturgicae* 98 (1984) 465.

Concordat of 1801 led to the replacement of the old bishops with new ones nominated by the state. Napoleon's "Organic Articles" of 1802 gave the government further powers over the Church, including regulation of processions and the dress of the clergy.

By that time, however, the most dramatic idolatry and bizarre practices of the Revolution were becoming a distant memory. The Revolution had frequently pitted the people and parish clergy against the bishops and affluent clergy, and took particular vengeance on monastics, who were regarded as contributing little or nothing to society. Monasticism virtually vanished in France and much of Europe. "It has been computed that of the thousand-odd monasteries of Benedictines and Cistercians extant in 1750" only about forty survived. Public opinion felt that "monasticism, a medieval survival, had vanished forever along with the other institutions of the *ancien régime*."[7] Monasticism was abolished in France in 1790. Its eventual revival in the nineteenth century was to be of tremendous importance in the history of liturgy.

At its most bizarre moments, the French Revolution had been equally profane and colorful. A prostitute dressed as the goddess of reason was placed on the altar at Notre Dame in Paris. The irony of this seems to have eluded the revolutionaries, and did not they wince at devotions directed to Voltaire and other philosophers. At the first anniversary of the fall of the Bastille, July 14, 1790, the statesman Charles Maurice de Talleyrand presided over a "Mass" wearing a tricolored sash as a vestment.[8] Royal and Church rites, even the secular calendar, were replaced temporarily by patriotic and occupational festivities. Few of these idolatries survived to the end of the century.

French innovations were not alone in this century. A movement in Germanic lands known as Febronianism was largely directed against the temporal power of the papacy. The name derives from the suffragan bishop of Trier, Johann Nikolaus von Hontheim, who in 1763 published a treatise on the power of the Roman pope under the pen name Febronius. Like Gallicanism, Febronianism advocated placing the locus of power in the hands of the bishops and civil state. A document of twenty-three articles entitled the "Punctuation of Ems" (1786)

7. David Knowles, *Christian Monasticism* (New York: McGraw-Hill, 1969) 170.

8. David I. Kertzer, *Ritual, Politics & Power* (New Haven: Yale University Press, 1988) 151–152.

would have reduced papal control over local matters, but it led to no lasting results.

More successful were the efforts of the Holy Roman Emperor Joseph II, emperor from 1765 to 1790. He sought to limit the powers of the pope to purely spiritual matters, granted religious liberty in the Toleration Edict of 1781, suppressed some religious orders, and transferred monasteries to the control of bishops rather than Rome. The Jesuits were successfully attacked in many countries, leading to the abolition of the order in 1773 by Clement XIV, although they survived for a while under the Protestant Frederick II in Prussia and the Orthodox Catherine II in Russia.

Without doubt, the leading liturgical event of the eighteenth century was the Synod of Pistoia, held in that Tuscan town in 1786, the same year as the meeting of the German archbishops at Ems. Much of the impetus came from Leopold II, grand duke of Tuscany from 1765 to 1790. In 1790 he succeeded his brother as emperor. But the principal figure was Bishop Scipio de' Ricci (1741–1810), bishop of Pistoia-Prato from 1780 until deposed in 1790. The Synod of Pistoia is of interest today because its reforms anticipated so much those of the Second Vatican Council; in its own time it was completely squelched by Rome and proved entirely abortive.

Many of the reforms of Pistoia bear the stamp of Gallicanism and its Austrian counterpart, Josephism. Pistoia adopted the Gallican articles of 1682, which affirmed the independence of diocesan bishops from the papacy and asserted that bishops ruled contingent upon the synodical assent of their clergy. The civil state was exalted in its powers. The liturgical reforms bear many of the earmarks of Jansenism, including opposition to the cult of the Sacred Heart.

Liturgically, it was two centuries too soon to advocate the abandonment of Latin for the vernacular, to argue for only one altar per church and only one Mass on a Sunday, to have the laity communicate during Mass from elements consecrated at that time, and to lessen exposition of the consecrated Host. Charles Bolton sums up the reforms as an attempt to restore liturgy as "an action common to priest and people . . . [through] greater simplicity of rites, by expounding it in the vernacular, and by pronouncing it in a clear voice."[9] Much of the conflict was against popular devotions in favor of liturgical action by the

9. Charles Bolton, *Church Reform in 18th Century Italy (The Synod of Pistoia)* (The Hague: Martinus Nijhoff, 1969) 82.

entire community. Ricci undertook improvements in clergy education to promote his liturgical reforms. He also favored reforms in the daily Office.

If all this sounds curiously modern, it did not sound very palatable to Rome at that time. Nor were the people of Tuscany ready for such reforms. In 1794, Pius VI soundly condemned eighty-five propositions extracted from the *Acts and Decrees of the Diocesan Synod of Pistoia* in his constitution *Auctorem fidei*. Over fifty of the condemned propositions dealt with sacraments and worship.[10] Many are condemned with such terms as rash, intemperate, favoring the heretics, leading to error, injurious to the Church, or injurious to the Apostolic See. Without support from the faithful of Tuscany or from Rome, nothing came of the reforms.

More successful were early nineteenth-century developments in Germanic lands, where the Enlightenment was not as vehemently anti-clerical as it had been in France. Indeed, many principalities were headed by prince-bishops, some of whom had imbibed positive principles of the Enlightenment, or *Aufklärung*. Leonard Swidler has shown that in southwestern Germany, especially in the diocese of Constance, many Enlightenment principles were effected.[11] The leader was Ignaz Heinrich von Wessenberg (1774–1860). The list of German proposals sounds redolent of Vatican II reforms: much of the liturgy in the vernacular, congregational participation and singing, emphasis on reading and preaching of the Scriptures, diminished devotions to the saints and Mary, eliminating private Masses, driving out superstitious practices, reforming the Breviary, and making the sacraments more accessible and pastorally effective. Rome was to have none of it, and by 1855 most of these reforms had disappeared. "Aufklärung Catholicism appeared to have been almost entirely obliterated in a short time after it appeared to have an unbreakable hold."[12] It was left to Vatican II to reinstitute these reforms on a lasting basis.

Some of this spirit animated Bishop John Carroll (1735–1815), the first Catholic bishop in the United States. Elected bishop by his clergy in 1789, he was ordained in 1790. Carroll advocated a lay voice in

10. Henry Denzinger, *Enchiridion Symbolorum*, 33rd ed. (Freiburg: Herder, 1965) 526–540.

11. *Aufklärung Catholicism 1780–1850* (Missoula, Mont.: Scholars Press, 1978) 51.

12. Ibid., 62.

choosing pastors and for national churches to select their own bishops for papal confirmation. At several times he advocated translating the Mass into the vernacular in order to function pastorally in this country. In a much more limited way, an English priest, John Lingard (1771–1851), through his book *A Manual of Prayers on Sundays and During Mass* (1833) and his work in a Lancashire parish, urged a closer union of priest and people in the Mass and discouraged the rosary at Mass.[13]

The most interesting liturgical figure of the eighteenth century was a pope, Benedict XIV, who reigned from 1740 to 1758. Coming before the anti-clericalism of the French Enlightenment had become fully manifest, Benedict endorsed much of the learning of the Enlightenment. As a priest, he had worked for several years in the Congregation of Sacred Rites and later wrote the classic work on the process of beatification and canonization (1734–1738). He wrote a treatise on the sacrifice of the Mass (1748), revised the Roman Martyrology in 1748 and the Roman Pontifical, the *Caeremoniale Episcoporum,* and the Roman Ritual, all in 1752. Benedict dealt with the Chinese Rites Controversy firmly in the bull *Ex quo singulari* (1742) and with a similar situation in India in *Omnium sollicitudinum* (1744). In the letter *Sollicitudini* he forbade the representation of the Holy Spirit in human form unless in a representation of the Trinity as "three men alike, of equal aspect." He disliked the over-elaborateness of baroque forms of devotions and church music, looking more to a "discreet simplicity in the Liturgy." A recent scholar concludes: "Benedict XIV is one of the most important Popes of modern times regarding the liturgical life in the Church because of his scientific works in that field, because of the revised editions of so many official books, and because of his pastoral care in liturgical matters."[14]

RHYTHMS OF TIME AND DEVOTIONS

Changes in seasons of celebration and devotions were at the center of many of the cultural and countercultural conflicts of the eighteenth century. Powerful spiritual forces were also in vehement conflict within Western Catholicism even at the time it was beset by dire

13. Joseph P. Chinnici, *The English Catholic Enlightenment: John Lingard and the Cisalpine Movement, 1780–1850* (Shepherdstown, W. Va.: Patmos Press, 1980).

14. J. Hermans, *Benedictus XIV en de Liturgie* (Bruges: Uitgeverij Emmaüs, 1979) 403.

threats from secular society in the form of the Enlightenment. The most obvious currents were represented by the Jansenists and the Jesuits, but there were many eddies of new and old spiritualities. Although condemned by Clement XI in the constitution *Unigenitus* (1713), Jansenism was still a strong factor in the Synod of Pistoia (1786). The Jesuits took their lumps, being suppressed "irrevocably" in 1773 by Clement XIV with the brief *Dominus ac Redemptor* because of the hostilities they had provoked and the controversies in which they were involved.

Despite these internal squabbles, the most interesting thing is how piety both reflected the larger culture and reacted against it. Much of the piety tended to echo the atomistic and individualistic concepts of autonomy so characteristic of the time. Piety was practiced alone in the intimacy of a personal relationship with God. The larger community might reinforce these practices, particularly in encouraging morality, but often the gathered community seemed more a distraction from, rather than a source of, encounter with God. The sovereign individual with his or her inalienable rights set the tone for both devotions and civics. Yet there were popular devotions that defied the stress on rationality and coherence, even if they operated in highly individualistic ways.

The cult of the Sacred Heart had developed greatly in the seventeenth century, especially in France. From 1672 on, it began to appear in Mass texts, and a variety of Propers were soon in use in various French dioceses and orders. In 1765 official Propers for the Mass and Office were enacted for Poland and Portugal under Clement XIII, and Pius VI provided other Propers for Austria, Spain, and Venice in 1778. Other texts were to follow in the nineteenth and twentieth centuries. Pierre Jounel detects a duality in these rites: first, "thanksgiving for the inexhaustible riches of Christ," and second, "reparative contemplation of the pierced heart."[15] Such a disparate approach Jounel traces to the differing emphases of St. John Eudes and St. Margaret Mary Alacoque.

The Sacred Heart liturgies and devotions were countercultural in that they went against so much of the eighteenth-century revulsion against cults of the saints, relics, indulgences, and processions. Over

15. "The Feasts of the Lord in Ordinary Time," in *The Liturgy and Time*, vol. 4 of *The Church at Prayer*, ed. A. G. Martimort (Collegeville, Minn.: The Liturgical Press, 1986) 106.

and over again these items were targets of reformers. The cult of the Sacred Heart was specially attacked at Pistoia and frequently criticized in Germany. The chief objection seems to have been that it was often so excessive as a devotional exercise as to detract from congregational worship. At the same time that the cult of the Sacred Heart was offensive to Enlightenment sensibilities, it fed on the same individualistic spirit of the culture. The exercises were intrinsically privatistic in such acts as attending Mass on Fridays, when one could avoid the crowded Sunday assembly and find time for private contemplation.

If, as is often said of King Edward VI that he had a "superstition of superstition," the Enlightenment tended to take this a great deal further in condemning legends and relics of the saints, especially when they seemed spurious. We have seen the disappearance of many saints' commemorations in the Neo-Gallican liturgies and revisions of legends of those retained. Outdoor processions, hardly a major practice today, were frequently condemned as superstitious. The general tendency of the culture was to regard things medieval as barbarous or "gothic," a term meaning "crude" or "uncouth" in the eighteenth century. The cult of the Virgin was often criticized, and even Benedict XIV condemned excesses proposed by a Franciscan, Z. de Somerie.

It is all the more amazing that one of the major new devotions of the eighteenth century, the work of St. Alphonsus Liguori, seems so explicitly countercultural. His work is crucial to understanding the mental baggage of most Western Catholics before the modern liturgical movement and much of the resistance to it.

Alphonsus Liguori (1696–1787) came from a noble Neapolitan family. He was trained and practiced as a lawyer, until, disillusioned with the law, he became a priest in 1726. In 1732 he founded the order of Redemptorists, and in 1762 he was named bishop of Sant' Agatha dei Goti. He became famous for his writings on moral theology. In opposition to Jansenist rigorism and Jesuit probabilism, Liguori developed a system known as equiprobabilism. He was canonized in 1839 and declared a Doctor of the Church in 1871.

Liguori's greatest impact, though, was in popularizing new devotions, which had a lasting influence. The most important of these came through his publications, especially *Visits to the Blessed Sacrament and the Blessed Virgin*, first published in 1745. Its popularity is attested by more than two thousand editions in the next two centuries, a record rarely, if ever, equaled. A product of his own personal life, it grew out of his experience of the special sanctity of prayer before the altar.

Much of the emphasis is on "spiritual Communion," that is, a desire to receive Jesus and a loving embrace of him through contemplation. It was implied that spiritual Communion was equivalent to sacramental Communion but had the advantage that it could be practiced more often, indeed, "as often as we please, without being observed by any one, without being fasting, and without leave of our director."[16]

The book consists of forms for each of thirty-one days of the month. They are to be used at visits to the reserved Sacrament and at Mass. Three spiritual Communions are recommended on these occasions, that is, at the beginning, middle, and end of the visit and of the Mass.[17] To these is conjoined a visit to an image of the Blessed Virgin. Liguori made a conscious effort at simplicity in order to "render the book more useful to all sorts of persons," and the pattern soon became familiar by repetition. Each visit began with a very affective, invariable act of contemplation or adoration before Christ in the Blessed Sacrament. Then followed a meditation, usually prefaced by a sentence from Scripture; next a short ejaculation, such as "My Jesus: Thou hast given Thyself entirely to me: I give my whole being to Thee";[18] and finally the spiritual Communion. Then came a visit to an image of the Blessed Virgin with a short meditation concluded by an ejaculation, such as "O Mary! show thyself a mother to us,"[19] and an invariable prayer.

The daily visits are followed in the book by "acts for Communion," including "acts before Communion" of faith, confidence, love, humility, sorrow, and desire. "Acts after Communion" consist of acts of faith, thanksgiving, oblation, and petition. Other acts of "aspirations of love to Jesus in the Holy Sacrament" are a mixture of Scripture, passages from various saints, and many exclamations, some of even mildly erotic flavor. "Directions for Spiritual Souls" encourages frequent, even daily Communion, with the suggestion that daily confession is not requisite in the absence of mortal sins.

Added to the *Visits* is "An Apologetic Reply on the Subject of Frequent Communion" in the form of response to a critic and obliquely to Arnauld, the Jansenist. Liguori concedes that from the tenth to the

16. *Visits to the Most Holy Sacrament for Every Day in the Month* (Dublin: James Duffy and Co., n.d.) 17.

17. Ibid., 16.

18. "Fifth Visit," ibid., 29.

19. Ibid., 30.

sixteenth century, six or seven Communions a year would have been considered frequent[20] but that now weekly and daily Communion ought to be advocated at least for those free of mortal sin and striving to conquer venial sins. Devotions for confession and "Maxims of Eternity or Meditations for Every Day in the Week" are also provided.

The whole tenor of Liguori's devotions is intensely emotional. It is very subjective and private yet has a great intensity, which, no doubt, accounts for its wide appeal. As a moralist, Liguori has great concern about shaping the will, and much of the prose is directed to transforming the will of the devout on the basis of the encounter with Christ in the visit. The constant theme is "Take from my heart whatever is not pleasing to Thee; convert it entirely to Thyself, that it may wish and desire only what Thou dost wish."[21] Even the Enlightenment could relish the moralistic application of such piety, though it rejected the highly emotional context. Much of Liguori's language sounds too sentimental and exuberant for the mind of the present, but it certainly struck a sympathetic chord for over two centuries.

Indeed, much of the resistance to the modern liturgical movement can be understood on the basis of the enduring popularity of the *Visits.* Liguori certainly advocated frequent sacramental Communion as well, but spiritual Communion became a popular substitute for reception of Communion. In making the visits a popular devotion, Liguori unwittingly set up a major obstacle to the efforts of the liturgical pioneers to emphasize liturgy as the communal life of the Church and to show that liturgical worship has priority over devotions. Ten generations or more were nourished by an individualistic piety that for them provided a satisfactory substitute for being a liturgical community. A one-sided diet produced what from today's perspective seems like a malnourished version of Christian worship.

Liguori also promoted several different novenas, a private or public devotion structured over nine days. The antecedent was the apostles' wait from Ascension to Pentecost, and the intent was to obtain some special grace. Novenas began to appear in the seventeenth century. Liguori wrote novenas for Christmas, on the Heart of Jesus, and for All Souls' Day. These contained prayers to be used for individual devotion on each day of the novena. They focus on the occasion at hand and usually draw a moralistic application for the individual.

20. Ibid., 169.
21. "Twenty-Fifth Visit," 73.

The Sacred Heart and a very strong Marian devotion are major forces in his novenas. Liguori also produced a number of other devotional works in addition to his writings on moral theology.[22]

THE MASS

As we have seen, devotions played a major role for the devout, often as something to occupy them during Mass. From the Council of Trent onwards there were a succession of efforts to promote frequent Communion, usually with weekly Communion as the goal. But there was also steady resistance: the obstacle of the apparent novelty of frequent Communion, the connection of reception to prior confession and the battles ensuing over the rigor of confession, and now the attractive alternative of spiritual Communion. Not until the twentieth century was the basic reform of frequent Communion widely accomplished. When received, Communion often was distributed at a side altar to kneeling communicants, who interrupted their devotions during the Mass to receive from a priest not engaged in the Mass. Our sense of Communion as an integral part and climax of the community's actions would have amazed most eighteenth-century worshipers.

Beneath all this lay an even deeper problem. The Enlightenment looked askance at mystery and miracle. Immanuel Kant spoke as a Protestant but summed up the attitude of the age in 1793 in condemning "illusory faith" in miracles, mysteries, and means of grace.[23] The Eucharist, he found, could be beneficial in memorializing Christ and in inculcating "the idea of a cosmopolitan moral community," but in no ways as a means of grace. The problem for all Western Christians was to live in the presuppositions of one world and to worship in another. This, of course, applied not just to the Eucharist but to all sacraments. But it hit the Eucharist with the greatest impact because of its miraculous basis.

How, then, could Christians live in a world that denied any divine intervention since biblical times yet at the same time keep a sacrament at the heart of which was God's intrusion into their very midst? Many Protestants, and probably not a few Enlightenment Roman Catholics, fell back on making the Eucharist almost exclusively a memorial of

22. Théodule Rey-Mermet, *St. Alphonsus Liguori: Tireless Worker for the Most Abandoned* (Brooklyn: New City Press, 1989) 641–650.

23. *Religion Within the Limits of Reason Alone* (New York: Harper & Row, 1960) 182.

the biblical events. Memorializing the life and death of Jesus Christ could be a strong incentive to moral endeavor. "Jesus died for us, so why can't we behave ourselves?" is still a frequent sermon theme. Eighteenth-century Christians could inhabit the world of everyday, in which nothing was more than it appeared to be, and bring the same world to church by making bread and wine only visual aids but not means of grace.

It is not comfortable to live in two worlds, but that was the choice most Roman Catholics had to make until recently with regard to the Eucharist. Everything outside church doors excluded the miraculous; once inside, one set aside familiar modes of understanding reality. There was a willing suspension of the disbelief that characterized all the rest of daily life. The result was a schizophrenic approach to reality in which the experience of Christ's presence was defined in unfamiliar terms borrowed from Greek philosophy.

Theologians took the course of defying the Enlightenment's challenge to rational discourse by simply reaffirming the old formulations of what the Church experienced in the Mass. This was different from Aquinas's willingness to use the most rational terms available in his age to express the same experience. In contrast to Aquinas's willingness to speak the language of even pagan philosophers, eighteenth-century Catholicism preferred to play it safe by retreating to a fortress mentality.

A good example of this was the concentration on validity. This concept is basically minimalistic: what is the least you can do and still have a valid sacrament? How little water suffices for a valid baptism? By today's standards, these are the wrong questions to ask, but they were the criteria of a besieged era concerned about the validity of celebration rather than the quality. The result was a legalistic and mechanistic approach to sacramental life. The concepts of validity were pushed to their extremes in a highly defensive manner.

For the average worshiper, the Mass was an almost completely passive act with almost no participation except to gaze at the elevation. With everything but the sermon in Latin—and Latin mostly whispered at that—there was little to interrupt private devotions, although the more devout might slip off to a side altar to receive Communion at a convenient time during the Mass. Prayer books and devotional manuals could make good use of the remaining time.

The attempts of Ems, Pistoia, and Constance to change this situation led to little amelioration. Most reforms were resisted in Rome, and the vernacular, congregational song, and other reforms attempted in the Mass had to wait for a later century and new priorities. Roman Catholicism dug in its heels during the Enlightenment, and nowhere as stubbornly as in the Mass.

RHYTHMS OF THE LIFE CYCLE

A good indication of sacramental minimalism was the type of baptismal fonts appearing in new churches. Known as pedestal fonts, they consisted of a bowl on top of a shaft. They worked fine for pouring, but immersion of infants was an impossibility and not even contemplated for adults. If a few drops of water sufficed for a valid baptism, no one worried about the deficiency of sign value when baptism was no longer a ritual act of cleansing. Original and actual sin were removed no matter the quantity of water involved, and our modern concern for signifying washing had no place in the eighteenth century.

The seventeenth and eighteenth centuries did see concerted efforts to instruct children before confirmation and first Communion. At first, confirmation initiated the age of instruction at about age seven, and first Communion completed it about five years later. In France a new custom developed in the eighteenth century, that of first Communion preceding confirmation.[24] In the early twentieth century this reversal of sequence became normal almost everywhere in the West. Thus instead of the Eucharist being the climax of initiation, it was a stage on the way to confirmation. Benedict XIV observed in the encyclical *Ex quo primum* that although the Greeks did not practice the laying on of hands, they did anoint, and therefore had a sacrament of confirmation.[25] He also restored the ancient gesture of the bishop's laying his hand on the head of an individual being confirmed rather than simply holding it over the confirmands, as Durandus had indicated in the thirteenth century.[26]

Marriage rites tended to be the most conservative of all, and local traditions remained vigorous. At the same time, the ever-widening scope of missions brought in a new array of local customs. The *Tametsi*

24. Robert Cabié, "Christian Initiation," in *The Sacraments,* vol. 3 of *The Church at Prayer,* ed. A. G. Martimort (Collegeville, Minn.: The Liturgical Press, 1988) 76.

25. Gerard Austin, *Anointing with the Spirit* (New York: Pueblo Publishing Company, 1985) 28–29.

26. Cabié, "Christian Initiation," 74.

decree of Trent had welcomed "other laudable customs and ceremonies," and such cultural traditions tended to be added worldwide. Various ceremonies not included in the Roman Ritual occurred in various places: the use of a canopy over the couple, the giving of crowns, the giving of precious coins, and blessings of the bed chamber. A wide variety of rites appeared in diocesan rituals in France. "These trends represent nothing very new, but rather show a continuation of medieval development and enrichment."[27]

As with marriage, the celebration of Christian death continued to manifest local customs. But there was also a growing uniformity in the more commercial aspects of death. In a sense, these represent a growing democratization of death as items once reserved for the wealthy and powerful became common: coffins and individual tombstones. These did not necessarily add to the Christian aspects of death although eighteenth-century tombstones often provided moralistic epigraphs. The secularization of death was beginning, even though most of the process of death and burial still remained in the context of family and church.

The Enlightenment was reflected in some appendices to various diocesan funeral rites. That proposed for the diocese of Constance in 1806 included hymns, prayers, and an exhortation in the vernacular, the "edification theology" of the Enlightenment.[28] Words of consolation were mingled with counsel of moral behavior in this life. Thus even death was enlisted as a means of urging high morality in this life.

The lifelong journeys through confession and healing rites also showed the shifts of the Enlightenment. Confession remained a source of contention among the moral theologians, with various degrees of laxity and rigor being advocated in dealing with penitents. The advent of historical research only complicated matters. Some advocated a return to the early Church's public forms of confession, in which penance for the few was long and rigorous; others championed the tariff penance, which involved everyone but was private. And many others chose to disregard any evidence either way from history. It should be kept in mind that confession was in some ways the central

27. Kenneth Stevenson, *Nuptial Blessing,* Alcuin Club Collections 64 (London: Alcuin Club/S.P.C.K., 1982; New York: Oxford University Press, 1983) 174.

28. Richard Rutherford and Tony Barr, *The Death of a Christian* (Collegeville, Minn.: The Liturgical Press, 1990) 107.

sacrament; the faithful received it more frequently than they received sacramental Communion.

Nevertheless, various reforms were attempted. Pistoia advocated a return to an order of penitents, postponing absolution until after satisfaction, and raised doubts about indulgences and too frequent Communion. *Aufklärung* Catholics argued for public preparation for confession and also confession in a communal way.[29] Such attitudes were often condemned as being too Protestant. Nevertheless, "Most of the liturgical reforms [of confession] sought by the Catholic Aufklärung, though rejected and condemned at the time, have been implemented since Vatican II."[30]

What we would prefer today to call the anointing of the sick persisted in its late medieval guise as extreme unction. If anything, pastoral practice tended to emphasize the sacrament in its eschatological dimension as preparation for imminent death. It was a replication of baptism and confession now occurring in finality. Benedict XIV in 1747 made "a plenary indulgence available to all those who had been anointed"[31] and included the apostolic blessing for the dying in his revised Roman Ritual.

CHURCH MUSIC

In one sense, this was an age of brilliant developments in church music; in another, much of this music belonged more in the concert hall than in the church. Some of the greatest composers of all times worked in this period. Bach, Handel, Mozart, Haydn, Beethoven, and a host of others flourished in the eighteenth and early nineteenth centuries. All of them wrote religious music, but certainly not all of it was liturgical music. Even when called a "Mass," works such as Beethoven's *Mass in C* and the *Missa Solemnis* were highly individualistic and lengthy works written for the concert hall.

The opera became one of the dominant musical forms of the period, and it was tempting for musicians to employ similar techniques in writing for the church. But this demanded high technical skills from

---

29. Swidler, *Aufklärung Catholicism,* 35–37.

30. James Dallen, *The Reconciling Community* (New York: Pueblo Publishing Company, 1986) 197.

31. James Empereur, *Prophetic Anointing* (Wilmington, Del.: Michael Glazier, 1982) 71.

the performers and further removed church music from participatory skills of the congregation.

Church music continued to be the most ecumenical of liturgical forms. Johann Sebastian Bach (1685–1750) in particular was welcomed by Roman Catholic musicians. His organ and instrumental works bore no denominational cachet. His use of the same Gregorian Lectionary, as Western Catholics did, his settings of the Propers of the Mass, and settings of the invariable Mass texts were generally useful. In Bach's music a deep strain of German pietism combined with high-quality musical workmanship. Written as meditations on the Sunday gospel, his cantatas, of which over two hundred survive, were a magnificent accomplishment.

In Bach's hands, music became a highly developed form for portraying dramatically the Passion narratives of St. Matthew and St. John. The oratorio came into its own in the eighteenth century, especially with George Frederick Handel's *Messiah*. Bach was rapidly forgotten after his death until rediscovered by Mendelssohn in the next century. Yet over the centuries Bach's instrumental and choral music has probably proved itself more durable than that of any other church musician.

The classical composers who soon followed him in popularity in the eighteenth century, especially Mozart and Haydn, wrote music of dazzling melodic brilliance full of personal expression. Vienna became the musical capital of Europe but little distinguished the orchestras and soloists hired to sing in churches from their music at court and in the theater. Indeed, it was the reforming Emperor Joseph II who restricted operatic concerts disguised as Masses at the same time he was closing monasteries. Liturgical music often became little more than a musical program. "Artistic expansion of church music led to a complete disregard of the music's usefulness for the service. . . . Personal art triumphed over ecclesiastical and liturgical considerations."[32] Ironically, even those who sought the continuation of Gregorian chant continued to alter the music so profoundly that little of the medieval melodies remained intact.

The most important document the eighteenth century produced on church music was the encyclical *Annus qui* of 1749 by the energetic Benedict XIV. It has been called second only in importance to the 1903

32. Karl G. Fellerer, *The History of Catholic Church Music* (Baltimore: Helicon Press, 1961) 165.

motu proprio on church music of St. Pius X. The chant was to be retained in singing the Divine Office in unison, and "the use of theatrical and profane chant must not be tolerated in Churches."[33] Even instrumental music was seriously questioned. The organ was given approval, a short list of other instruments might be allowed, but none "that give a theatrical swing to music." When instruments "do nothing else but bother and drown out the choir voices and the meaning of the words, then the use of instruments does not reach the desired end; it becomes useless, rather, it is forbidden and condemned."[34] It must be remembered that this was written, not by Puritans or John Wesley, who made similar statements, but by a very sophisticated pope. The bifurcation of high art and ecclesiastical music had become profound.

A more affirmative note for an entirely different kind of church music appeared in the German *Aufklärung* in the encouragement of vernacular hymnody at Mass. The last part of the eighteenth century and first third of the nineteenth saw a number of German Catholic hymnals in the vernacular. The leading figure in *Aufklärung* Catholicism was the vicar general of the vast diocese of Constance, Ignaz Heinrich von Wessenberg. A poet himself, Wessenberg decreed in 1809 the singing of German hymns "at all communal Masses" and wrote a number of hymns for the diocesan hymnal published in 1812.[35] Frequently Protestant hymns were borrowed, both tunes and texts. The character of many of the hymns written for Catholic hymnals tended to be didactic and heavily ethical. They were at home in an Enlightenment culture.

PREACHING

It should not be surprising that preaching had a great appeal to the Enlightenment mind. It was directed to the mind, not to the senses; it did not claim to be mysterious or miraculous, and it could be used to teach morality. On the other hand, the type of preaching the Enlightenment despised was the highly emotional and affective kind, which encouraged the enthusiasm that the cultured despised. Preaching was used to support or oppose every religious group from Jansenists to Jesuits.

33. Full text in Robert F. Hayburn, *Papal Legislation on Sacred Music* (Collegeville, Minn.: The Liturgical Press, 1979) 96.
34. Ibid., 104.
35. Swidler, *Aufklärung Catholicism*, 21.

Jansenists found preaching useful in encouraging the strict morality they felt necessary to devout Christianity. Jesuits found it equally useful to support loyalty to the hierarchical Church and a necessity in winning converts in the missions. Alphonsus Liguori was a noted preacher, seeking to state the faith in simplest terms possible to reach the poor and unlearned.

Every reform movement seemed to find preaching a necessary part of its agenda. It must be realized that preaching was by no means frequent in many parish churches, many having a sermon no more often than once a month. Nor was the quality necessarily very high even on such relatively rare occasions. Part of the problem was the notion that preaching was basically a Protestant thing (especially in English and Germanic countries). However, a distinctive Roman Catholic trait was that preaching generally would occur in the context of the Eucharist.

Wessenberg, in Constance in 1803, "issued a circular to all the priests of his diocese requiring that at all Masses celebrated before noon on Sundays and major feast days a sermon be preached."[36] That was much more of a novelty than we might expect and was not easy to enforce. The purpose of the sermon was to instruct about the mystery present. In order to reverse a prevailing custom of preaching, when it did occur, before or after the Mass but not during it, Wessenberg issued a further directive in 1809 that "the main parish worship service on all Sundays and required feastdays shall consist of a Mass in the forenoon with German Mass hymns and a sermon, which must take place during the Mass immediately after the first gospel."[37] Part of his intention, besides liturgical appropriateness, was to thwart those who timed their arrival at church with the end of the sermon preached prior to Mass! Wessenberg's intent was that the sermon expound the gospel for the day (read in German) and ordered that such instruction last a quarter of an hour.

That was the ideal; how much it was reached even in Constance is debatable. Most of Wessenberg's agenda was defeated deliberately by Rome, which finally stripped him of all power in 1827. All too often, one suspects, preaching was more directed to teaching than to proclamation, to instructing humans how to behave rather than proclaiming what God has done. Even sermons on civic virtue or the need for vaccinations could supplant the preaching of the gospel, but to the

36. Ibid., 14.
37. Ibid., 14–15.

Enlightenment mind this seemed a laudatory use of the pulpit. Preaching as moralistic harangue was prevalent in much of the Catholic world, and threats of eternal damnation were taken seriously even by the Enlightenment. Even Voltaire admitted that without such counsel his servants would likely slit his throat. The concept of duty, religious, civil, and social, was inculcated in sermons with monotonous regularity. The Enlightenment considered this a commendable function for clergy.

PUBLIC PRAYER

The Breviary continued to be a source of controversy during this period. The Neo-Gallican editions sought to make the Breviary more edifying to the mind of the time. This was especially true of the dioceses with Jansenist leanings and those bishops who had appealed against the constitution *Unigenitus*. These reformed Breviaries had many common features, especially the desire to replace ancient texts with Scripture. They include, among others, the Breviary of Troyes (1718), the Breviary of Auxerre (1726), the Breviary of Rouen (1728), and the Breviary of Paris (1736). The last was adopted or adapted by many other French dioceses.

Opponents could find indication of Jansenist leanings in the texts and prayers provided, but many of the same theological statements occur in non-Jansenist sources.[38] It has been shown that the Paris Breviary, sometimes known as the Vintemille Breviary after the cardinal archbishop of Paris, was soundly orthodox in its teachings. It did soft-pedal somewhat the sanctoral cycle in order to fortify the temporal, and it involved a greater use of Scripture than the Tridentine Breviary. Items of great value were added in the readings, hymns, and prayers.[39]

There was clearly in the minds of many sophisticated Roman Catholics a fear that some things bordered on superstition. These included processions, the use of relics, indulgences, and the cult of saints, including that of the Virgin. Emperor Joseph II considered monasticism itself basically unproductive and closed monasteries to use their revenue to establish educational institutions. Many others were terminated by the French revolutionaries. So the tradition of the

38. Weaver, "The Neo-Gallican Liturgies Revisited," 62–65.

39. Michael Kwatera, "Marian Feasts in the Roman, Troyes and Paris Missals and Breviaries and the Critique of Dom Prosper Guéranger" (Ph.D. diss., University of Notre Dame, 1993).

choir Office sung daily in community almost vanished off the map of Europe for a period of about fifty years. "Bare ruined choirs" were not just an English peculiarity.

Of course, diocesan clergy were obliged to read the Breviary daily, but numerous proposals arose for its reform, including its complete abolition. Beginning with Cologne in 1780, various German dioceses published Breviaries in line with some of the French examples. Radical reformers advocated simply requiring clergy to read daily from Scripture; more moderate ones argued for a greatly reduced Breviary or selective use of it due to the pastoral obligations of the clergy. A four-volume German Breviary published by J.T.A. Dereser in 1792 was structured in four daily Offices and consisted largely of Scripture. It was used in many German dioceses in preference to the Latin Roman Breviary. Swidler presents evidence that a large number of clergy in Germany, perhaps the majority, had abandoned the Latin Breviary by 1830 in favor of Dereser's Breviary or simply the reading of Scripture.[40] All this has a curiously modern ring about it, but then the Enlightenment shaped us in many ways.

The ever industrious Benedict XIV started work on a revised Breviary and, dissatisfied with the work of others, resolved himself to do "an honest correction of our breviary" (1755) but died without having accomplished it.[41]

40. Swidler, *Aufklärung Catholicism*, 43.
41. Pierre Batiffol, *History of the Roman Breviary* (London: Longmans, Green and Co., 1912) 282.

Chapter Four

The Romantic Era

There are many ways to define Romanticism. The simplest is to see it as the inevitable reaction to the exaltation of reason so characteristic of the Enlightenment. It is easy to list the adjectives describing Romanticism in opposition to those employed for the Enlightenment. Yet that misses the endurance of many Enlightenment traits throughout this period and right up to the present, especially scientific methodology, individual liberty, and a belief (that now seems naive) of inevitable progress in human affairs.

Yet there is much justification in seeing Romanticism as rocking the boat to the other side, away from the extreme tilt of the Enlightenment. Where the Enlightenment stressed reason, Romanticism valued feeling and emotions. Romantic architecture stressed grandeur and the picturesque as preferable to fine finishes and classical proportions. Music was to use a wide range of dynamics and to express passions and fantasies. Literature dwelt upon legendary heroes, often on a journey, in some wondrous or marvelous world. Everything conspired to stimulate the imagination, especially of a fanciful golden age far removed from the problems of the present.

Romanticism invaded every sphere of life as an all-pervading cultural phenomenon. An important aspect was a new interest in history, particularly that of one's own nation. One's own national culture tended to fascinate people. It was an uphill battle for John Ruskin to advocate the beauties of Venice to English readers. Folk legends and lore gripped the popular imagination, nowhere as successfully as in the novels of Sir Walter Scott. Romanticism meant new respect for the history of the Church, as François Chateaubriand demonstrated in 1802 with his *Génie du Christianisme, ou beautés de la religion Chrétienne*.

Here was a strong defense of Christianity as the source of Western civilization. It was directed against the rationalists of his time. The tide had not yet turned from Enlightenment to Romanticism, but it would within a generation.

By the 1830s it was no longer an insult to describe something as quaint or primitive. In England, Victorians found escape from the social problems of the Industrial Revolution by reassembling a fancied golden age and building gothic railroad stations. As G. K. Chesterton remarked, Victorians saw the Middle Ages "by moonlight." But that was close enough to launch a revolution in taste and to reverse two hundred years or more of preference for replicating the past of classical Greece and Rome. The neo-medieval spirit encompassed Europe and spread to colonies overseas.

It also was a time of strong conservative currents in both Church and state. For many, this meant an attempt to reestablish the power of Rome, the Church, and the clergy. All these had suffered drastically under such progressive monarchs as Joseph II or the French revolutionaries. In France, Napoleon had virtually nationalized Catholicism by adding to the Concordat of 1801 his "Organic Articles" (1802), which gave the state far-reaching control over the Church. Ironically, this meant that liberals in French Catholicism became Ultramontanes, that is, champions of the powers of Rome against a secular state. It is ironical that Gallicanism and Ultramontanism were both liberal causes, but with opposing aims in different centuries. But the only way for the French Church to exercise freedom from the state now appeared to rest in the hands of a strong papacy independent of the government.

It is not surprising that such views were welcomed by Rome. For much of this period the papacy was occupied by two of the most reactionary of popes, Gregory XVI (1831–1846), who decried the notion that the Church needed reform, and Pius IX (1846–1878), who issued the *Syllabus of Errors* in 1864 condemning a wide swath of "progress, liberalism, and modern civilization." Many of the liturgical developments of this period need to be seen in the light of a generally conservative papacy, until John XXIII (1958–1963) threw open the windows of the Church to the modern world and spoke of *aggiornamento*.

We shall take the position that there were essentially two phases to the liturgical movement. The earlier liturgical movement began in the early 1830s and lasted through World War II. Its landmark document of termination might well be the encyclical *Mediator Dei* of Pius XII in

1947. The later liturgical movement began soon after World War II and culminated in Vatican II's Constitution on the Sacred Liturgy of 1963.

Our position is that the two phases of the liturgical movement had different objectives and that quite different personnel were involved. For the earlier liturgical movement, the term "restoration" is crucial. It looked back to restoring treasures lost or overlooked but not to changing the liturgy itself. For this reason, we can call the earlier movement the "Romantic" liturgical movement. It might also be called the "monastic" liturgical movement, since its chief promoters were usually monastics, from Prosper Guéranger (1805–1875) to Odo Casel (1886–1948). The later liturgical movement revolved around the word "reformation" and planned significant changes in the liturgy. Its chief promoters were diocesan priests and a considerable number of lay people. They dreamed of things that the earlier liturgical movement never dared. This phase could justly be labeled the "reformist" or "parochial" liturgical movement.

Obviously, both movements overlap at a number of points: participation is mentioned in the nineteenth century, and restoration is championed after World War II. But there seemed to be a clear shift as *Mediator Dei* marked the end of one era in 1947 and new ideas and leaders took over. Not all the ideas were new (the importance of Scripture) nor the leaders (Romano Guardini). But the ideas were advocated with a new style and vehemence that ultimately led to success at the Second Vatican Council. The distance from *Mediator Dei* to the Constitution on the Sacred Liturgy is great, even though the time-span is but sixteen years.

In this chapter we shall explore the period 1833 to 1947 under the title "The Romantic Era." Much happened during these 114 years, so we must move swiftly, but we shall note the most significant developments.

BACK TO THE SHRINE AND ONWARDS

The liturgical architecture of this period began with a long look back to medieval church buildings; it ended with the first plunge into modern architecture. And just about everything in between was repeated at least once.

The clearest sign of a change came about through the work of an English architect, Augustus Welby Northmore Pugin (1812–1852). Ironically, his writings were probably more influential than his buildings, and he was taken far more seriously by Anglicans than by his fellow Roman Catholics. The serious study of English gothic architecture had been launched by Thomas Richman, a Quaker, who published in 1817 *An Attempt to Discriminate the Styles of Architecture in England*. Pugin's father published similar books with his son's help, and this launched the younger Pugin on a career as an architect. He is best known for the gothic details of the Houses of Parliament, everything from façades to inkwells.

Pugin soon developed a monomania for gothic architecture, coupled with his passion for Catholicism. A visit to Rome was a severe test of his faith because he found so little gothic there. He took up writing forceful treatises on gothic as the only true Christian architecture. His *Contrasts* (1836 and 1841) is probably the most devastating architectural caricature of all time. It contrasts the buildings of his time with their medieval antecedents, and the superiority in beauty and humane character of the latter is graphic. The principle is clear: in gothic "alone we find *the faith of Christianity embodied, and its practices illustrated. . . .* all revived classic buildings . . . are evidences of a lamentable departure from true Catholic principles and feelings."[1]

What Pugin proclaimed in writing, he embodied in his buildings, and these were completely designed down to the last ornament, tile, and chalice. There was nothing wishy-washy about these buildings. They flew in the face of a now long tradition of theatrical churches after the baroque plan. Instead, Pugin plugged for the full medieval church, preferably of thirteenth- or fourteenth-century style, with an elongated chancel and roodscreen. The church was to be again a shrine, with the high altar shielded from view as the holy of holies. Most priests balked at the idea of a roodscreen, so pervasive had the baroque concept of clearly visible church space become.

But Pugin taught a large segment of English and Irish Catholicism to think gothic. His St. Giles, Cheadle, 1840–1846, is a magnificent example of what Pugin could do when he had a generous patron. St. Barnabas Cathedral, Nottingham, England, and in Ireland, St. Mary's Cathedral, Killarney, and St. Aidan's Cathedral, Enniscorthy, are magnificent examples of large-scale buildings combined with exquisite detail.

Pugin was not alone, although it seemed a lonely struggle in his lifetime, and he died insane, toward the end eating only food shaped

---

1. *Contrasts: or, A Parallel between the Noble Edifices of the Middle Ages, and Corresponding Buildings of the Present Day; Shewing the Present Decay of Taste,* 2nd ed. (Edinburgh: John Grant, 1889) 7.

in gothic molds. In France, Eugène-Emmanuel Viollet-le-Duc became the high priest of medieval church architecture both as a writer and restorer of ancient churches. He was intrigued by the structural engineering of gothic churches but, unlike Pugin, relished the possibilities that the emerging use of iron was providing in his own time. In the United States gothic revival flourished especially during the 1840s and 1850s. The best-known example is St. Patrick's Cathedral, New York (1853–1857) by James Renwick, but one has only to think of the cathedrals of Boston, Chicago, or the old cathedral in San Francisco to see how prevalent this style became.

It was an audacious act to turn back the clock six hundred years and to build churches that functioned well for medieval worship while ignoring how much worship had changed in intervening centuries. But proponents were unwilling to concede any advances since a fancied golden age of worship. This set the agenda for much else in nineteenth-century worship. Restoration of past glories, real or fancied, became a priority in music as well. Not everyone gave up on the baroque concept of church space; Cardinal Newman preferred baroque, and eventually Brompton Oratory (1884) and Westminster Cathedral (1903) were built in styles other than gothic. Roodscreens were rarely included and, in some cases where installed, removed in the course of time. But the church as theater was challenged by a return to the church as shrine, with holy things kept at due distance from the people. Anglicans took the type of church Pugin advocated very seriously and built it in British colonies all over the world, even in Athens and Rome.

A battle of styles ensued for the last half of the nineteenth century and well into the twentieth. A drive through the inner suburbs of any major North American city will attest to this conflict, with baroque usually the most prevalent style. For a time Richardsonian romanesque was in the forefront but quickly gave way to eclectic styles. Goths vied with those who built baroque or renaissance buildings, which the goths labeled as "neo-pagan." In most of these late nineteenth-century churches, baroque concepts of space prevailed, with the high altar clearly visible, adjacent to the nave, even though the details might be gothic. The twentieth century saw a second gothic revival, presided over by Ralph Adams Cram, with a much more academically correct gothic. Although Cram designed only five Roman Catholic churches, his writings and examples convinced many that church architecture had to start again where it left off in the sixteenth century.

Frank Lloyd Wright built the first modern church in 1906, but it was a generation and more before modern architecture appealed to Roman Catholics in this country. Rather, the lead went to France with Auguste Perret's Notre Dame at Le Raincy near Paris in 1923. A greater sophistication began to appear with the founding of the Liturgical Arts Society in 1928, which was guided for four decades by Maurice Lavanoux (1894–1974).[2] The early issues of the Society's periodical, *Liturgical Arts,* heralded the sophistication of such recent gothic revival buildings as St. Vincent Ferrer's in New York City. James J. Walsh's *The Thirteenth: Greatest of Centuries* (1907) still held the imagination of most American Catholics. His effusions on gothic architecture (Chapter VI) are Pugin rewarmed. It was not until the 1950s that any conversion to modern art was evident and the half-century time lag in the United States between living art and the Roman Catholic Church began to be bridged.

The leadership fell instead to France and Germany, although even there the widespread acceptance of modern art and architecture came only after World War II. From the standpoint of liturgy, the developments in Germany in the 1920s and 1930s were well ahead of their times. Much of this stemmed from the work of a German priest, Romano Guardini (1885–1968), whose fingerprints are all over the German liturgical movement for forty-five years. Guardini rose to leadership in the German Catholic youth movement, the Quickborn, and in the 1920s he made Burg Rothenfels, a sixteenth-century castle, a vibrant conference center. Guardini worked with an architect, Rudolf Schwarz (1897–1961), to remodel the chapel and knight's hall in 1927. They conceived of white-walled spaces, with the congregation seated on three sides of a freestanding altar, the presider seated behind it.

Schwarz went on to be a pioneer in church architecture, building over sixty churches. These are a revolution, totally unlike any churches before. His Corpus Christi Church at Aachen was consecrated in 1930. It is a rectangular building with no decoration whatsoever—just the altar at one end and a pulpit projecting from a wall. There is nothing to distract from the Mass; everything has been banished but the two liturgical centers. The church is no longer devotional space but entirely focused on the liturgy. In 1938 Schwarz wrote *Vom Bau der Kirche,* articulating his principles: "We cannot continue on from where

---

2. Susan J. White, *Art, Architecture, and Liturgical Reform* (New York: Pueblo Publishing Company, 1990).

the last cathedrals left off. Instead we must enter into the simple things at the source of the Christian life. We must begin anew and our new beginning must be genuine." All that is necessary is a "large, well-proportioned room [and] . . . a table. . . . That is all. Table, space and walls make up the simplest church."[3]

Schwarz lived to build a number of churches after World War II. His contemporary, Dominikus Böhm (1880–1955), also experimented with a variety of entirely new forms, such as parabolic arches and a circular floor plan in St. Engelbert, Riehl (1932). He moved to bringing the congregation around a freestanding altar, as in the church in Ringenberg (1935).[4] Böhm and other architects were experimenting with trapezoidal, elliptical, and circular forms when the war ended church building for a decade. They had clearly thrown off the baggage of historical styles and were starting with the liturgy itself to find the best expressive form to house it.

An early attempt in America was St. Mark's in Burlington, Vermont. Built in 1944, it reflects the liturgical ideas of the pastor, William Tennien, and was designed by the local firm of Freeman, French, and Freeman. St. Mark's is a Greek-cross plan, with the altar at the center. The congregation is on three sides, the choir and pulpit on the fourth. Clerestory windows above the central space flood the sanctuary with light. Twenty years later similar plans would become common; St. Mark's was well ahead of its time.[5]

Architecture was slowly moving beyond the Romanticism of the earlier liturgical movement here and there on a local basis. Once architects were freed of the shackles of historical revivalism, they could begin to build from the liturgy itself rather than from preconceived notions as to how churches should look. Particularly in Germany, where new concepts as to the meaning and purpose of the liturgy were fermenting, it was possible to start over at the beginning and to develop a new architecture based on a clear understanding of the priority of the liturgy over devotions. The buildings were no longer to be distractions to occupy a passive laity while a solitary priest said

3. English edition: *The Church Incarnate,* trans. Cynthia Harris (Chicago: Henry Regnery, 1958) 35–36.

4. Peter Hammond, *Liturgy and Architecture* (London: Barrie and Rockliff, 1960) 60–61.

5. James F. White, *Protestant Worship and Church Architecture* (New York: Oxford University Press, 1964) 153–154.

Mass on their behalf. Instead, the people were there to be part of the action, a reality achieved only several decades later. These early experiments were prophetic architecture!

LITURGICAL EVENTS AND PERSONS
The Romantic liturgical movement had a long pre-history in Germanic lands, where theologians had been discussing the nature of the Church. Much of this new approach was prompted by the rapidly developing discipline of Church history, which had, at long last, stopped being a polemical science for defeating opponents and had begun a careful transcription of what happened in history. The Protestant historian Johann Neander was particularly concerned with the inner life of the Church as the divine life affected persons within it. A convert from Judaism, it was natural for him to write a history of a people, not of institutions or dogmas. Johann Möhler (1796–1838), influenced by Neander, wrote an important treatise, the *Unity of the Church or the Principle of Catholicism* in 1825, in which he stressed the life of the Spirit in the Church as paramount and not the institutional hierarchical Church. One can draw a line from Möhler to Pius XII's *Mystici Corporis* (1943) or the Dogmatic Constitution on the Church (1964), but it is a very zigzag line. Möhler's early work reflects the *Aufklärung*, but he made major contributions to the Romantic liturgical movement and beyond.[6] Möhler marks the beginning of a quite different ecclesiology that places emphasis on the whole Body of Christ as defining the Church and not just the juridical and institutional apparatus, ideas finally officially promulgated at Vatican II, a hundred and forty years later.

The generally accepted launching of the liturgical movement was the formation of a new Benedictine community at Solesmes, France, by Prosper Guéranger in 1833. The timing was significant. John Henry Newman marked the beginning of the Oxford Movement in the Church of England as a sermon preached by John Keble on July 14, 1833, and for a dozen years Newman provided vigorous leadership before leaving the Church of his baptism. In Bavaria, Wilhelm Loehe began a long pastorate in Neuendettelsau in 1837, devoted to making frequent confession and Communion a reality among Lutherans. Nikolai F. S. Grundtvig led a sacramental revival in the Lutheran

6. Nathan Mitchell, "Church, Eucharist, and Liturgical Reform at Mercersburg, 1843–1857" (Ph.D. diss., University of Notre Dame, 1978).

Church of Denmark. Already, on the American frontier, the Disciples of Christ had been formed in 1831 and achieved lasting success in making weekly communion for all the baptized a permanent norm for worship. Something dynamic was in the atmosphere worldwide in the 1830s. This was truly the liturgical decade, exceeded only by the 1960s.

Prosper Guéranger (1805–1875) is a controversial figure. He was first to coin the term "liturgical movement" and often is called its father. He is justly blamed for eliminating the Neo-Gallican liturgies that were thriving in France, and Louis Bouyer speaks derisively of the "amateurish kind of scholarship of Dom Guéranger,"[7] used to caricature and ridicule the Neo-Gallican rites. Bouyer flays him for believing that "to go back to the authentic liturgy meant to go back to medievalism," while what he actually accomplished was to perpetuate the baroque focus on the Real Presence with medieval trappings.[8] Certainly there is much in Guéranger's writings that would be disputed today.

But he is not without vigorous defenders,[9] and much of this becomes understandable in the context of his times. French Catholicism was certainly at a low ebb after the era of Napoleon. The state virtually controlled the Church, monasticism was nonexistent, and piety was at low ebb. Guéranger adopted the Ultramontanism of the liberal Félicitê de Lamennais, with the premise that only firm, centralized papal control could set the Church in France free to be the Church. In doing this, he firmly opposed Gallicanism and Jansenism, which lay behind the liturgical liberties the French Church had enjoyed for two centuries. In the eighty-one French dioceses, more than a score of Missals were in use in the 1830s. Guéranger set out to restore liturgical unity by asserting the necessity of conformity to the Roman liturgical books of 1568 to 1614.

He began publication of *Institutions liturgiques* in 1840 as a liturgical history, but it became propaganda against the Neo-Gallican rites in volume two. Volume three (1851) resumed a more dispassionate

---

7. *Liturgical Piety* (Notre Dame: University of Notre Dame Press, 1966) 65.
8. Ibid., 15.
9. Especially Cuthbert Johnson, *Prosper Guéranger (1805–1875): A Liturgical Theologian* (Rome: Studia Anselmiana, 1984) and R. William Franklin, *Nineteenth-Century Churches* (New York: Garland Publishing, 1987), and a series of articles in *Worship*, 1975–1985.

stance. Pius IX took an active part in squelching the Neo-Gallican rites and strengthening the Solesmes program in the 1853 encyclical *Inter multiplices*. The resistance of the French bishops was overcome; in 1860 the archbishop of Toulouse regretfully wrote: "Because of the pontifical bulls, in the matter of liturgy a bishop has no rights. . . . Seventy-two dioceses of France have already adopted the Roman liturgy. The others have promised to accept it very shortly."[10]

Guéranger began publishing *L'Année liturgique* in 1841, and it eventually reached ten thousand pages. It contains historical and spiritual information and meditations on each day of the year and became an immensely popular work in French and other languages.

Under Guéranger, Solesmes became the center for the study and revival of medieval plainsong. We shall return to this subject.

Perhaps Guéranger's most important work was the restoration of monasticism, for it was the Benedictines who proved to be the first apostles of the liturgical movement. Upon his purchase of the ruined medieval abbey at Solesmes in 1833, Guéranger and five other priests began life in community. In 1837, Gregory XVI made Solesmes an abbey, with Guéranger as abbot and head of the French Benedictine congregation. From the first, Guéranger determined that liturgy was the center of monastic life, and Solesmes was to exemplify this at its best. The Wolter brothers, Maurus and Placid, visited Solesmes and took the advice of Guéranger in refounding the German abbey of Beuron, which in turn founded Maredsous in Belgium and Maria Laach in Germany. Monasteries were revived all over Europe, although as late as 1835 Spain suppressed all monasteries. In 1846, Bavarian monks from Metten Abbey came to America to found St. Vincent's Archabbey at Latrobe, Pennsylvania. Swiss monks founded St. Meinrad's Archabbey in Indiana in 1855. Monks from St. Vincent's founded St. John's Abbey, Collegeville, Minnesota, in 1856, recently the largest Christian monastery in the world. From the start, the liturgy was a basic part of revived monastic life in Europe and America.

As we fast forward into the twentieth century, we encounter two extraordinary individuals, St. Pius X, (pope from 1903 to 1914), and Lambert Beauduin. Both have also been called founders of the liturgical movement; both contributed, but in entirely different ways. In 1903 Pope Pius published a *motu proprio* on sacred music, *Tra le sollecitudini*.

10. Quoted by Franklin, *Nineteenth-Century Churches*, 442.

The "foremost fount" of "the true Christian spirit," he tells us, "is the active participation" in public prayer.[11] As patriarch of Venice, Pius had collaborated with a church musician trained at Solesmes. Pius lays down in the *motu proprio* that Gregorian chant is "the supreme model for sacred music," which "most recent studies have so happily restored to their integrity and purity."[12] Pius mandated the restoration of "the use of the Gregorian chant by the people, so that the faithful may again take a more active part in the ecclesiastical offices, as they were wont to do in ancient times."[13] Operatic-style church music from Italy of the previous century was particularly censured (Rossini, Verdi, etc.). Furthermore, "the language of the Roman Church is Latin. It is therefore forbidden to sing anything whatever in the vernacular in solemn liturgical functions . . . of the Mass and office."[14]

Two years later the decree *Sacra Tridentina Synodus* picked up on the sixth chapter of the twenty-second session of the Council of Trent, which advocated that the faithful receive Communion at each Mass at which they are present. The decree blamed the lapse on the "widespread plague of Jansenism," not on medieval precedent. Frequent, even daily Communion is to be made open to all who are "in a state of grace, and who approach the holy table with a right and devout intention," as long as "they be free from mortal sin."[15]

The importance of this document cannot be overestimated. It led gradually to an ever increasing number of laity receiving Communion on a weekly basis. This was the most important reform in Roman Catholic worship in centuries, although it is almost taken for granted today. Pius X is sometimes known as "the Pope of frequent Communion." By all odds, this is a relatively recent reform. In 1910, Pius enacted that children who had reached the age of reason should receive first confession and first Communion. In another sphere, a rearrangement of the Psalter in the Breviary was mandated by his apostolic constitution *Divino afflatu* in 1911. Pius also attempted to drive out Modernism in biblical and theological work with edicts of 1907 and 1910 and promoted the study of Thomism.

11. Text in R. Kevin Seasoltz, *The New Liturgy: A Documentation, 1903–1965* (New York: Herder and Herder, 1966) 4.
12. Ibid., 5.
13. Ibid., 5–6.
14. Ibid., 6.
15. Ibid., 13.

Lambert Beauduin (1873–1960), by contrast, was an outsider for most of his career, indeed living in ecclesiastical exile from 1931 to 1951, largely because of his fledgling ecumenical activities with the Eastern Churches and with Anglicans. It was a lifetime of powerful opponents and significant friends, including one Angelo Roncalli (later Pope John XXIII), whom he met in 1925.

Some would argue that the twentieth-century liturgical movement really began with a talk Beauduin, as a monk of Mont César, Louvain, gave at Malines, Belgium, in 1909. This led to a liturgical week the next year at Mont César and the publication of the periodical *Liturgical Life*. Beauduin was soon embroiled in controversy because of the one central message he had. This is echoed in the title of his only book, *Liturgy the Life of the Church* (in English translation), published in French in 1914. Liturgy is the central act of the Church and shapes the theology of the laity. While this may seem obvious today, it was disturbing to his contemporaries. If the first rule of politics is "Don't hit their hustle," then Beauduin had offended by challenging all who had a vested interest in promoting various devotions to occupy the laity. The Jesuits felt that their apostleship of prayer was being slighted; proponents of the rosary were equally offended.

Beauduin's "liturgical piety" seems so commonplace today that we take for granted sentences such as "the active participation in the liturgical life of the Church is a capital factor in the super-natural life of the Christian."[16] Vatican II hardly said it better. But Beauduin spent his life defending and spreading such dangerous ideas. "His major contribution was to have put into the hands of the people and their pastors what had been the private domain of a few specialists. Under his deft guidance the liturgical movement became solidly grounded in theology."[17]

If Beauduin had a talent for popularizing theological ideas, he soon had collaborators of substantial theological abilities, especially two Germans, Romano Guardini and the Benedictine Odo Casel. Guardini had produced in 1923 one of the classics of the liturgical movement, *The Spirit of the Liturgy*. Asserting that "it is to liturgical worship that pre-eminence of right belongs," he goes on to discuss the emotional

16. *Liturgy the Life of the Church,* trans. Virgil Michel (Collegeville, Minn.: The Liturgical Press, 1926) 8.

17. Sonya A. Quitslund, *Beauduin: A Prophet Vindicated* (New York: Newman Press, 1973) 30–31.

restraint of public worship. In a chapter named "The Playfulness of the Liturgy," Guardini compares liturgy to a child's play, which has no purpose. In the "supernatural childhood before God" the Christian community acts "not for the sake of humanity, but for the sake of God."[18]

Odo Casel was a monk of Maria Laach Abbey, which under Ildefons Herwegen (abbot from 1913 to 1946) became the great German center of the liturgical movement. The study of the mystery religions of ancient Greece and Rome led Casel to a different vision of Christianity than the Scholastics had. For him, Christianity is a mystery that the liturgy makes present. Instead of a space mystery—that is, how does Christ become present in bread and wine?—he concentrated on liturgy as a time mystery—that is, how do the events of salvation history become our contemporaries? Casel pointed the way toward new foundations for thinking about liturgy, foundations on which others were to build.[19] He did not favor the use of the vernacular. Casel's death on Easter morning in 1948 marked the end of the monastic or Romantic liturgical movement.

These European developments were largely imported to the United States by Virgil Michel (1890–1938), a monk of St. John's Abbey, Collegeville, Minnesota. Michel not only kept communications open with the European liturgical pioneers but contributed a distinctively American flavor in linking liturgy to social justice. "More than any other U.S. Catholic of the twentieth century, Virgil Michel reminded the Church of the intimate bond between liturgical worship and social justice."[20] Keith F. Pecklers adds that "it was precisely its social consciousness that became its [the American liturgical movement's] hallmark when viewed from other parts of the world."[21]

While studying at Sant' Anselmo in Rome, Michel met Beauduin, who inspired him with the concept of the Mystical Body of Christ. After visiting various Benedictine abbeys in Europe, Michel returned to St. John's in 1925. That year he called a Christmas conference of two others interested in the liturgical apostolate, a diocesan priest, Martin

18. (New York: Sheed and Ward, 1935) 177.

19. *The Mystery of Christian Worship and Other Writings* (Westminster, Md.: Newman Press, 1962).

20. William Franklin, *The Social Question: Essays on Capitalism and Christianity by Fr. Virgil Michel, O.S.B.* (Collegeville, Minn.: St. John's University, 1987) ii.

21. *The Unread Vision: The Liturgical Movement in the United States of America: 1926–1955* (Collegeville, Minn.: The Liturgical Press, 1998) 149.

Hellriegel of St. Louis (1890–1981) and Gerald Ellard (1894–1963), a Jesuit who had been exposed to the same ideas as Michel during study in Europe. Hellriegel, who had been inspired by Guardini, Casel, and visits to Maria Laach, spent twenty-two years as chaplain to nuns in O'Fallon, Missouri, and pastored Holy Cross parish from 1940 on. He made Holy Cross into a model liturgical parish.[22] Ellard was the most scholarly of the American leaders but combined this talent with popular books, such as *The Mass of the Future, The Mass in Transition, Christian Life and Worship,* and *Men at Work at Worship.* He spent his career teaching at St. Mary's College in Kansas and St. Louis University.[23]

This triumvirate launched in 1926 the periodical *Orate Fratres,* which became the flagship of the American liturgical movement. It attracted a loyal following and supported the morale of the weary and discouraged. It was controversial (some bishops forbade seminarians to read it), but not radical as to changes in the liturgy. St. John's Abbey also established The Liturgical Press. Michel kept in close contact with Dorothy Day and the Catholic Worker Movement and fervently stressed the links between genuine worship and social justice. Michel died, exhausted, in 1938, but by then there were many to inherit his mantle. In 1940 the Liturgical Conference was founded at a meeting in the basement of the Chicago Cathedral. The twenty-fifth annual meeting attracted twenty thousand people to St. Louis in 1964. The small group of conspirators who had begun in 1926 had picked up many valuable coworkers along the way.

In 1943 Pius XII issued two very important encyclicals. *Mystici Corporis* stresses the corporate nature of the Mystical Body of Christ, although with considerable emphasis on the hierarchical nature of the Church. *Divino afflante Spiritu* unlocked Catholic biblical scholarship from the deep freeze in which Pius X had locked it almost forty years before in his fight against Modernism. Henceforth the original texts rather than the Vulgate were to be the basis of scholarship. This encyclical prompted a major biblical movement within Catholicism that contributed in many ways to the advancement of the liturgical movement.

22. Noel Hackman Barrett, "The Contribution of Martin B. Hellriegel to the American Catholic Liturgical Movement" (Ph.D. diss., St. Louis University, 1981).

23. John Leo Klein, "The Role of Gerald Ellard (1894–1963) in the Development of the Contemporary American Catholic Liturgical Movement" (Ph.D. diss., Fordham University, 1971).

Pius XII brought out the first encyclical devoted entirely to worship in *Mediator Dei*, published in 1947. It was a cautious, basically conservative document, taking one step backward for every two forward. But the important thing was that it acknowledged the existence of the liturgical movement, even crediting it to "the devoted zeal of certain monasteries of the renowned Benedictine Order."[24] But it viewed "with anxiety and some apprehension" innovation and lack of prudence. It admitted the historical development of the liturgy, defended the use of Latin as "an imposing sign of unity," and condemned returning to such ancient customs as a table-like altar. It denied that the laity "possess the power of the priesthood," since the priest is "lower than Christ, but higher than the people." But the laity do indeed "offer the Sacrifice *through* the priest and . . . in a certain sense, they offer it *with* him." Private Masses were defended and the idea that "the general Communion of the faithful is to be regarded as the culminating point of the whole celebration" was denied. Communion before or after Mass was seen as unavoidable, if not particularly desirable. Various eucharistic devotions, especially Benediction, were commended.

Mediator Dei made it clear that the liturgical movement had arrived and was now given official, if cautious, blessing. But it was more a backward-looking document over the terrain the restorationist liturgical movement had traversed so far. The encyclical gave no indication that much more drastic reforms were soon to be advocated and shortly thereafter enacted by the reformist liturgical movement.

RHYTHMS OF TIME AND DEVOTIONS

The nineteenth century saw an accentuation of those feasts and devotions that had so horrified the Enlightenment. The cult of the Sacred Heart, for example, reached its highest following as various popes extended its observance. Pius IX made the feast a day of universal observance in 1856. His successor, Leo XIII, made it a double of the first class in 1889 and in 1899 consecrated all humanity to the Sacred Heart. And Pius XI gave it a privileged octave in 1928. New texts for the Mass and Office were provided by both Pius IX and Pius XI. An optional feast of the Eucharistic Heart of Jesus was added in 1921.

Another feast was the Most Precious Blood. Pius IX had fled Rome in 1848 in the face of efforts for a free and united Italy. He took refuge in Gaeta along with the superior of the Congregation of the Most

24. (London: Catholic Truth Society, 1954) 8.

Precious Blood. When, at Pius's behest, the French occupied Rome on June 30, 1849, Pius choose out of gratitude to make the next Sunday a universal feast of the Most Precious Blood.

This was also the period in which Marian devotions reached their highest peak in recent history. The central aspect of many of these devotions seems to have been Mary's submissiveness to the will of God. How much this was a subtle statement of woman's role in nineteenth society can be debated, but Mary's subservience rendered her an ambiguous image for empowerment.

Two important Marian dogmas were proclaimed: the Immaculate Conception in 1854 and the Assumption in 1950. Despite the opposition of St. Bernard and St. Thomas Aquinas, the doctrine that Mary was conceived without taint of sin had become widespread by the fifteenth century and had acquired a Mass and Office by 1476. Clement XI made the Immaculate Conception a feast of universal obligation in 1708. By the bull *Ineffabilis Deus,* Pius IX promulgated the Immaculate Conception as dogma on December 8, 1854. Referring to a tradition of commemorating the death of the Virgin, Pius XII promulgated the dogma of the assumption of Mary "body and soul into heavenly glory" in *Munificentissimus Deus* on November 1, 1950, and provided new Mass texts for the feast. An account of Mary's death had appeared in the Roman Breviary of 1568, and the feast and octave of August 15 had been observed in the West since the ninth century.

This was also a period in which various Marian apparitions occurred. Most famous was that of Lourdes, France, in 1858 to St. Bernadette Soubirous. That led to millions of pilgrims and miraculous cures of the sick. The feast of Our Lady of Lourdes was made universal by Pius X in 1907. A twentieth-century apparition occurred in Fatima, Portugal, in 1917 to three children, encouraging penance, the rosary, and devotion to the Immaculate Heart of Mary. Pius XII in 1944 made the Immaculate Heart a universal feast for Catholics of the Latin Rite. A whole host of other Marian feasts had been added to the calendar from the late seventeenth century through the time of Pius XII. Our Lady of Mercy, the Seven Sorrows of the Blessed Virgin, and the Motherhood of Mary are just a few.[25]

25. Pierre Jounel, "The Veneration of Mary," in *The Liturgy and Time,* vol. 4: *The Church at Prayer,* ed. A. G. Martimort (Collegeville, Minn.: The Liturgical Press, 1986) 144–147.

Quite a different history lies behind the feast of Christ the King, instituted by Pius XI in 1925 in the context of a jubilee year. It was meant to stress the lordship of Christ over all humanity. Lacking the background of long tradition, it has yet to become the center of much liturgical or devotional life.

A major theological focus in the 1930s and 1940s was the theological work of Odo Casel, monk of Maria Laach. He devoted much scholarly writing to the mystery of time as the means of encounter with Christ. As a monk, he observed a daily cycle of time as well as weekly and yearly ones. In his theological writings he explored how the Christian community rehearses liturgically the events of salvation history and thereby recaptures them in their saving power. The primeval saving act is again made present to us in our liturgical celebration of it. "The church does what the Lord did, and thereby makes his act present. Christ himself is present and acts through the church, his *ecclesia*, while she acts with him. Both carry out the action."[26] This is both communal and personal; we relive sacred history by making the events again available in their power to save. Casel never specifies exactly how this happens, but he introduces an important understanding of time as mystery. Today we see the Hebrew Scriptures as full of this same concept; Casel, instead, looked for analogies in the pagan mystery religions of the first Christian centuries.

THE MASS

An anomaly was the addition of three prayers at the end of the Mass by Leo XIII in 1886. Jungmann puts it delicately: "We cannot affirm that these additions have any intrinsic relationship to what has gone before."[27] These so-called Leonine prayers address the Virgin and St. Michael. They provide a good mirror of late-nineteenth-century piety. During this period the Mass was seen as something the priest did for the people while they occupied themselves in various devotions. There were even directives in some dioceses forbidding the giving of Communion during the Mass. For the early liturgical pioneers, much of the crusade centered on making the liturgy itself the focus rather

26. "The Meaning of the Mystery," in *The Mystery of Christian Worship and Other Writings by Odo Casel, O.S.B.,* ed. Burkhard Neunheuser (Westminster, Md.: Newman Press, 1962) 141.

27. Joseph A. Jungmann, *The Mass of the Roman Rite* (New York: Benziger Brothers, 1955) 2:458.

than such devotions as the rosary. As late as 1900 it was still forbidden to translate the Missal. The devout had to be content with spiritual Communion, Benediction, or novenas. In 1913 one leading Jesuit called the liturgical renewal a "Benedictine innovation."[28]

It was extremely helpful to be able to cite Pius X as authority for a much more participatory approach to the Mass. After all, he had clearly stated, a decade before, that "the faithful assemble for acquiring this [true Christian] spirit from its foremost and indispensable fount, which is the *active participation* in the holy mysteries and in the public and solemn prayer of the Church."[29] The 1905 decree promoting daily Communion (in the absence of mortal sin) was a major turning point. The habits of a thousand years were in the process of being reversed. Hitherto the average Western Catholic had received Communion every Easter and, perhaps, at Pentecost and Christmas. The especially devout might receive more often, but usually visits to the Blessed Sacrament sufficed. Alphonsus Liguori had popularized the notion that this could be done in private at almost any time at anyone's convenience.

Frequent Communion for the majority of Roman Catholic laity dates only from the beginning of this century. It received considerable resistance from many priests as an unnecessary delay in saying Mass. Furthermore, an emphasis on frequent Communion appeared to conflict with prevailing devotions to Mary and the Sacred Heart of Jesus.[30] Only slowly was frequent Communion achieved. Until Vatican II it was the chief liturgical innovation of the twentieth century. Other means of participation began to open up under Pius X, especially the attitude to "pray the Mass." The restoration of Gregorian chant was not chiefly for aesthetic reasons but to add another dimension of participation by replacing the highly professionalized operatic music of the time with congregational singing.

A major assist in praying the Mass was *My Sunday Missal,* which a Brooklyn priest, Joseph F. Stedman (1896–1946), published in 1932. Prohibitions against translations had lapsed after 1900. The Stedman missal was a model of clarity in helping thread one's way through the

28. Quitslund, *Beauduin,* 18.

29. *Tra le sollecitudini,* translation in Seasoltz, *The New Liturgy,* 4. Italics added.

30. Joseph Dougherty, "From Altar-Throne to Table: The Campaign for Frequent and Daily Communion in the American Roman Catholic Church: 1894–1926" (Ph.D. diss., University of Notre Dame, 1999), especially 389–440.

Mass, aided by art work drawn by Adé Bethune (1914–2002). Father Stedman was "the apostle of the missal," making its contents known in English (and eventually in many other languages) to millions of worshipers to whom it had previously been an unknown book.[31]

Pius XII gave fresh impulse from Rome. Bernard Botte claims that "the liturgical reform begun by Pius X seemed to have come to a halt, and the Congregation of Rites was immobilized by rigid rubricism. . . . [Mediator Dei] was received as an encouragement to the liturgical movement, and the possibility of restarting the reform begun by Pius X."[32] Part Two, the longest section, dealt exclusively with the Eucharist. It strongly promoted frequent Communion, though it encouraged spiritual Communion and other devotions.

Mention was made of "the dialogue Mass," which by this time was beginning to appear in some avant-garde parishes. The priest would lead, with Latin greetings and responses by priest and people. This provided a much higher level of participation than simply silently reading *My Sunday Missal* or the *St. Andrew Missal* in order to "follow the priest." If the dialogue Mass seems like a small step today, it was hailed as a great leap forward in the 1940s and 1950s. The epistle and gospel were often read in the vernacular after the Latin readings. Writing in 1954, Ernest Koenker still regarded the dialogue Mass as a rarity in the United States, though common in Germany (75 percent of parishes).[33] It was still newsworthy when found in American parishes. The dialogue Mass was, however, a portent of what was soon to come.

RHYTHMS OF THE LIFE CYCLE

Much less concern was evident during this period over the rites of initiation. Indeed, such concerns had to await rediscovered interest in the nature of the Church. Equally important, although unrecognized at the time, was the slow subversive work of modern liturgical scholarship. The identification of an ancient document in 1910 by the German E. Schwartz, and the confirmation in 1916 of this discovery by the English monk R. H. Connolly, was momentous. For this document

31. Frances Krumpelman, "Joseph Stedman: My Sunday Missal," in *Leaders of the Liturgical Movement* (Chicago: Liturgy Training Publications, 1990) 217–224.

32. *From Silence to Participation* (Washington: Pastoral Press, 1988) 78–79.

33. *The Liturgical Renaissance in the Roman Catholic Church* (Chicago: University of Chicago Press, 1954) 158.

was the long-lost *Apostolic Tradition,* attributed to the third-century writer Hippolytus of Rome. This discovery of ancient practice was to give enormous impetus to reforming the process of initiation fifty years later.[34]

In 1897, Leo XIII advocated confirmation before first Communion as better preparing one for the Eucharist. The Code of Canon Law of 1917 provided for confirmation at about seven years of age (Canon 788) or, if death was imminent, at an earlier age. Yet the general practice was to have first Communion precede confirmation,[35] and Pius X's encouragement in 1910 of the reception of Communion by children strengthened the priority of first Communion. Even today a satisfactory fitting together of initiation rites lies in the future for the West.

Many more of the colorful local marriage customs (see *Madame Bovary*) were lost as the Roman Ritual came into full vigor in France in the second half of the nineteenth century. The 1917 Code did prescribe "the rites approved and prescribed by the Church or laudable customs" (Canon 1100). Less uniformity was achieved in marriage rites than in any others. Stevenson cites several unusual nineteenth-century rites in Romania and Poland.[36] Rome added in 1914 an appendix to the Roman Ritual with special prayers for occasions of "mixed marriage" and during Lent. A massive amount of regulation appeared in the Code with regard to marriage, but most of it dealt with moral rather than liturgical concerns.

The death of a Christian continued to devolve more and more into the commercial sphere. Embalming became common in America during the Civil War, and the Christian community's care for the dead became less and less tangible. The rise of Victorian cemeteries instead of churchyards shows in magnificent necropolises in Glasgow, London, and Cambridge, Massachusetts (Mount Auburn). If all were equally dead, they were not equal in death as far as monuments were concerned. Henceforth the dead would rest in the suburbs of the community's consciousness rather than surrounding them in the churchyard.

---

34. Bernard Botte, *La Tradition apostolique de Saint Hippolyte* (Münster: Aschendorffsche Verlagsbuchhandlung, 1963) x–xi.

35. Gerard Austin, *Anointing with the Spirit* (New York: Pueblo Publishing Company, 1985) 29.

36. Kenneth Stevenson, *Nuptial Blessing* (London: Alcuin Club/ S.P.C.K., 1982) 176–177.

The increasing frequency of Communion under Pius X naturally led to an increase in the number of confessions, "probably reaching its peak in the early 1950s."[37] Already there was a growing anxiety about prevailing practice as scholarly research probed the early practices of public penance and wondered whether such a drastic shift as the medieval Church of the West had made had been well advised. It became more apparent why the Fourth Lateran Council of 1215 had tied confession so closely to the Eucharist, but was a penitential Eucharist desirable? Pius XII promoted the prevailing practice of devotional confession as a means of cleansing the soul. Awareness of the Eastern Churches' stress on the role of the Spirit and knowledge of the new science of psychology raised questions about Western practice. During the time of Pius XII, unofficial experiments with communal forms of reconciliation had begun in the Low Countries.

Much less changed was extreme unction, which continued to live up to its name, even though the Code of 1917 did admit the possibility that the sacrament could be repeated if the recipient recovered (Canon 940). Charles Gusmer concludes of this period, "In all truth, extreme unction became a pastoral failure."[38] It had gone as far as possible in one direction, and no evolution was possible without radical redirection.

CHURCH MUSIC

Church music became a particularly important item in this period. The Romantic era had seen the rise of composers as popular idols, most notably Richard Wagner. Their tone painting focused on emotional music, achieved by exaggerated dynamics and chromaticism, to produce music that was highly dramatic. These very technical demands removed much Romantic music from the capacity of all but highly trained professionals.

In the mid-nineteenth century a reaction in the form of the Cecilian Movement, which saw sixteenth-century polyphony as the golden age of Catholic music, set in and sought to imitate polyphony. But this soon proved to be a dead-end road.

The operatic style eventually became so pervasive that tunes from Donizetti or Bellini operas were being adapted for the ordinary parts

37. James Dallen, *The Reconciling Community* (New York: Pueblo Publishing Company, 1986) 186.
38. *And You Visited Me* (New York: Pueblo Publishing Company, 1984) 36.

of the Mass. Hector Berlioz, Franz Liszt (who eventually became a priest), Charles Gounod (who intended to become a priest), César Franck, and Camille Saint-Saëns all wrote religious music in operatic style. Two notable exceptions were Gabriel Fauré and Anton Bruckner, who avoided the sentimental overkill of their contemporaries and wrote music of liturgical integrity.[39]

An alternative direction was developing. Medieval plainsong had the same Romantic appeal as did gothic architecture. In the aftermath of Trent, Palestrina and others had contributed to the Medicean edition of the Gradual, confusing much of medieval chant with the musical conventions of their own time, a confusion only amplified by eighteenth-century revisions. As late as 1871, the musicologist Friedrich Pustet published a corrupt edition, which won official approval and a thirty-year monopoly for publishing rights of chant. But those slow patient termites, the scholars, working out of sight within the Church, finally brought down these false conceptions of plainsong. The monks at Solesmes compared hundreds of medieval manuscripts to show that the overly elaborate melodies, metrical rhythms, and instrumental accompaniments that had been grafted onto chant in recent centuries were as fallacious as rococo plaster ceilings.

Pius X had been deeply interested in music as a young priest and as pope wrote more on sacred music "than all the popes together."[40] A Jesuit, Angelo De Santi, had been moved by the reforms proposed at Solesmes. These were in drastic conflict with the Ratisbon editions published by Pustet, which had hitherto been sanctioned by Rome. De Santi had helped formulate many of the principles that appeared in Pius X's *motu proprio* on church music, *Tra le sollecitudini*. Only three months after his election as pope, Pius X began the reform of church music with this *motu proprio*, on which De Santi collaborated.[41]

Pius X demanded a return to Gregorian chant as recovered by the monks of Solesmes and made it clear that this was the "chant proper to the Roman Church" and that "the more closely a composition for Church approaches in its movement, inspiration and savor the Gregorian form, the more sacred and liturgical it is; and the more out

---

39. Andrew Wilson-Dickson, *The Story of Christian Music* (Oxford: Lion Publishing, 1992) 124–129.

40. Robert F. Hayburn, *Papal Legislation on Sacred Music* (Collegeville, Minn.: The Liturgical Press, 1979) 195.

41. Ibid., 219–231.

of harmony it is with that supreme model, the less worthy it is of the temple."[42] Not only was Gregorian chant given the highest priority but the Solesmes method triumphed over the lush Ratisbon approach. André Mocquereau of Solesmes became the twentieth-century authority, and Solesmes supplied the sources of subsequent Vatican editions of the chant books.

A major effort soon developed to make these texts available to all churches everywhere. Many were enlisted in the effort to make Gregorian chant available in even the smallest of churches around the world. The chief exponent in the United States was Justine Ward (1879–1975), who with Mother Georgia Stevens, R.S.C.J., founded in 1916 the Pius X Institute of Liturgical Music at Manhattanville College of the Sacred Heart. Her "Ward Method" was taught to millions of Roman Catholic school children. She and Mother Stevens may well be the most important woman liturgical reformers of this century.

In retrospect, it all seems to have been a good run down the wrong road. Except for a few monastic communities, Gregorian chant virtually vanished in the wake of Vatican II. It had been kept resolutely in Latin, and it was an entirely alien musical form in a dead language for the cultures in which it was introduced. After Vatican II, Justine Ward wrote in disgust: "They want to lower the prayer of the Church to mud level in order to attract the most ignorant people."[43] The change of the name of the Gregorian Institute of America in 1968 to G.I.A. Publishers was a sign of changed times. A mighty effort had been made for sixty years to make Gregorian chant the usual music of Roman Catholics, but it was an impossible task.

PREACHING

Preaching has taken many forms in different cultures. The nineteenth and first half of the twentieth centuries have seen continual adaptation. As an Anglican, John Henry Newman had led the Oxford Movement largely by his appeal to students as a preacher while vicar of St. Mary's Oxford. His sermons were published as *Parochial and Plain Sermons*.

Much of Catholicism in this country had been shaped by the experience of immigrants from countries other than England. It was an extraordinary challenge and opportunity. In many cases priests

42. *Tra le sollecitudini*, translation in Seasoltz, *The New Liturgy*, 5.

43. Quoted in Pierre Combe, *Justine Ward and Solesmes* (Washington: The Catholic University of America Press, 1987) 134.

adapted the same revival techniques that Protestant circuit riders used so successfully in the nineteenth century to Christianize a continent. A favorite device was the parish mission. In a sense this was not uniquely American; Alphonsus Liguori had been famous as a mission preacher in eighteenth-century Italy, and the Franciscans and Dominicans long before that. Liguori's missions ran for two or three weeks at a time, with preaching morning and evening. His favorite theme was punishment for sin.

Somewhat similar techniques were used in this country but were given an American flavor partly because of the Frontier Tradition in Protestant worship. Its greatest evangelist, Charles G. Finney, spoke of one of his converts, Charles Walworth, a lawyer from Rochester, who became a priest: "He has been for years laboring zealously to promote revivals of religion . . . holding protracted meetings; and, as he told me himself, . . . trying to accomplish in the Roman Catholic church what I was endeavoring to accomplish in the Protestant church."[44] Many members of religious orders, especially Jesuits, Redemptorists, Paulists, and Passionists, operated in fashions similar to those of the itinerant Protestant circuit riders and with similar successes.

Indeed, the type of preaching often was what we would today call hellfire and damnation (which certainly has not vanished from either tent revivals or television). Jay Dolan concludes that the sermons at parish missions changed little over the years and "followed a similar plan, preaching the great truths of salvation which aimed at a religious revival by bringing people face to face with the evil of sin and the harshness of God's judgment."[45] It produced a lasting strain in American Catholicism as revival religion "became the most popular religious experience of Catholic Americans in the second half of the nineteenth century."[46]

A major factor in shaping Roman Catholic preaching was the growing biblical movement. Pent-up forces were released in 1943 when Pius XII, in *Divino afflante Spiritu*, freed Catholic biblical scholarship from the bonds with which Pius X had tied it. In the next decades enormous strides were made in Catholic biblical scholarship. This

44. Quoted from Finney's *Memoirs* by Jay P. Dolan, *Catholic Revivalism: The American Experience, 1830-1900* (Notre Dame: University of Notre Dame Press, 1978) xv.
    45. Ibid., 76–77.
    46. Ibid., 89.

encouraged a growing practice of the laity reading the Bible and the increasing popularity of biblical study groups.

The consequences for homiletics took time to be realized, but the way was being prepared for a much more exegetical style of preaching after Vatican II instead of the moralistic homilies so common before the Council. In a sense, it was a switch from "Don't do this" to "Christ did that for us," from condemnation to proclamation. The new focus on the Bible as central in the life of all Christians has had enormous consequences. Three movements—biblical, ecumenical, and liturgical—found many common aims and began to coalesce.

A pioneer in bringing these movements together was the Austrian priest Pius Parsch. His monthly, *Bible and Liturgy,* was popular in Germany, but he is best known in the English-speaking world for his five volumes, *The Church's Year of Grace,* which offered meditations on the texts for Mass and the Office for each day of the year. Parsch saw an intrinsic unity in liturgy as commentary on Scripture and Scripture as central in liturgy.[47]

PUBLIC PRAYER

Very little had changed in the Roman Breviary since 1568 except for minor tinkering. Benedict XIV's attempt to revise it was cut short by his death. But under Pius X, the bull *Divino afflatu,* published in 1911, made major revisions. Ironically, many of them came from the Neo-Gallican Parisian Breviary of 1736, which Guéranger had done so much to abolish. Much of the reform had to do with the distribution of the psalms according to the hour and day. Indeed, Batiffol calls this "the one truly innovating part of the reforms of Pius X."[48] Robert Taft finds this "a shocking departure from almost universal Christian tradition"[49] but admits that major improvements were pruning the growth of the sanctoral cycle and restoration of the primacy of Sunday. The length of the Offices was shortened somewhat. The Psalter was recited on a weekly basis, with far fewer interruptions except for the most major of feasts.

---

47. Michael Kwatera, "Pius Parsch, Evangelist of the Liturgy," in *Leaders of the Liturgical Movement* (Chicago: Liturgy Training Publications, 1990) 29–35.

48. Pierre Batiffol, *History of the Roman Breviary* (London: Longmans, Green and Company, 1912) 325.

49. Robert Taft, *The Liturgy of the Hours in East and West* (Collegeville, Minn.: The Liturgical Press, 1986) 312–313.

The average lay person could not have cared less; the Breviary was only for clergy and religious. And except for those living in monastic communities, it was usually read in private. Although Guéranger had succeeded in restoring choral recitation of the Office as the heart of monasticism, this was generally regarded as a monastic peculiarity. But the plainchant, so carefully cultivated at Solesmes, was to have a major impact on attempts to introduce congregational singing at parish Masses.

Another possibility had been proliferating on an unofficial basis, namely, devotional manuals and prayer books for lay people. Especially after 1830, these books enjoyed widespread popularity, particularly as immigration swelled the numbers of Roman Catholics in America. Many of these books included traditional items, such as the seven penitential psalms, the litany of the saints, morning and evening prayer, and prayers at Mass. Most included the rosary and Benediction, and the amount of devotional materials tended to increase with time: "prayer books published after 1840 were more likely to include other Marian devotions (e.g., the seven dolors, the Immaculate Conception, the Immaculate Heart of Mary, and one or more scapulars) and other devotions to the Blessed Sacrament (e.g., the forty hours devotion and visits to the Blessed Sacrament) as well."[50] To many of the prayers, indulgences had been attached, especially under Pius IX. The *Raccolta* had initially been published in 1807. It contained all the indulgenced prayers and devotions, and many of these were passed on in various vernacular translations.

The use of the prayer books was mostly in private, but increasingly novenas (nine days of public or private devotions) came to be an important part of Church life. They were arranged for special events in the Church year or special occasions in the community's life. Most asked for particular favors. Many had indulgences attached. Since they were generally in the vernacular, they had a more direct grip on the imagination of many people than the incomprehensible (and often inaudible) Latin of the Mass. Louis Bouyer vehemently criticizes these devotions: "These new devotions involved a mentality not only foreign to that of the liturgy but almost irreconcilable with it. It is when people are no longer in touch with the authentic spirit of the

50. Ann Taves, *The Household of Faith: Roman Catholic Devotions in Mid-Nineteenth Century America* (Notre Dame: University of Notre Dame Press, 1986) 24.

liturgy that such devotions are developed; but once these are in possession, a return to the liturgy is almost impossible."[51] Or so it seemed when Bouyer's *Liturgical Piety* first went to press in 1954. But much was to change in a very short time.

51. *Liturgical Piety* (Notre Dame: University of Notre Dame Press, 1966) 248.

Chapter Five

The Journey to the Second Vatican Council

In 1951, after twenty-five years of publication, the name of the leading North American liturgical periodical was changed from *Orate Fratres* to *Worship*. This name change received some negative comment and a few cancellations because "worship" was still a Protestant word at that time.[1] (The sexist problem of the title had not yet become apparent.) It was a significant shift: Latin contradicted what was fast becoming the end of the liturgical movement, active participation, and what was obviously the means, the vernacular.

Our thesis is that the sixteen years between *Mediator Dei* (1947) and the Constitution on the Sacred Liturgy (1963) are the pivot between a liturgical movement that was largely restorationist and the revolution that occurred after the Second Vatican Council, in which every item in Roman Catholic worship was taken apart and reassembled. We describe the spirit of this sixteen-year interval as that of "reformation," again a word once a Protestant monopoly. The reformist ethos of this period was so different from the 114 years preceding it that we refer to it as the later liturgical movement. The Middle Ages had fallen from being idealized as the high tide of the liturgy to being looked down on as the lowest ebb of public worship. Scholarship had prepared the way for much of this shift, but even more was dictated by the realities of parish life. Some even sensed the humor of trying to get Americans to participate in worship by singing in Latin and using a musical form just as foreign.

Equally important was the change in postwar culture as the world slowly recovered from the trauma of World War II. America entered a

1. Kathleen Hughes, *The Monk's Tale: A Biography of Godfrey Diekmann, O.S.B.* (Collegeville, Minn.: The Liturgical Press, 1992) 119.

booming economy, and the West began to experience an optimistic can-do mentality only slightly clouded by Sputnik in 1957. Rising standards of living, high educational possibilities, and the entry of Roman Catholics into the mainstream of American social, economic, and political life were reflected in the religious boom of the 1950s and 1960s. The times gave birth to an optimistic atmosphere and an impatience with resistance to change.

This was the era in which the background work for Vatican II was being prepared. No one knew a council was imminent, although Lambert Beauduin predicted in 1957 that his friend Angelo Roncalli would be elected pope and would call a council. We now can see how much crucial work had gone on in the years immediately prior to Vatican II. Most of the changes in worship could never have happened had not a new agenda arisen in the years since *Mediator Dei*. Our purpose in this chapter is to explore how these changes came about. Much of this section deals with changes in attitudes and the vigorous promotion of (and opposition to) new ideas. A whole new personnel entered the picture; in the previous chapter the story was almost entirely that of roles exercised by clergy in religious orders. Now diocesan clergy and laity, even women, became leaders. These liturgical pioneers, many of whom represented a second generation on the American scene, often lived to see their work crowned with success after Vatican II. A few (for example, Reynold Hillenbrand, William Busch) were appalled at the excesses of the late 1960s. And some are still rejoicing with the Church on earth for the fruits produced from the seeds they planted in the forties, fifties, and sixties.

One cannot deny that the later liturgical movement adopted essentially a Protestant agenda for worship. Much of the opposition came from those who claimed that the changes proposed were Protestant and hence unacceptable, sometimes on that basis alone. The same concept of popular participation in the common prayer of the Church had motivated almost everything Luther, Calvin, and Cranmer accomplished in worship in the sixteenth century, and maybe even more the things they had hoped to achieve. Use of the vernacular, congregational hymnody, an emphasis on preaching the Word of God, frequent communion, and a general raising of the priestly role of all the baptized—all these had also been priorities for most of the Protestant reformers of that century.

It should not be overlooked that the later liturgical movement caught fire primarily in countries like the United States and Germany, where there was a Protestant majority. In countries such as Spain and Ireland, it was little heard of. The leaders often had close Protestant contacts. Beauduin had spent time in England during World War I and was deeply involved in ecumenism with leading Anglicans. As a boy, H. A. Reinhold recounted "a favorite pastime was to visit Protestant churches on Sunday afternoons,"[2] where the preaching and church music left a lasting impression. The American liturgical movement was largely a Midwestern phenomenon in the midst of the Protestant heartland. Despite prohibitions, Catholics went to weddings and funerals of Protestant relatives and were aware of alternatives to Latin Masses.

If we argue that the second liturgical movement bought largely into a Protestant liturgical agenda, espousing many of the worship ideals of the sixteenth-century Reformation, we must also point out that the compliment was quickly returned in the years after Vatican II, when many of the new reforms in the Roman Rite were quickly adopted by mainline Protestants, especially the changes revolving around the Sunday Lectionary, multiple options, and contemporary speech. The degree of confluence in the last thirty years has been amazing.

BEGINNING OVER AGAIN IN ARCHITECTURE

The period after World War II saw the rebuilding of much of Europe, including the repair and rebuilding of thousands of churches. The war-torn countries and especially Germany provided a vast laboratory for new experiments in liturgical architecture. In many cases this was an architecture of poverty, resources being extremely limited. A church was built for ragpickers in France out of scrap lumber for $150. Rainer Senn, a Swiss architect, wrote in 1963, *"The limitation of financial means generally has a positive effect on the appearance of a building . . . for in this way the architect learns the 'discipline of conditions of privation':* to examine thoroughly the requirements of a building in order to find fundamentals."[3]

2. *H.A.R.: The Autobiography of Father Reinhold* (New York: Herder and Herder, 1968) 8.

3. "The Spirit of Poverty," *Churchbuilding* 9 (1963) 23. *L'Art Sacré* devoted the issue of January–February 1958 to "La transparence de la pauvreté." For a brief survey of the scene as it appeared in 1963, see James F. White, *Protestant Worship and Church Architecture* (New York: Oxford University Press, 1964) 143–156.

A common factor in many of these churches was exclusion of the devotional centers—the Stations of the Cross, images, side altars—or relegation of them to side chapels. The focus of the building concentrated entirely on the Mass. One architect even suggested a whitewashed wall behind the altar, with the priest's vestments in strong colors. The wall, after all, is unnecessary for the Mass; the altar and actions of the priest are central. In the past the wall was often more eye-catching than the priest. This concentration on essentials often resulted in buildings of extreme simplicity but amazing emotive power. An honest and sincere effort to make the building function as the best setting for the Mass often also produced buildings of considerable beauty.

Both Rudolf Schwarz and Dominikus Böhm survived the war to build a number of churches in Germany. Cologne, especially, became famous for its new churches. Schwarz built St. Michael's in Frankfurt in 1954 as basically an ellipse with the altar near one focus. The altar was freestanding and could function in two directions: for the whole church and for a weekday chapel.

In France, too, there was a return to beginnings. A common factor was the return to centrally planned buildings: square, round, hexagon, etc. Or the altar might be at the center of the long side of a rectangular building. These buildings exemplified simplicity by excluding anything not essential to the Mass. Utility was expressed in providing exactly what was needed and nothing more. And intimacy was achieved by the sense of togetherness about a common center, that is, the altar placed as close to as many people as possible. A problem remained in these churches: the tabernacle still had to be on the main altar. Various experiments were already being tried in order to make a freestanding altar suitable for celebration facing the people.

In the United States the period was one of prosperity for many, and church building by the end of the 1950s was a billion dollar annual industry. All too many of these churches were built on the premise that liturgy was unchanging, and therefore no new architectural settings would ever be necessary. These buildings provided stubborn resistance when change became necessary in the 1960s. Whatever the architectural style, they usually were based on a baroque concept of space, with a highly dramatic altar visible to all but defended from the congregation's approach by a moat of excessive height and solid Communion rails.

But experimentation had also begun in the United States. The most obvious was the gradual acceptance of modern architecture. This was a long and weary battle. Most priests and bishops knew what they liked, which meant they liked what they knew. A major breakthrough came with the Church of Assy in France, consecrated in 1950. Here, with the persistent encouragement of Marie-Alain Couturier, O.P., the best of modern artists, unbelievers as well as believers collaborated to build a completely contemporary building. Beginning that same year, "the Liturgical Arts Society became increasingly direct and unequivocal in advocating modern art for the Church."[4] The best of liturgical art and architecture appeared in the pages of its quarterly, *Liturgical Arts,* to the consternation of many. This was the McCarthy era, and modern art was somehow considered Communist by some people. *Mediator Dei* had been deliberately ambiguous on style, and both sides could quote it with relish. A more conservative instruction from the Holy Office in 1952, *De arte sacra,* pleased some; progressives were encouraged by the purchase of contemporary masters by the Vatican Museum.

Already a few contemporary Roman Catholic churches had been built in the United States by Barry Byrne, a disciple of Frank Lloyd Wright. In the 1950s, Frank Murphy was making the St. Louis area something of a mecca for modern Roman Catholic church architecture. The transition to modern architecture was important because it opened up new structural and spatial possibilities, but many of these early modern buildings still operated basically with a baroque floor plan.

Reconceiving liturgical space had begun, especially with St. Mark's in Burlington, Vermont, in 1944. A more radical step was Blessed Sacrament Church in Holyoke, Massachusetts, built in 1953. Here the altar was dead center in an octagonal church and surrounded by eight rows of pews. This soon turned out not to be the answer, but it did herald the movement to reconceiving the relationship of congregational space to the sanctuary. All was still in flux when events after Vatican II soon gave new directions to church building.

LITURGICAL EVENTS AND PERSONS

As the process of liturgical change began to accelerate, the distinctive contributions of various individuals became more apparent. Much of the history of liturgy is anonymous, but specific roles have become

4. Susan J. White, *Art, Architecture, and Liturgical Reform* (New York: Pueblo Publishing Company, 1990) 158.

more conspicuous in recent times. Nowhere is this more obvious than in scholarly contributions, especially among historians of liturgy and theologians. Their influence usually dates from when they made new facts and concepts public through major publications in articles and books.

Much had been spurred on by the identification of the *Apostolic Tradition* attributed to Hippolytus. It was felt that this document gave the first clear information of what Christian worship had been like in Rome in the late second and early third centuries. Knowledge about the Eucharist, initiation, ordination, and daily prayer was expanded enormously. Editions appeared in English in 1934 (Easton), 1937 (Dix), and in French in 1963 (Botte) and gave urgency to the calls for reforms. It became increasingly apparent how much worship in the West had changed from its roots.

One of the most influential historians of liturgy was the Anglican monk Gregory Dix (1901–1952). Dix's work affected all liturgical revision in the 1950s and 1960s. In his classic work *The Shape of the Liturgy* (1945), Dix situated early Christian worship in the context of what was known at that time of Jewish worship, showing a high degree of continuity. Beyond that, he traced a definitive pattern of early eucharistic rites and concluded that they revolved around four basic actions: the offertory, the [Eucharistic] Prayer, the fraction, and the Communion. He also gave us, for better or worse, such concepts as the "historicization" of liturgy as the Church "became reconciled to time" and substituted the "sanctification of time" for imminent expectation of Christ's return.[5]

Dix had spent the war years writing his "fat green book" in England, while Joseph Jungmann (1889–1975) was compiling his massive two-volume *Missarum Sollemnia* at the same time in Austria. Essentially a conservative, Jungmann's meticulous narrative of the history of the Roman Rite and all that had gone wrong in its long journey made changes inevitable. By narrating in careful detail the origins and development of the Mass and then examining each portion of the Tridentine rite, he took away any excuses for not making reforms. The so-called last gospel would be a good example. The relatively late development of the latter Jungmann carefully chronicled, then gently suggested that "there is something incongruous, something dis-

5. (Westminster: Dacre Press, 1945) 103, 305.

cordant about this last point of the Mass-liturgy."[6] The last gospel disappeared after Vatican II. Balthasar Fischer correctly remarked: "Probably more than any other single book, *Missarum Sollemnia* prepared the way for the conciliar reform of the liturgy."[7] Conservatives in the 1990s accused Jungmann of undue bias against medieval developments and believed that this had prejudiced post-Vatican II reforms.[8]

Dix and Jungmann were far from alone, but they certainly were the most influential historians of the liturgy of this period. Equally important developments were happening in sacramental theology at the same time. The influence of Odo Casel continued to grow after his death in 1948. He was most important for having helped to break the grip of Scholastic categories for doing sacramental theology. Increasingly these terms were found to be insufficient to express modern realities.

That is especially true as theologians turned to the human sciences: anthropology, sociology, communications theory, and phenomenology. Here were dimensions of human experience that could not be contained within the static terms of matter, form, or minister. Rather, the concern was with how humans relate to one another and the words and gestures by which they establish and destroy relationships. There was also beginning to be a degree of ecumenical dialogue.[9]

The most significant single product of this period, although not widely known to the English-speaking world until later, was the publication of Edward Schillebeeckx's (1914–) *Christ the Sacrament of the Encounter with God* (Dutch, 1960; English, 1963). In passages reminiscent of John Calvin's insistence that humans need signs to believe the promises of God, Schillebeeckx depicts the sacraments as means of personal encounter with God. Jesus Christ is the primordial sacrament who establishes the sacraments in his Church: "The sacraments are

6. *The Mass of the Roman Rite: Its Origins and Development (Missarum Sollemnia)*, trans. Francis A. Brunner (New York: Benziger Brothers, 1955) 1:450.

7. Quoted by Robert Peiffer, "Josef Jungmann: Laying a Foundation for Vatican II," in *Leaders of the Liturgical Movement* (Chicago: Liturgy Training Publications, 1990) 62.

8. Eamon Duffy, "The Stripping of the Altars and the Modern Liturgy," *Antiphon*, vol. 2, no. 3 (1997) 3–12.

9. Joseph M. Powers, *Eucharistic Theology* (New York: Herder and Herder, 1967) 112–121.

not things but encounters of men on earth with the glorified man
Jesus by way of a visible form. . . . They are his [Christ's] saving
action itself in its availability to us; a personal act of the Lord in
earthly visibility and open availability."[10]

The impact of this was to put much emphasis on the sign value of
sacraments, so that, as in all human actions, they communicate to the
fullest. This aspect gives a new dynamic quality to the sacraments as
sign acts and places quality of celebration as a major category along-
side of validity. The obsession with what is the least one can do to
have a valid sacrament was replaced with a concern as to how a sacrament can signify grace as effectively as possible. A whole new
approach to the theology of the sacraments was evolving in Europe
during the years before the Council. Schillebeeckx was a *peritus* at
Vatican II, and his work and that of many others brought a major shift
in conceiving of what the Church experiences in the sacraments. The
consequences were to become apparent in the decades after Vatican II.
For the first time in centuries, sacramental theology was being done in
terms congenial to the mind of modern people. No longer was a
schizoid division necessary between sacramental life and daily life.

The contribution of Roman Catholics in the United States was less
emphatically on the academic and scholarly plane, but it was no less
important. In the United States it was a matter of building a climate
for liturgical reform. A wide cast of characters came into play. For the
most part, the later liturgical movement was largely a Midwestern
affair, and many of the chief names were of German extraction:
Michel, Hillenbrand, Diekmann, Busch, Hellriegel, and Laukemper.
Ellard and Shehan were exceptions. As the movement progressed,
an increasing number of lay people took leadership roles: John Ross-
Duggan, Mary Perkins Ryan, Adé Bethune, Dorothy Day, Maurice
Lavanoux, and Justine Ward all contributed in distinctive ways.

A sign of the growth of the movement was the National Liturgical
Week, which had been first held in 1940 under the auspices of the
Benedictine Liturgical Conference. In 1943 it was taken over by the
Liturgical Conference. The new president and vice president were
diocesan priests, Joseph P. Morrison and Joseph F. Stedman, replacing
two abbots. The first meeting outside the Midwest occurred in 1944 at
St. Patrick's in New York City.

10. *Christ the Sacrament of the Encounter with God* (New York: Sheed and Ward,
1963) 44.

Many leaders played diverse roles. Godfrey Diekmann (1908–2002) took over the editorship of *Orate Fratres* after the death of Virgil Michel in 1938. For twenty-five years Father Godfrey led this (then) monthly journal as a roundup of the best scholarly and pastoral information. He managed to attract the most distinguished writers in Europe and North America. Diekmann became a most engaging activist for liturgical reform as speaker, teacher, and editor.[11] Along with the National Liturgical Weeks, *Worship,* the vernacular title that replaced *Orate Fratres* in 1951, upheld the faint-hearted and gave strength to the bold.

Another course was taken by Reynold Hillenbrand, a priest of the Archdiocese of Chicago. As early as 1941, Hillenbrand organized a summer school on liturgy for priests at Mundelein Seminary. He chose the best North Americans as lecturers: Busch, Diekmann, Ellard, Hellriegel, and Reinhold.[12] In the summer of 1947 the first American degree program in liturgy began at the University of Notre Dame under the leadership of Michael Mathis (1885–1960).[13] After 1965 this led to the graduate program in Liturgical Studies, which so far has produced over sixty Ph.D's. In the early years Mathis relied heavily on European scholars. He invited such men as Joseph Jungmann, Louis Bouyer, Jean Daniélou, and Johannes Hofinger. Many of their lectures were published in book form by the University of Notre Dame Press, helping to establish a tradition of solid liturgical scholarship among American publishers. The most scholarly of the American activists was Gerald Ellard, who published a widely used textbook, *Christian Life and Worship,* in 1933 and seven others books combining scholarly and pastoral concerns.[14]

If these were all liturgical activists, there was still considerable resistance. Even though the movement had shed its skin of being a

11. See Hughes, *The Monk's Tale.*

12. Robert L. Tuzik, "The Contribution of Msgr. Reynold Hillenbrand (1905–1979) to the Liturgical Movement in the United States" (Ph.D. diss., University of Notre Dame, 1989).

13. Robert Kennedy, *Michael Mathis: American Liturgical Pioneer* (Washington: Pastoral Press, 1987). Also LaVerne Thomas, "Michael A. Mathis, C.S.C., Liturgical Education and Practice in Service of Renewal" (Ph.D. diss., University of Notre Dame, 2003).

14. John Leo Klein, "The Role of Gerald Ellard (1894–1963) in the Development of the Contemporary American Catholic Liturgical Movement" (Ph.D. diss., Fordham University, 1971).

monastic fad, it was still suspect in many quarters. Not the least objection was that so many of the things being advocated sounded definitely Protestant and were in common practice right down the street in every American town. Nevertheless, the conspirators persevered. A sign that the bishops were being educated was the formation in 1958 of what was to become the Bishops' Commission on the Liturgical Apostolate. The Church's most important activity was finally to be bureaucratized on a national level.

Events progressed meanwhile in Europe. In England, the Society of St. Gregory had been founded in 1929 but devoted most of its efforts to church music in the pre-war years. In 1944 the title of its journal, *Music and Liturgy,* was shortened to *Liturgy,* and then changed in 1970 to *Life and Worship.* Liturgical weeks and various workshops were held, but the English clergy, J. D. Crichton reported, were "reluctant" and "lukewarm" to the ferment going on in France and Germany and "it made little or no impression in England."[15]

International congresses appeared on the Continent beginning in 1951. The most important were those held at Lugano (1953) and Assisi (1956). Part of the procedure was to draw up resolutions asking for certain changes from Rome. Not all the resolutions were welcome in Rome, especially an appeal for the vernacular engineered by Americans at Assisi. Pius XII addressed the Assisi delegates in Rome, thus giving the congress an official blessing. In his concluding "allocution," Pius XII rejoiced in the progress of the liturgical movement and gave credit to the hierarchy as "the chief driving force." He maintained "the unconditional obligation" to use Latin in the Roman Mass and in Gregorian chant.[16]

Another issue was beginning to emerge in a silent way: liturgy and the missions. Bernard Botte recalls the intervention of Johannes Hofinger, the first missionary invited to one of the congresses, at the Lugano Congress in 1953, as awakening in his mind the question "Are we working for Europe or for the universal church?"[17] The question never went away thereafter. Hofinger had been a missionary in China and the Philippines. He was known for his portions of *Worship: The Life of the Missions,* which included "several urgent requests to be

15. "The Liturgical Movement from 1940 to Vatican II," in *English Catholic Worship* (London: Geoffrey Chapman, 1979) 71.
16. *The Assisi Papers* (Collegeville, Minn.: The Liturgical Press, 1957) 236.
17. *From Silence to Participation* (Washington: Pastoral Press, 1988) 82.

made to Mother Church if the liturgy is to regain that missionary effectiveness which it enjoyed in the early missionary Church."[18] Three requests stand out: "greater freedom in the use of the vernacular," "modification of the rites for greater simplicity," and "a more flexible conformity." Henceforth the voice of mission countries could not be ignored in liturgical circles. Missionary requests were made at the Assisi Congress in 1956.

Progress was becoming more evident in Rome itself despite the long tradition of foot-dragging by the Congregation of Sacred Rites. A secret Commission for the Restoration of the Liturgy worked within the Congregation from 1948 to 1960 on general liturgical reforms. The first evidence of their work was the restoration in 1951, on an experimental basis, of the ancient Easter Vigil as the climactic celebration of the Church year. Four years later followed the restoration of all of Holy Week. The high drama of Christian worship was once again being expressed in ancient form.[19]

The Roman Ritual had already been translated into French and German when in 1953 the American bishops petitioned Rome for permission to allow a bilingual ritual. The translation was done at the University of Notre Dame by Michael Mathis and others. Legend has it that the manuscript was slipped onto Pius XII's bedside reading table by his housekeeper. The Pope approved the translation in 1954, before a furious Cardinal Spellman could dissuade him. Bilingual rituals had been approved even before World War II for Poland (1927), Austria (1935), and, after the war, for France (1947), Germany (1950), Spain (1950), and Italy (1953).

In 1953 an evening (after 4:00 p.m.) celebration of Mass without obligation to fast was issued for the benefit of workers. This was meant to aid factory workers, persons traveling, and others for whom a morning Communion was impossible. Within limits, food and drink could be taken before an evening Communion. A simplified code of rubrics was completed and finally issued in 1960 under John XXIII. These dealt with the Roman Missal and the Roman Breviary. The general purpose was to bring the rubrics into accord with modern

---

18. Johannes Hofinger and others (Notre Dame: University of Notre Dame Press, 1958) 282–301.

19. Annibale Bugnini, *The Reform of the Liturgy 1948–1975* (Collegeville, Minn.: The Liturgical Press, 1990) 7–10.

practice, but the code soon became irrelevant after Vatican II.[20] Things were already moving slowly in Rome before the precipitous jolt of Vatican II.

Patience was not always easy, especially for some of the American leaders. Easily the most interesting of these was H. A. Reinhold (1897–1968), an immigrant from Germany in 1936. Reinhold had been inspired by Guardini's *Spirit of the Liturgy*. After various ministries in this country, he landed for a while as pastor of a church in Sunnyside, Washington. But his real ministry was nationwide, especially through his "Timely Tracts" in *Orate Fratres/Worship*. Altogether he contributed 183 items. These were often the rallying points of the American liturgical movement. Eventually, through a misunderstanding with his bishop, his canonical status made him too controversial even for *Worship*, and Reinhold was dropped as a contributor. This shift allowed him time for writing books. Despite much harassment, he persisted in his advocacy of reform. His autobiography is written in a mellow and forgiving tone.[21] Through his writing and speaking he made an irrevocable impact on North American Catholicism.

One of Reinhold's chief causes was the vernacular, and this soon became the main agenda of much of the reformist liturgical movement in the United States. Reinhold was one of the chief promoters, although even he did not yet dare dream of the Canon in the vernacular when he wrote "My Dream Mass in 1940."[22] He formed the St. Jerome Society in 1943 and at a conference in 1945 asked for others to join the crusade for the vernacular. Seventeen people met to form the Vernacular Society. A few years later, a news item in *America* could note: "The remarkable growth of interest in congregational participation in divine worship is evidenced by the growth of the Vernacular Society. Founded in 1946, it now has 2000 members, including 16 bishops as well as priests and laity."[23] After 1951 this group published a periodical, which, ironically, bore the Hebrew name *Amen*. For many years the secretary and chief promoter was a layman, Lt. Col. K. John Ross-Duggan (1888–1967), who had retired in 1949 from publishing a peri-

20. Frederick R. McManus, *Handbook for the New Rubrics* (Baltimore: Helicon Press, 1961).

21. *H.A.R.: The Autobiography of Father Reinhold* (New York: Herder and Herder, 1968).

22. "Timely Tracts: My Dream Mass," *Orate Fratres* 14 (1940) 265–270.

23. *America* 88 (December 13, 1952) 293.

odical, *Quick Frozen Foods*, to work full time to thaw out the liturgy.[24] Under his energetic leadership a membership of 110,000 was built up. It had by this time become obvious that the only way the "active participation" that Pius X had spoken of could be achieved was by having the Mass in a language understood by the people. The advances in the Ritual and the reading of the lessons in the vernacular were only stages on the way.

The way came much faster than anyone anticipated. On January 25, 1959, John XXIII announced the calling of a council, which came to be known as Vatican II. The result was a mad scramble to prepare documents before the Council opened in October 1962. A Preparatory Commission on the liturgy was summoned from around the world, including Frederick McManus (1923–) and Godfrey Diekmann from the United States. The Commission produced a progressive schema, to the horror of the Roman Curia, which attempted to substitute its own version for the bishops to discuss at the Council. Many have argued that the turning point of the Council was when the bishops requested that the original schema be submitted for their debate. When the Pope signaled his approval, the Council came alive. After considerable debate, the Constitution on the Sacred Liturgy (hereafter Constitution) was approved, 2,147 to 4, and was promulgated on December 4, 1963, the four-hundredth anniversary of the conclusion of the Council of Trent.

Just as Trent inaugurated one liturgical age, the Constitution began another. The Constitution commences with "General Principles for the Reform and Promotion of the Sacred Liturgy," then turns to the Eucharist, the other sacraments and sacramentals, the Divine Office, the liturgical year, sacred music, and sacred art and sacred furnishings. Arguably, the sections on music and art are the weakest; the American Bishops' Committee on the Liturgy remedied this with documents in the 1970s. In the "General Principles" of the Constitution, the statement that "the liturgy is the summit toward which the activity of the Church is directed; it is also the fount from which all her power flows" (reminiscent of Pius X) has been perhaps the most often quoted passage (no. 10). Second in frequency has been probably the phrase "full, conscious, and active participation" (no. 14).[25] Liturgy was to be

24. Obituary, *New York Times* (February 4, 1967) 27.

25. Translations are from Austin Flannery, O.P., *Vatican Council II: The Conciliar and Post Conciliar Documents*, new rev. ed. (Collegeville, Minn.: The Liturgical Press, 1992).

taught as a major subject in seminaries (no. 16). The liturgical books were to be revised with "noble simplicity" (no. 34). Scripture was to be emphasized and preaching promoted as part of the liturgy (no. 35). The culture of mission lands was to be respected in "legitimate variations and adaptations" (no. 38).

The Constitution was a far more progressive document than anyone dreamed possible before 1963. And it unleashed impetus to carry things a good deal further than that anticipated in the tepid paragraph (no. 54) on the vernacular in the Mass. The complete abandonment of Latin was clearly not envisioned but soon happened.[26]

RHYTHMS OF TIME AND DEVOTIONS

During several centuries the liturgical calendar had operated under a complex system of priorities that now seems extraordinarily awkward. Festivals were ranked as simple feasts, semi-doubles, doubles, greater doubles, doubles of the second class, and doubles of the first class. In addition, some major feasts had octaves, which involved an eight-day observance. Both Pius V and Pius X had reduced the number of octaves observed. In 1955, as part of the simplification of rubrics, octaves were eliminated except for the three greatest feasts in the West: Christmas, Easter, and Pentecost. Semi-doubles were reduced to simple feasts. These changes in the Breviary and Missal dealt largely with the Propers for daily use, permitting a few options.

The Constitution soon sorted out priorities in firm fashion. Sunday is to have precedence over all but the greatest celebrations, since it is "the foundation and kernel of the whole liturgical year" (no. 106). The sanctoral cycle was clearly to be made subservient so that it did not interfere with the salvation events commemorated in the temporal cycle (nos. 108, 111). And Lent was to prepare for the paschal mystery by emphasizing Lent's character as a time of preparation for baptism and for penance (nos. 109–110).

In Germany during the war years, moves had already begun in hopes of restoring the Easter Vigil and the rest of Holy Week.[27] This tied in very much with growing awareness of the paschal mystery as

26. Many commentaries soon appeared. Notable is that by Frederick R. McManus, "The Constitution on Liturgy Commentary," *Worship* 38 (1964) 314–374; 450–496; 515–565.

27. Anne C. McGuire, "The Reform of Holy Week, 1951–1969: Process, Problems, and Possibilities (Ph.D. diss., University of Notre Dame, 2001).

the essence of Christianity and of a pressing pastoral need to help Western Catholics focus their life and worship on the resurrection. Odo Casel and Romano Guardini had laid the groundwork for a renewed sense of paschal festivity. Cautious steps had been taken to recover some of the forms of celebration that the pilgrim Egeria had described as existing in fourth-century Jerusalem.

After many petitions, "Pius XII restored the liturgy of the sacred vigil of Easter in 1951 . . . at the discretion of the ordinary and as an experiment."[28] Local experiments had been highly successful and led to demands for the restoration of the whole of the ancient Holy Week observances. On November 16, 1955, the Congregation of Sacred Rites issued a decree and instruction on the restoration of the full order of Holy Week. This ordo was to become obligatory on Palm Sunday, 1956. In prior centuries the services had been celebrated in the morning. This had the effect of reducing lay attendance to such a point that in 1641 Urban VIII declared the last three days of Holy Week no longer days of obligation. The restoration was expedited because evening Masses, allowed in *Christus Dominus* of 1953, had been so well received.

The restoration of Holy Week involved a major pastoral transition. Not only did the laity have to become familiar with an entirely new schedule for Holy Week but they had to be taught the meaning of the restored rites. Also, the clergy had to appropriate the new rites and the preparation they required. A massive campaign of education for both clergy and laity was necessary. Godfrey Diekmann, for example, wrote the lead article to interpret Holy Week for an issue of the popular journal *Jubilee*.[29] Some sense of the novelty of the decree appears in the Instruction that accompanies it, delineating "the chief points of instruction that should be given to the Christian people."[30] Detailed instructions to clergy on following the rubrics are also provided. A major component of the Church year had been recovered.

Of a different character was the dogmatic definition of the Assumption of Our Lady by Pius XII on November 1, 1950. Pius cites as proof

28. "The Restoration of the Holy Week Order," translation of *Liturgicus Hebdomadae Sanctae Ordo instauratur*," in R. Kevin Seasoltz, ed., *The New Liturgy: A Documentation, 1903–1965* (New York: Herder and Herder, 1966) 211.

29. "Liturgy of Holy Week: Palm Sunday, Holy Thursday, Good Friday, Easter Vigil, and Easter Mass," *Jubilee* 3 (April 1956) 2–24.

30. Seasoltz, *The New Liturgy,* 213.

of this dogma the many liturgical formulas used over history, such as that in the Sacramentary of Hadrian I in the eighth century. Accordingly, it was defined as "divinely revealed dogma" that Mary "was assumed body and soul into heavenly glory."[31] Pius also provided new Mass Propers for the feast. This period saw the highwater mark of Marian devotions in the twentieth century.

THE MASS

In 1956 Gerald Ellard published *The Mass in Transition*.[32] He began by acknowledging that his 1948 book, *The Mass of the Future*,[33] was already out of date, so rapidly had liturgical practice progressed. People were beginning to grasp the difference between praying at Mass and praying the Mass itself. Various practices were becoming common. Vernacular missals were now in the hands of millions of lay people. In a few places the altars had already been pried loose from walls, and priests were celebrating facing the people, albeit with a tabernacle in their way. The so-called dialogue Mass was well on its way to being no longer a rarity in the United States and was prevalent in Germany. In some places Communion was beginning to be received "if possible" during Mass and from hosts consecrated at that Mass rather than previously. Evening Mass had become a possibility, and the fasting requirements were alleviated. Easter and all of Holy Week had been "made over." There was much in which to rejoice.

The penultimate chapter of *The Mass in Transition* broaches a touchy topic—ecumenism. This was still dangerous ground; Roman Catholics had been forbidden to attend the World Council of Churches assembly in Evanston in 1954, although apparently a few priests did so without their clerical collars. But just as missions had already intruded into the liturgical consciousness, so did ecumenism. This was to become irrevocable. A major event was the publication of "An Order for the Lord's Supper or the Holy Eucharist" of the Church of South India in 1950. It was the first liturgy to be based on Dix's scholarship, and although some parts of Dix's study may seem a bit shaky today, the South India liturgy was immediately recognized as a new star in the liturgical sky. It blunted the Anglican claim of "our incomparable

31. "The Dogmatic Definition of the Assumption of Our Lady," translation of *Munificentissimus Deus*, in Seasoltz, *The New Liturgy*, 174.

32. (Milwaukee: Bruce Publishing Company, 1956).

33. (Milwaukee: Bruce Publishing Company, 1948).

liturgy," for South India was state of the art as far as liturgical scholarship had then progressed. It was viewed with great interest and not a little envy by liturgical experts of all Churches.

The climate was changing rapidly. John XXIII shocked the world in 1959 by calling a council. An event that is little remembered during his short pontificate was a highly significant portent. On November 13, 1962, Pope John announced that he was adding the name of St. Joseph to the Canon of the Mass, presumably unchanged in a thousand years. "This act of John XXIII was at the same time a response given to those who considered absolute the immutability of the canon of the Mass as a dogma."[34]

The Constitution, approved a year later, was much less reticent than it might have been. "The rite of the Mass is to be revised . . . the rites are to be simplified. . . . Parts . . . are to be omitted. Other parts . . . restored" (no. 50). An oft-quoted line read: "The treasures of the Bible are to be opened up more lavishly so that a richer fare may be provided for the faithful at the table of God's word" (no. 51). Homilies were to be normal at Masses with congregations present (no. 52); the intercessions were to be reinstituted, (no. 53); the mother tongue might be used for parts of the Mass, for example, the readings and intercessions and maybe eventually more (no. 54); the faithful should receive after the priest's Communion, and the possibility of reception in both kinds was contemplated (no. 55); people should be present for the entire Mass (no. 56); and concelebration (two or more priests celebrating together) was to be allowed in carefully limited cases (nos. 57–58).

Concelebration had been a hot issue, especially after Karl Rahner had written on the issue in "Many Masses and the One Sacrifice" of Christ, questioning whether the multiplication of Masses added to God's glory and grace.[35] After Vatican II concelebration became common in religious communities, on diocesan occasions, and for important parochial Masses, almost to excess. Other theological debates were to proliferate, but this one seems to have been resolved at the theological level, if not in practice. Thus the Council exceeded the fondest hopes of men such as Reinhold, Guardini, Hellriegel, and

34. Herman Schmidt, *La Constitution de la Sainte Liturgie* (Brussels: Editions Lumen Vitae, 1966) 93.

35. Karl Rahner and Angelus Häussling, *The Celebration of the Eucharist*, trans. W. J. O'Hara (New York: Herder and Herder, 1968).

many others who lived to see their dreams realized. Others, such as Ellard, who died April 1, 1963, rejoiced from another shore.

RHYTHMS OF THE LIFE CYCLE

The most significant change in the pastoral rites before Vatican II came to be widespread permissions to have the Roman Ritual in the vernacular. Requests for these had already been approved for most of Europe when the first official American translation was approved in 1954. Technically, these were bilingual rituals, with the Latin and vernacular often printed on opposite pages or in double columns. Latin alone prevailed for some sacramental formulas, and key prayers, such as the confirmation of the marriage bond, "Ego conjungo vos," in the American marriage rite, or the exorcisms, anointings, blessings, and baptismal formula. The rubrics were not translated. But it was a major step forward, one that the Neo-Gallican rituals had looked to three centuries previously. Now the rites of life's passages and journeys could be marked in words that those most involved could understand. It was a major pastoral advance.

Nearly a decade later, the Constitution pushed things a great deal further. Recognizing the edifying function of the sacraments of the life cycle, it stated that it was "of the greatest importance that the faithful should easily understand the sacramental signs" (no. 59). Their importance was underscored in that "the liturgy of the sacraments and sacramentals sanctifies almost every event on their [the faithfuls'] lives" (no. 61). In order to adapt these sacraments to "present-day needs," the Ritual could be in the vernacular and adapted linguistically to "the needs of the different regions" (nos. 62–63).

Major changes were proposed for most of the sacraments of the Ritual. In initiation, the adult catechumenate was to be revived with distinct stages, as in the *Apostolic Tradition* (no. 64). Customs in mission lands of initiation could be "adapted" (no. 65). Adult baptismal rites were to be revised (no. 66), as well as infant rites, "taking into account the fact that those to be baptized are infants" (no. 67). A new rite for converts to Catholicism who are already validly baptized was to be compiled (no. 69). And the rite for confirmation was to be revised so that it comports more clearly with the whole process of initiation (no. 71).

The marriage rite was treated with the greatest freedom, building on the decree *Tametsi* from Trent. The rite in the Ritual was to be revised. No longer was the bride singled out as the one more likely to stray

116

from fidelity (nos. 77–78). Matrimony was normally to be in the context of Mass, after the gospel and homily, but the epistle, gospel, and blessing were to be retained when celebrated outside of Mass (no. 78).

The Constitution devoted only three sentences to burial of the dead, but they were potent. The rite "should express more clearly the paschal character of Christian death" rather than the fearsome panoply of hell. Regional "circumstances and traditions" should be honored as well as local liturgical colors (no. 81). And the rite for infant burial was to be revised and a special Mass provided (no. 82). The impact of the missions was apparent in stressing adaptability to various cultures.

Confession got the shortest notice of all: "the rite and formulae of Penance are to be revised so that they more clearly express both the nature and effect of the sacrament" (no. 72). Perhaps the brevity was due to the fact that scholarly research and pastoral experiment had not yet jelled. For some time the Dutch had been trying out communal services that included general confession and communal absolution or only a prayer for forgiveness. In France a combination of private confession within a communal service was preferred. A range of controversies arose from differing practices, especially as to the sacramentality of communal absolution.[36]

The renaming of confession as "reconciliation" had not yet happened, but just such a renaming and a real revolution did occur with regard to extreme unction. It may "more fittingly be called 'Anointing of the Sick' [and] is not a sacrament for those only who are at the point of death" (no. 73). When danger of death "from sickness or old age" approaches, the time for anointing has arrived. A continuous rite for the dying is to be devised, with anointings coming between confession and Viaticum (no. 74). The anointings were to be made more adaptable to pastoral situations (no. 75). Among the "General Principles" of the Constitution, a distinction was made between "unchangeable elements divinely instituted, and of elements subject to change" (no. 21). Obviously, the changes that had occurred over the centuries to produce extreme unction as a rite only for the dying could be reversed and the primitive purpose of healing revived. But it was to take a full generation before most people understood that an offer to anoint a sick person was not a prelude to calling the undertaker.

36. James Dallen, *The Reconciling Community* (New York: Pueblo Publishing Company, 1986) 190–191.

It is difficult to trace a consistent pattern in church music during this period, and even the fathers of the Council appear a bit confused when legislating for musicians. The Gregorian quest was still in full swing. The year 1941 had seen the founding of the Gregorian Institute of America by Clifford Bennett. Later it was to be camouflaged as G.I.A. and to become a major publisher of hymnals. Joseph Gelineau began in 1947 to introduce into French parishes a new method of singing the psalms in the vernacular. The Gregorian Institute of America eventually became the leading publisher of the Gelineau psalms in this country.

A particularly brilliant period in the history of church organ music occurred in France in a long succession of brilliant composers: Louis Vierne and Charles Marie Widor both died in 1937; Jean Langlais and Oliver Messiaen lived into the 1990s. Messiaen in particular wrote brilliant concert pieces inspired by the liturgy, but as his personal interpretations of faith to be presented in the concert hall. Vatican II had certainly not given up on the Gregorian chant but praised it in rather reserved terms: "specially suited to the Roman liturgy. Therefore, other things being equal, it should be given pride of place in liturgical services" (no. 116). But other things were rarely equal, and the same paragraph went on to commend "other kinds of sacred music, especially polyphony." The *editio typica* of the Gregorian books was to be completed and "a more critical edition" issued of those already published, plus an edition for small churches (no. 117).

Cracks had already appeared in the Gregorian wall during the pontificate of Pius XII. These rifts multiplied as the 1950s progressed, and the unlikeliness of Gregorian chants succeeding on a popular level, especially in Latin, became clear to some musicians. Implicit recognition of this came in an encyclical of Pius XII, *Musicae sacrae disciplina*, of 1955. He acknowledged that in some localities there was a custom of vernacular hymnody after the Mass, such as the German *singemesse*. Vernacular song were not to intrude on the Mass itself, where all singing was to be in Latin. Hymns have a valuable purpose, namely as "a powerful aid in keeping the faithful from attending the Holy Sacrifice like dumb and idle spectators."[37] "Popular religious singing" was encouraged, provided it did not occur at solemn high

37. Robert F. Hayburn, *Papal Legislation on Sacred Music* (Collegeville, Minn.: The Liturgical Press, 1979) 353.

Masses. On occasions other than Mass, popular hymnody was to be readily welcomed. And the gamut of musical instruments used at such non-liturgical services could be wider than hitherto. Shortly before the death of Pius XII, the Congregation of Sacred Rites in 1958 issued a decree, *De musica sacra,* spelling out some of the practical details. Popular religious song and religious music were commended, although their place was not in the liturgy itself. And radio, television, and film were given standards.

The Constitution thus picked up on a growing liberalization of the dominance of Gregorian chant and a wider range of musical instruments. What it had to say was clouded in generalities: "sacred music is to be considered the more holy, the more closely it is connected with the liturgical action" (no. 112). Choirs were to be promoted, music was to be taught in seminaries, and schools of sacred music were to be established. The people were to be encouraged to sing, and in mission lands local "musical tradition" was to be respected and followed "in adapting worship to their native genius" (no. 119). The pipe organ was preeminent in worship, but "other instruments also may be admitted" as long as they were suitable for worship (no. 120). Composers were to be encouraged, provided they wrote for suitable texts and were invited to write for small choirs and the faithful as well as large choirs (no. 121). There was a new openness that was important, although the text basically says music should be good and appropriate. Probably no more could be expected at the time. At least it did not close any doors. Sometimes ambiguity is a blessing.

Already experiments were being tried in church music. One has only to think of Alexander Peloquin (1918–) in Providence or Omer Westendorf (1916–) with World Library Publications in Cincinnati. Both were already championing congregational song and were ready to lead in moving to the use of the vernacular. These musicians were preparing for a new era that became possible soon after Vatican II.

PREACHING

A new attitude was developing about preaching, propelled by many forces. The encouragement given to scientific biblical studies by *Divino afflante Spiritu* (1943) was beginning to have its effect in a sudden spurt in Catholic biblical scholarship. With studies based on the Greek and Hebrew texts, all the tools of biblical criticism could be employed for a deeper understanding of Scripture. From being almost a closed book for the faithful, Bible reading was being encouraged on a vast popular level. In 1957 a Scripture section became a prominent part of *Worship* and eventually led to the popular journal *The Bible Today,* both published by The Liturgical Press at Collegeville, Minnesota.

The Constitution was full of references to the importance of the Scriptures in the liturgical life of the Church. We have already mentioned the famous passage about a "richer fare" (no. 51). A hope that remained unfulfilled after the Council was that there would be widespread development of so-called "Bible services" (*Verbi Dei celebratio*— no. 35). The Constitution suggests that these would be a further opportunity for the expounding and preaching of Scripture on the weekdays of Advent and Lent as well as on Sundays and feast days.

Another factor was the growing use of public media such as radio and television as vehicles for preaching. This opened a whole new doorway to apologetic preaching. Beyond doubt, the leading Roman Catholic figure in this venture was Bishop Fulton J. Sheen (1895–1979). He was a prominent speaker on the "Catholic Hour Broadcasts" on the NBC network from 1930 to 1952, which led to the televised series "Life Is Worth Living" from 1951 to 1957 on ABC. He had become the greatest Catholic evangelist in American history, blending Christian faith, doctrine, social justice, and anti-Communism. Sheen set a style that was folksy, whimsical, and highly engaging. He popularized a style for much preaching, both Catholic and Protestant, in the years before the Council.

Various periodicals sought to guide and improve the level of preaching, especially *The American Ecclesiastical Review* and *The Homiletic and Pastoral Review.* Much in them seems tame today. "The evidence of actual pastoral sermons contributes to the homogeneous and predictable reputation of American Catholic homiletics. That is to say, for the most part, preachers delivered for their assemblies Sunday after Sunday short courses in doctrinal or moral instruction. This focus on the perennial questions and universal concerns of Catholic life extended the formalist, didactic character of U.S. Catholic preaching into the 1960s."[38] Probably each generation looks back in horror at the preaching of its predecessors, but memories of this period tend to focus on moralistic harangues that, at least, were usually brief.

---

38. Mary E. Lyons, "Preaching, Catholic, in the United States," in *A New Dictionary of Sacramental Worship* (Collegeville, Minn.: The Liturgical Press, 1990) 990.

Vatican II set out to remedy some of these deficiencies. The Decree on the Ministry and Life of Priests states it clearly: "It is the first task of priests as co-workers of the bishops to preach the Gospel of God to all men" (no. 4).

The liturgy Constitution spells out the character of the sermon. It "should draw its content mainly from scriptural and liturgical sources, for it is the proclamation of God's wonderful works in the history of salvation, which is the mystery of Christ ever made present and active in us, especially in the celebration of the liturgy" (no. 35). In the Eucharist, "the guiding principles of the Christian life are expounded from the sacred text during the course of the liturgical year. The homily, therefore, is to be highly esteemed as part of the liturgy itself." In Masses with congregations "it should not be omitted except for a serious reason" (no. 52).

Two things seem to stand out in Vatican II's image of preaching. Preaching is to be biblical, that is, drawing its message from the biblical text read at Mass and from the Scriptures as a whole. Second, it is to be liturgical, that is, conceived as an integral part of the liturgy itself and not as some words of wisdom or a personal chat interrupting the Mass. It takes its place in the flow of the liturgical year, just as do all the Propers. Like them, it is an element of the liturgy that should not be omitted, since it, too, builds up the faith of the assembly.

When seen as liturgical preaching, the sermon almost by necessity became biblical preaching in explicating the appointed readings. This did not vitiate its relevance for daily living, but it put it in a different context than simply a diatribe against birth control. The sermon became part of the proclamation of the Word of God and not just the preacher's word. Trent, too, had said fine things about preaching, but the message of Vatican II seems to have been much more effective.

PUBLIC PRAYER

For many years popular devotions had some of the functions of public prayer. At least until World War I, Latin Vespers and Benediction were attended on Sunday in some places. "For the ordinary Roman Catholic in the period roughly between 1920 and 1955, the only regular opportunity for communal prayer in church apart from the Mass was some form of popular devotion."[39] Latin Vespers eventually

39. Carl Dehne, "Roman Catholic Popular Devotions," in *Christians at Prayer* (Notre Dame: University of Notre Dame Press, 1977) 88.

disappeared, but Benediction remained joined to a popular devotion. There appeared to be an enormous gap in public prayer life long before Vatican II.

The Constitution made a timid gesture with regard to the Divine Office: "The laity, too, are encouraged to recite the divine office, either with the priests, or among themselves, or even individually" (no. 100). But it was clear from the rest of the chapter on the Divine Office that the principal consumers were meant to be clergy and religious. The reforms were engineered to make their prayer life richer and more convenient.

The Constitution says that "the traditional sequence of the hours is to be restored so that, as far as possible, they may again become also in fact what they have been in name," that is, related to the time of day at which they are prayed (no. 88). Returning to ancient tradition, Lauds and Vespers were seen as "the two hinges on which the daily office turns. They must be considered as the chief hours and are to be celebrated as such" (no. 89). Compline was to accord better with the end of the day; Matins (the night Office) could be prayed at any time of the day; Prime was suppressed; and outside of choir, any one of the Little (Midday) Hours suited to the time of day could be selected (no. 89). The psalms were to be distributed over a longer period than a single week (no. 91). As to the readings, more of "the riches of the divine word" was to be provided, better selections from the writings of the fathers were to be chosen, and the "lives of the saints were to be made more historically accurate" (no. 92). Hymns were to be "restored to their original form" and mythological elements purged (no. 93). Religious communities with a choral obligation were bound to recite the Office in choir; clergy in major orders were to pray the Office "either in common or individually" (nos. 95–96). And finally, "the Latin language is to be retained by clerics in the divine office" although the vernacular might be used when this was a "grave obstacle" to clergy and religious alike (no. 101).

By the end of 1963 liturgical reformation had become not just something to dream of and to promote but was the official agenda of the Latin-rite Church. We will see in the next chapter how these reforms were accomplished in the years following the Council.

Chapter Six

The Legacy of the Second Vatican Council

The twenty years after 1963 saw the accomplishment of most of the
agenda of the liturgical movement. In retrospect, many things went
further and faster than anyone would have believed possible. Not
everything turned out as expected; the overnight victory of the
vernacular caught even the most optimistic off guard. The virtual
cessation of most public devotions was unexpected, and little was
available in their place. Nor could anyone have foreseen that a
reformed Church would also face a serious shortage of priests, who
were essential to its whole sacramental system.

The liturgical reforms mandated by the Second Vatican Council, as
far as "practical norms" were concerned, applied specifically to the
Roman Rite (Constitution on the Sacred Liturgy, no. 3; hereafter
Constitution). Other Catholic rites frequently underwent their own
reforms: the Eastern Rites, the Milanese Rite, and various religious
orders. Often these rites followed the Roman reforms; sometimes the
Roman reforms borrowed from them, for example, the words of distribution: "The Body of Christ." Thus there were a number of reforms
going on at the same time in different rites and orders, although we
shall note only the Roman ones. The Cistercians, like the Protestants,
had an observer at the meetings of the Consilium for the Implementation of the Constitution on the Sacred Liturgy.

Internationally, this was a period of great stress as the cold war raged
and became very hot in Vietnam until 1975. It saw the civil rights
movement in the United States and the abrupt ending of political
colonialism around the world. In the United States the 1960s were an
era of heightened social consciousness and impatience with old conventions. Feminism became a major player in struggles for economic
and social justice. Democracy broadened as more disenfranchised

minorities and women played a greater role in determining their destinies. Perhaps inevitably, the 1980s saw a lapse into complacency.

Our story in this chapter essentially reaches from the [First] Instruction for the Proper Implementation of the Constitution on the Sacred Liturgy (1964) to the last major liturgical books to be revised, the Ceremonial of Bishops and the Book of Blessings, both issued in 1984. More changed in Roman Catholic worship in these twenty years than in any previous century. So much happened that we must be brief in cataloging the events. Such brevity should not conceal the importance of the results. It is astounding that so much was accomplished in such a short time, especially when we recall that the revision of the liturgical books after Trent took more than half a century for rather modest changes. These were exciting years, unequaled in the previous four hundred years in liturgical change.

Many of the post-Vatican II reforms were frankly borrowed by various Protestant Churches. This is especially true of items revolving around the liturgical year and the Lectionary. For nearly four centuries after the death of Luther (1546), Roman Catholic and Protestant worship had operated in almost airtight isolation from each other except in music. Now the barriers to sharing suddenly were dismantled. Today eucharistic celebrations in most Lutheran and Episcopal churches and some Methodist and Presbyterian churches are hard to distinguish from those in neighboring Roman Catholic parishes. Only issues of power and control (clergy) remain distinct. Catholic charismatics could easily be confused with their Protestant neighbors. Liturgy, once a dividing force, has now often become unitive.

THE HOUSE OF GOD BECOMES
THE HOUSE OF GOD'S PEOPLE

The most dramatic changes in Roman Catholic worship in the post-Vatican II era may well have been spatial rather than linguistic. The church buildings of this period came to reflect a whole new concept of what it is to be the Church. The built environment may be the best index of this shift. It is as if the church building shifted from being a theater, with stage and house clearly distinguished, to a structure in which everyone found himself or herself on stage. No spectator space was left over. (Something similar happened in the theater itself in thrust-stage design.)

The result was that thousands of churches were found unsatisfactory for reformed worship and underwent drastic renovation. New churches were built on an entirely different principle. God was now imaged, not as somewhere out beyond the east window, but as present in the midst of God's people. This produced buildings whose focus said more about immanence than about transcendence. Attention shifted from the church building as the house of God to the church as the house of God's people. Some of these changes had preceded the Council in advanced churches in Germany and a few bold attempts in the United States.

The first sign that something major was happening came in the [First] Instruction for the Proper Implementation of the Constitution on the Sacred Liturgy *(Inter Oecumenici)*, dated September 26, 1964, and effective March 7, 1965. Chapter V was devoted to church architecture to facilitate "the active participation of the faithful." It enacted that "the main altar should preferably be freestanding, to permit walking around it and celebration facing the people."[1] It still contemplated the tabernacle, "in the middle of the main altar," but other possibilities were mentioned and soon became common as celebrating with a tabernacle on the main altar while facing the people proved awkward. Gregory Dix once mentioned his Wesleyan grandmother, who believed that the priest had a crab on the altar, and all his fiddling around with his back to the people was to prevent the crab from crawling off![2] Now the priest was facing the people and no crab was in sight! It was hard to think of ever again turning one's back on the people of God while at the altar. The personal encounter of facing the people of God may be the most important shift of all, for it proclaimed louder than words that the action now belonged to the whole community and was not something the priest did *for* the community. Now it was *with* the community.

Other changes followed swiftly. There were to be "fewer minor altars," and many were eliminated altogether, especially what were once known as "His and Hers" (Christ and the Virgin) altars. Suitable ambos or pulpits were mandated. A new liturgical center appeared in what came to be known as the presider's chair, which was to "occupy a place that is clearly visible to all the faithful and that makes it plain that the celebrant presides over the whole community."[3] The cross and

---

1. International Commission on English in the Liturgy, *Documents on the Liturgy 1963–1979: Conciliar, Papal, and Curial Texts* (Collegeville, Minn.: The Liturgical Press, 1982), no. 91, p. 108. Hereafter *DOL.*

2. *Shape of the Liturgy* (Westminster: Dacre Press, 1945) 145.

3. *DOL,* no. 92, p. 108.

candlesticks could be placed next to the altar rather than on it. Congregational seating was to be arranged to maximize participation. And baptismal space was to enable communal celebration.

This triggered an avalanche of changes. It is likely that the 1960s saw as much iconoclasm in Roman Catholic churches as the Reformation had in some Protestant lands. Thousands of plaster images bit the dust or ended up at flea markets. Secondary altars were discarded wholesale. Communion rails and confessionals disappeared. Stations of the Cross and all kinds of devotional images were removed. This is not to say that there was much aesthetic loss; indeed, much of the housecleaning proved Mies Van der Rohe's dictum "Less is more." In some churches nostalgia brought some of these images back in the 1980s. What emerged in the 1970s was a severe Catholic "plain style."[4] These buildings make it quite clear that the community gathers for the liturgy, not for devotions. Devotional centers—tabernacle, stations, images—had all been relegated to side chapels.

The arrangement of the sanctuary underwent a major shift. At first a modest table was brought in to be used for Mass, and the impression given was that this was the "provisional" altar, but the "real" altar still loomed above at the end of the sanctuary. In many cases it took several years for the provisional altar to become the real altar and for the old high altar to be dismantled. But gradually a ministerial altar close to the people won out and the old heavy-laden altar was retired and removed. Secondary altars, no longer being used for private Masses, quietly vanished.

Congregational space underwent a revolution. Instead of the longitudinal church, stretching like a tunnel away from the sanctuary, central plans were in vogue. These brought as many people as close to the altar as possible. Immaculate Conception Cathedral, Burlington, Vermont, placed everyone within eight rows of the altar. Often fan-shaped designs, similar to the Akron plan popular in Protestant churches, 1880–1905, were adopted. The plan of the New England Puritan meetinghouse of 1700–1770, with the congregation on three sides of the altar and pulpit, also had great appeal. Frequently churches underwent a drastic reorientation, so that the altar, pulpit, and chair appeared in the middle of a long side instead of in a secluded sanctuary.

4. See Anthony Garvan, "The Protestant Plain Style before 1630," *Journal of the Society of Architectural Historians* 9 (1950) 5–13.

A major assist came from *Environment and Art in Catholic Worship,* published by the Bishops' Committee on the Liturgy in 1978 and said to be largely the work of Robert Hovda. It declares forthrightly that "among the symbols with which liturgy deals, none is more important than this [the baptized] assembly of believers."[5] Consequently, "the norm for designing liturgical space is the assembly and its liturgies."[6] The photographs that accompanied the text (significantly, beginning with a Shaker interior) were even more compelling than the eloquent text.

It is not entirely accidental that the illustrations of the first edition all represent the work of one man, the liturgical designer Frank Kacmarcik (1920–), who turned out to be the leading form-maker of Roman Catholic churches in the United States in this period. His renovations of older buildings and his work on new buildings showed a deep knowledge of the liturgy and were expressed in terms of directness and simplicity. One can call his work "ascetic." In churches he helped design, everything focuses the community's attention on three liturgical centers about which they do their work together: altar, pulpit, and presider's chair. There is nothing to distract from the liturgical action. Other liturgical designers who have had a major impact are Robert Rambusch (Syracuse Cathedral), William Schickel (Gethsemani Abbey), and Richard Vosko (Nashville Cathedral).[7]

Among architects, Pietro Belluschi (1899–1994) did some remarkable churches, such as Portsmouth Priory Church and the Chapel at the University of Portland.[8] One of the most influential church architects of this period was the Lutheran Edward Sövik (1918–). His St. Leo Church in Pipestone, Minnesota, built in 1968, in its frankly secular form, reflects the theology of Dietrich Bonhoeffer. Sövik developed the concept of the "non-church" church, in which he simply built the best possible space using the same architectural idiom as a warehouse or other secular buildings.

5. (Washington: National Conference of Catholic Bishops, 1978) 18.
6. Ibid., 25.
7. Michael E. DeSanctis, *Renewing the City of God: The Reform of Catholic Architecture in the United States* (Chicago: Liturgy Training Publications, 1993), contains many illustrations.
8. Meredith Clausen, *The Religious Architecture of Pietro Belluschi* (Seattle: University of Washington Press, 1992).

Two concepts emerged in these decades, neither of them mandated in official documents but both emerging from local experience of the liturgy. One of these was the sense of the importance of "gathering space."[9] Architecturally, this underscores the process of becoming a community through leading worshipers from the private space of their automobile to the public space of the pew. Both exterior and interior spaces were being designed to express this part of worship. Some newer liturgies acknowledge gathering as part of the liturgy.

The other development has been with regard to baptismal space. Baptismal fonts were relocated, sometimes appearing next to the altar (St. John Brebeuf, Niles, Illinois), sometimes at the entrance, but visible to the whole congregation.[10] They also grew in size, reflecting a new importance for baptism.

LITURGICAL EVENTS AND PERSONS

So much happened and so many people were involved in this twenty-year period that we can only mention the most noteworthy events and persons.[11] But there may be value in trying to be both concise and comprehensive in showing how the pieces fit together. This should not mask the intricate maneuvering that often lay behind the accomplishment of the proposed reforms or that tried to thwart them.

The first public act of the new reform was a *motu proprio* of Paul VI, *Sacram Liturgiam*, of January 25, 1964, exactly five years after John XXIII had called the Council. If this launched the reform, it also "granted little of the much that the Constitution had promised."[12] It soon became apparent that there would be ongoing tension between the Churches of various nations, which wanted to proceed at their own pace, and the Congregation of Sacred Rites, which insisted on retaining tight control over the entire process. Recent decades have done nothing to resolve these tensions.

9. James F. White, "Coming Together in Christ's Name," *Liturgy* (Fall 1981) 7–10.

10. Regina Kuehn, *A Place for Baptism* (Chicago: Liturgy Training Publications, 1992).

11. A detailed account from an insider's perspective occurs in the monumental history by Annibale Bugnini, *The Reform of the Liturgy 1948–1975* (Collegeville, Minn.: The Liturgical Press, 1990). This should be supplemented by *DOL* (see note 1 above).

12. Bugnini, *The Reform of the Liturgy*, 58; text of *Sacram Liturgiam* in *DOL*, pp. 84–87.

Already an Italian priest, Annibale Bugnini, C.M. (1912–1982), had been working at the urgent request of Paul VI to organize what came to be known as the Consilium for the Implementation of the Constitution on the Sacred Liturgy *(Consilium ad exsequendam Constitutionem de Sacra Liturgia)*. This was to consist of a staff, headed by Bugnini, of never more than ten people, with offices in Vatican City, plus members (bishops and abbots) and consultors (experts), who did most of the study and research. Top scholars were included, but it is indicative of the times that of the 148 official consultors, Christine Mohrmann was the only woman and almost the only lay person. Seven names from the United States appear: musicians Clifford Bennett and Francis Schmitt; liturgists Godfrey Diekmann, Frederick R. McManus, John Miller; patrologist Johannes Quasten; and Abbot Primate Rembert Weakland.

The work was divided up into study groups, or *coetus* (plural *coetus*), each with a relator, secretary, and usually five or six consultors. The thirty or so groups were organized on the basis of the chief Roman liturgical books: Missal, Breviary, Ritual, Pontifical, Martyrology, and Ceremonial of Bishops. The consultors could call in additional advisers, for example, Roland Murphy or Patrick Skehan from the United States. Each *coetus* was assigned a portion of a liturgical book and set to work to produce a *schema,* which then went to the Consilium (of bishops), which could ask for further revisions or pass it on to the Pope for approval.

The consultors set to work energetically, with the result that the last of the major books were issued in 1984: the Book of Blessings and the Ceremonial of Bishops. The approved English translations of these two books for the dioceses of the United States of America appeared in 1989, the same year as the revised Order of Christian Funerals. Most of the work of revision had actually been finished by 1972. Plenary meetings of the Consilium members convened semi-annually for several years to approve the work of the *coetus.* In the meantime, not always comfortable relations ensued between the Consilium and the Congregation of Sacred Rites. Basically, the Consilium was in charge of preparation of the liturgical books and experimentation; the Congregation was charged with promulgation. In time, the Congregation was renamed the Congregation for Divine Worship (1969) and in 1975 was combined with the Congregation for the Discipline of the Sacraments as the Congregation for Divine Worship and the Discipline of the Sacraments. This entity published the official documents on liturgy. The Consilium ceased to function as a separate entity in 1972, but by then its major work had been done.

Even before the Council ended (1965), what may best be described as the period of liturgical euphoria began. This was the time when pent-up energy for reform burst the bounds of legitimate change and erupted in unofficial experimentation. The late 1960s were an era of pushing the limits of authority in all aspects of life, including liturgy; only the Netherlands exceeded the United States in daring. All assumptions and conventions were tested. At some Newman Centers it was found that the best time for Mass was midnight Saturday, after dates. Everyone tried banners and balloons. Many went further; so-called underground Masses were anything but secret because the media paid so much attention to them. Several volumes of Mass liturgies were published in the United States.[13] They seem a bit tame compared with some Dutch and French experiments of the time, such as those of Huub Osterhuis or Thierry Maertens.

For many, the twenty-fifth Liturgical Week, held in Kiel Stadium, St. Louis, in 1964 was the height of euphoria as crowds rejoiced that so much they had anticipated was now reality. By 1966, in Houston, there were excited rumors as to the experimental Masses being celebrated in hotel rooms. The following year, in Kansas City, despite the topic, "Experiments in Community," participants were greeted with a stern episcopal warning to restrain themselves. By 1968, things in Washington were much more low key, despite the appearance of liturgists of another sort, such as social activists Saul Alinsky or Will Campbell. Dr. Spock and other activists made it to the 1969 meeting in Milwaukee, where many marched with picketing workers. But after a disappointing session at Princeton in 1970, the Liturgical Weeks sputtered out. Perhaps it was just as well; euphoria can last only so long before it becomes exhaustion.

Partly out of concern for regulating things and partly to open up legal possibilities, three general Instructions were issued in the early years of the reform (1964, 1967, 1970). In addition, specific Instructions on eucharistic worship and on sacred music came out in 1967.

13. John Barry Ryan studied three of these: Robert F. Hoey's *Experimental Liturgy Book*; John Gallen's *Eucharistic Liturgies*; and Stephen W. McNierney's *The Underground Mass Book*, all published 1968–1970. John Barry Ryan, *The Eucharistic Prayer* (New York: Paulist Press, 1974).

The [First] Instruction for the Proper Implementation of the Constitution on the Sacred Liturgy *(Inter Oecumenici)* mandated that "those measures that are practicable before revision of the liturgical books go into effect immediately."[14] It called for instruction of the laity in preparation for changes underway, for the teaching of liturgy in seminaries, and for founding pastoral liturgical institutes to do continuing education for the clergy. Obviously, retraining for everyone was a necessity. Frederick McManus once remarked that it was as if after an entire childhood of being warned never to cross the street, a parent suddenly said: "Okay, everyone cross the street today!" Strict warnings occurred against any individual changing any part of the official liturgy on his or her own account; authority was reserved to the Holy See "to approve or confirm the *acta* and decisions of territorial authorities" consisting of national or regional associations of bishops. Procedures for determining the use and extent of the vernacular language were provided; some ceremonies were dropped; Bible services were encouraged; and national and diocesan liturgical commissions were promoted. Changes made in the Mass included omission of the last gospel and the prayers added by Leo XIII (last in first out); a homily was to be mandatory at Sundays and feast days when a congregation was present; the prayer of the faithful might be introduced; and the vernacular could be used for the readings, the sung chants of the Ordinary, and in dialogue portions. No mention was made of the Canon, which remained in Latin for the time being. Various reforms were indicated for the other sacraments, the Divine Office, and church architecture.

This was pretty heady stuff when it first came out, although often not enough to satisfy more impatient priests, who were frequently taking matters into their own hands. The Second Instruction *(Tres abhinc annos)* of 1967 consisted mostly of minute regulations of things now allowed, such as "the maniple is no longer required." Maniples soon flooded flea markets. The Third Instruction *(Liturgicae instaurationes)* of 1970 took a much sterner approach, warning that "the private recasting of ritual introduced by an individual priest insults the dignity of the believer and lays the way open to individual and idiosyncratic celebrations that are in fact the property of the whole Church."[15] Things that may not be done loom large. But women could

14. *DOL*, no. 3, p. 89.
15. *DOL*, no. 1, p. 161.

read the lessons (except the gospel), pray the intercessions, play the organ, make announcements, serve as commentators and ushers.

As the work of the Consilium proceeded, gradually the revised liturgical books appeared. The period 1967 to 1972 was one of feverish excitement as each issue of *Notitiae* brought news of new documents approved in the Latin *editio typica*. Various portions of books appeared at different times: the ordination rites of the Pontifical were approved in 1968 and confirmation in 1971. Portions of the Ritual came out in 1969: marriage, funerals, baptism of infants. The new rite for Christian initiation of adults came out in 1972 and the reformed rite of reconciliation not until 1973. The reformed Liturgy of the Hours made its appearance in 1971. The Roman Missal was approved on Holy Thursday, 1969, effective at the beginning of the next liturgical year, that is, 1970. It replaced the Missal of Pius V of 1570.

But there was a problem that the Tridentine era did not have to face: the vernacular. What the Consilium produced was in Latin; what the Church now needed had to be in hundreds of different languages. An extraordinary congress was held in Rome in November 1965, sponsored by the Consilium, on the translation of liturgical books.[16] Guidelines on translations were established in a 1969 document of the Consilium, *Comme le prévoit*. It notes: "A translation of the liturgy . . . requires cautious adaptation."[17] A variety of topics became relevant: the history of translation, the style of liturgical language, etc. At this point there was much to be learned. Already it had been agreed that work would proceed on an international basis, namely, French: Québec, Belgium, France, and Switzerland; German: Austria, Germany, and Switzerland. Already in 1963, Paul Hallinan, progressive archbishop of Atlanta, had led the way in the formation of the International Commission on English in the Liturgy, usually referred to as ICEL. ICEL was established to accomplish the translation of the reformed Latin books into English.

That task was not easy, because not many people had done it since Thomas Cranmer did it in 1549, and Cranmer, perhaps, did it too well. The Roman Catholic bishops from England wanted a translation that sounded just like Cranmer's Book of Common Prayer; Americans

---

16. *Le Traduzioni dei libri liturgici* (Vatican City: Libreria Editrice Vaticana, 1966).

17. *DOL*, no. 21, p. 287.

demurred but had no ready example.[18] Research and debate went into deciding just what was good, contemporary liturgical English. The texts produced have functioned satisfactorily, but few people have expressed much enthusiasm over them. National and regional variances in English have gone unheeded. The issues of inclusive language were still ahead when the early texts were finalized. Ecumenism played a major part in the ecumenical International Consultation on English Texts (ICET), which translated jointly items such as the Lord's Prayer, the Creeds, *Gloria in excelsis*, etc.[19] ICET was replaced by the English Language Liturgical Commission (ELLC) in 1985.

The process was straightforward but the results were not always simple. Experts prepared the translations. They were then sent in "green book" form to all the bishops of English-speaking countries for comment. Revisions were made on the basis of these comments, and then a "white book" was sent out to be voted on by the bishops of each country. If they approved it, the text was sent to Rome for confirmation. Then it could be published and go into effect at a designated time for the whole episcopal conference.

What happened in an extraordinarily short time was that liturgical Latin became as dead as legal Latin, remembered only in brief snippets. Almost overnight Latin disappeared as a liturgical language, and young priests were as ignorant of it as their flocks. The Constitution on the Liturgy did not anticipate this, but, once allowed, the vernacular became irreversible. And a new liturgical language emerged in contemporary English.

With all the changes underway, academic training became necessary to form those who were to educate or re-educate priests. Balthasar Fischer (1912–2001) had become professor of liturgy at Trier in 1947. In 1956 the Institut Supérieur de Liturgie was established at Paris under the direction of Bernard Botte,[20] and soon the Pontifical Liturgical Institute at Sant' Anselmo in Rome followed. Many North American seminary professors of liturgy were trained in these institutes. In 1965

18. Jeffrey Kemper, "Behind the Text: A Study of . . . The International Commission on English in the Liturgy" (Ph.D. diss., University of Notre Dame, 1992).

19. *Prayers We Have in Common* (Philadelphia: Fortress Press, 1970, 1971, and 1975).

20. Bernard Botte, *From Silence to Participation* (Washington: Pastoral Press, 1988) 93–106.

a doctoral program in liturgical studies was begun at the University of Notre Dame, and another soon followed at The Catholic University of America. These European and American institutions and the doctoral programs in liturgy at Drew University and Graduate Theological Union in Berkeley have trained most liturgy professors now teaching in North America. In 1973 the North American Academy of Liturgy was organized by John Gallen so that liturgical scholars could share their research with one another and benefit the Churches. Originally mostly Roman Catholic in membership, the Academy has become nearly half Protestant and Jewish.

The new liturgical books as they appeared contained some radically new features. General instructions spelled out carefully the theological reasons underlying the new changes and gave pastoral dimensions. For the first time in many instances, a pluralistic approach was provided in which there were a number of different options: four Eucharistic Prayers appeared instead of one. Priests were now to make decisions based on local circumstances and occasions. After four centuries of more or less liturgical uniformity, pluralism had asserted itself. But to be used to best advantage, a trained imagination was necessary. So the teaching of liturgy in seminaries was taken out of the hands of canon lawyers and entrusted to people with advanced degrees in liturgical studies.

In all these changes, a new image of what it means to be the Church was both emerging and being expressed. These were not mere matters of tinkering with texts but means to enable the whole people of God to understand themselves as the Church and to be able to worship accordingly. Participation, "full, conscious, and active," was the motto, but it demanded participation of a baptized, informed, and committed community. Slowly people were beginning to comprehend the priestly nature of all the baptized. It now took far more people to celebrate Mass than when a single priest did everything. But even those not up front (wherever that might be) could see themselves on stage performing worship rather than as passive spectators.

Early on it was recognized that there were cultural barriers other than just language. Early issues of *Notitiae* speak of the problems of indigenization; for example, mention of a sacrificial lamb did not go over well in a Hindu land once the *Agnus Dei* was translated, and later permission was given to omit it. Over the years cultural issues moved closer to the forefront of liturgical controversy. The Immani Temple schism of black Catholics in Washington gave an immediate focus in the United States, but the problem was worldwide. In 1982, Anscar J. Chupungco began speaking of the need for "cultural adaptation," claiming that it was an imperative in light of the Incarnation.[21]

A major development of the 1960s, quite independent of Rome or any authority save the Holy Spirit, was the advent of Catholic Pentecostals, or charismatics. The Holy Spirit broke out where one might least expect it, among middle-class Roman Catholics at Duquesne University in 1966 and at Notre Dame in 1967.[22] Since then the various gifts of the Spirit—speaking in tongues, interpretation, prophecy, and healing—have manifested themselves to millions of Roman Catholics, lay and ordained. After an initial reaction of panic, the bishops welcomed the charismatic movement and encouraged priests to become involved. Charismatic Masses and prayer meetings became common. Studies have shown that charismatics tend to duplicate their peers in terms of social, economic, education, and psychological profiles.[23] Cardinal Leo Joseph Suenens of Belgium shepherded the movement on a worldwide basis. Leaders constantly made it clear that charismatic worship was not to replace the sacraments but to complement them.

Several names stand out in this whole process of liturgical reform. St. Hippolytus of Rome may not have effected any liturgical changes in third-century Rome, but that staunch conservative (or whoever actually compiled the *Apostolic Tradition*) engineered plenty of change in the twentieth century. Reforms of the Mass, the ordination rites, and the process of initiation are heavily indebted to his compilation.

Annibale Bugnini showed how essential the skillful liturgical bureaucrat is to the Church of our times. A master of diplomacy, he ended his days as pro-nuncio apostolic in Iran during the days of the Iran hostages. But his skills as a negotiator were never lacking in keeping the process of liturgical reform from being derailed. He well deserved the epitaph he chose: "He served the Church."

Little would have been possible without the strong encouragement of Pope Paul VI. As archbishop of Milan, he was formed in the Milanese or Ambrosian Rite, not the Roman. His actions and speeches

21. *Cultural Adaptation of the Liturgy* (New York: Paulist Press, 1982) 87.

22. Edward D. O'Connor, *The Pentecostal Movement in the Catholic Church* (Notre Dame: Ave Maria Press, 1971).

23. Kilian McDonnell, *Charismatic Renewal and the Churches* (New York: Seabury Press, 1976).

before and after he was elected pope showed a keen desire for liturgical reform.[24] This was fulfilled after his election, and he pushed the reform forward, giving it constant and detailed attention, so that much of the reform anticipated by Vatican II was essentially complete by the time of his death in 1978. A great host of others contributed to liturgical reform during this period of great surge forward.

RHYTHMS OF TIME AND DEVOTIONS

One of the biggest surprises to many people when it first appeared was the new calendar, the foundation of so much in the Missal and the Breviary. The new calendar and norms were published on March 21, 1969, although a *motu proprio* of February 14 had already approved the norms, all to become effective on January 1, 1970. The first norm was that "Sunday must be ranked as the first holyday of all," taking precedence over everything but "solemnities or feasts of the Lord."[25] Holy days were to be ranked as solemnities, feasts, and memorials. A thorough sorting out of saints' days occurred, those of universal importance being made universally obligatory; conversely, those of local significance were relegated to local observance. Easter and Christmas alone had octaves. The Easter Triduum was the culmination of the entire liturgical year. A new development was naming the seasons beginning on the Monday after the Sunday following January 6 and likewise on the Monday after Pentecost as "Ordinary Time." Some of the Marian feasts were terminated; others are placed in new contexts as feasts of the Lord. A new introduction was the Baptism of the Lord on the Sunday after January 6, and the feast of Christ the King was moved to the last Sunday of the liturgical year.

The end result was to reemphasize the priorities of the work of the Lord and to recover the priorities of the oldest calendars. A major simplification had occurred, especially in reducing the obligatory commemorations of lesser saints. Pierre Jounel was credited by Bugnini as the "principal author of the work." Yet there were negative reactions, especially from those who missed such feasts as the Most Precious Blood or saints of their nation or religious order. Some popular saints about whom nothing is known with historical certainty—

---

24. *Dialogo con Dio: Riflessi liturgici nei discorsi di Paolo VI* (Vatican City: Libreria Editrice Vaticana, 1966).

25. "General Norms for the Liturgical Year and the Calendar," *DOL*, nos. 4–5, p. 1156.

Sts. George, Christopher, Catherine of Alexandria—were dropped or made optional commemorations despite protests. Also to disappear were the season of Septuagesima, the term "Passiontide," and the octave of Pentecost. There was some juggling of the dates of the remaining saints in order to avoid conflicts, to be historically accurate, and to show universality. Particular calendars were to be added by national conferences, dioceses, and religious orders. The old oxymoron "holy days of obligation" was given some flexibility in allowing episcopal conferences to ask for changes.

All in all, the changes were sweeping and long overdue. A major shift for many people was permission given in 1964 to fulfill the Sunday obligation on Saturday evening. This became unexpectedly popular, perhaps too much so as emphasis on the day of resurrection was lessened.

The changes in the calendar both reflected and created new tendencies in devotions. There had been a reconsideration of Marian feasts, with some such as Mary, Mother of God, transferred to January 1, the feast of the Name of Mary suppressed, and others seen as primarily feasts of the Lord. This reflected an intention to see Mary in the context of the model of the Church. But it also was reflected over the next few decades in a significant slackening in Marian devotions: the rosary became largely the devotion of older Catholics, Marian altars tended to disappear, and most younger people hardly knew such hymns as *Salve Regina*. There are significant exceptions, such as the Marian apparitions at Medjugorge, but these have proved to be divisive in a way that Lourdes and Fatima never were. Pilgrims go to Medjugorge, and other Catholics make jokes about those who do so.

The same decrease also occurred in the cult of saints. If the very existence of Philomena was in doubt, what does that say about invoking her? The pruning of obligatory saints' commemorations was thorough, although Paul VI reinstituted some that were to have been made optional: Sts. Patrick, Charles Borromeo, and John of the Cross.[26] A whole array of saints' cults simply fell by the wayside. The invocation of St. Jude as patron of lost causes or St. Blaise for protection of throats would puzzle many younger Catholics today.

In similar fashion, many of the popular devotions evaporated almost overnight. Novenas came to be largely things of the past. The Stations of the Cross still held some appeal, especially during Lent,

26. Bugnini, *Reform of the Liturgy*, 313.

but when the stations were shuffled off to a side chapel, their hold was lessened, perhaps for good reasons. Even Friday abstinence, once the most conspicuous aspect of Roman Catholic identity, largely vanished. Exposition and Benediction of the Blessed Sacrament tended to disappear, although they made some comebacks in the 1980s.

Some of this loss of devotions has given more focus to the community and to the Eucharist. But there are voices that regret the impoverishment that the cessation of much devotional life has brought. There continues to be an impasse, especially given the failure of the Liturgy of the Hours to reach real people or, for that matter, many clergy and religious.[27] Return to the past seems unlikely, but future directions have not yet become plain.

THE MASS

Obviously, the most important revisions came in the Mass, although the calendar affected some of these. The Consilium provided seven *coetus* (study groups) to work on its revision. Early on, a schema for the *Missa normativa* experimented with the Order of Mass, that is, structure, and was tried out at the 1967 Synod of Bishops. Queries were addressed to the 183 bishops voting, and further input came from Paul VI. Eventually the Order of Mass was the basis for the new Roman Missal, which Paul VI promulgated in the apostolic constitution *Missale Romanum,* dated April 3, 1969.

Included in the reform besides the Order of Mass was a General Instruction, much of it written by Pierre Jounel. In the apostolic constitution *Missale Romanum,* Pope Paul VI pointed out that "the chief innovation in the reform concerns the eucharistic prayer." Citing the examples of the varied Eastern Canons, he says, ". . . we have decided to add three new canons to the eucharistic prayer."[28] All were to have uniform words of consecration based on the biblical texts. A second change was in the Order of Mass, and the third change mentioned was a three-year cycle of readings for Sunday Masses. An Old Testament reading was added. Changes in the Order included the opening penitential rite and the general intercessions. The homily was restored, as was the responsorial psalm and various Propers and votive Masses. All this was to go into effect on November 30, 1969, the first Sunday of

27. Carl Dehne, "Roman Catholic Popular Devotions," *Christians at Prayer* (Notre Dame: University of Notre Dame Press, 1977) 83–99.

28. *DOL,* p. 459.

liturgical year 1970. Actually, the new Roman Missal was not published until May 17, 1970.

The General Instruction was, in essence, a crash course in liturgical practice. It dealt with ministries, church arrangements and altars, rubrics, sacred vessels, and vestments. Various options appeared, so the priest had to make choices to be most pastorally effective. The number of prayers more than doubled from the Missal of Pius V, and wise selections were necessary.

The Sunday Lectionary was a major shift away from the one-year Lectionary with a thousand-year history. The Constitution had indicated a "richer fare" of God's Word, but it only specified "in the course of a prescribed number of years" (no. 51). A four-year cycle was considered but rejected. Nor did the Constitution mention the return of the Old Testament reading after an absence of over a millennium. It was left to episcopal conferences to determine what translation might lawfully be used in their regions. A vast array of scholars, some eight hundred in number, was consulted in choosing the pericopes.[29] In those days before computers, hundreds of pericopes were catalogued on three-by-five-inch cards in the Vatican City office of the secretary of *coetus* 11, Father Gaston Fontaine. It was the most thorough study and revision of a Lectionary in all Christian history and greatly expanded the number of texts appointed to be read. The basis adopted for each year was a synoptic gospel. Each Sunday (except in the Easter season) has an Old Testament reading related to the gospel for that day. The second reading (from the Epistles and Revelation) are read in course except on major festivals. It was all amazingly new, and one major American archdiocese, assuming that 1970 would start with year A, was out of phase until it discovered 1970 was actually year B.

The chief criticism now seems to be that the Old Testament reading is often distorted by having to backstop the gospel, and so the narratives of the Old Covenant are lost. Father Fontaine participated in a meeting of the Consultation on Common Texts (CCT) in 1978 in an effort to create a common Lectionary for all Christians that would remedy these faults and include a larger representation of passages involving women. The resulting Common Lectionary[30] (1983) and the

---

29. The author argued, apparently persuasively, for the addition of one verse to the epistle on the Second Sunday of Advent in Year A!

30. (New York: Church Hymnal Corporation, 1983).

Revised Common Lectionary[31] (1992), despite the appeals of the American bishops, have not been approved for liturgical use by Rome.

Easily the most controversial action was the creation of three new Eucharistic Prayers and revision of the venerable Roman Canon. There was a concern that when the Roman Canon was put into the vernacular, in the words of one of the consultors, "people would see what a mess it is." Historical scholarship had shown the early and continued existence of multiple Eucharistic Prayers, even though the Roman Rite (and most Protestant rites) allowed only one. There were also theological concerns, such as the neglect in the West of reference to the instrumentality of the Holy Spirit, so prominent in Eastern Rites. Important preparatory work had been done by Cipriano Vagaggini.[32]

The result was a modified Roman Canon, somewhat abbreviated, as the first Eucharistic Prayer. The second one was based on that found in the *Apostolic Tradition*. The third was a modern composition along lines suggested by Vagaggini. Number four was based on a more leisurely recital of salvation history in biblical terms, similar to the ancient prayer of St. Basil. The first three used variable prefaces, the fourth was invariable. After so many centuries of no invocation of the Holy Spirit, the new prayers now have two. A preliminary epiclesis (invocation of the Spirit) apparently was added to allay the suspicions of the Holy Office that the words of institution were being downplayed, but it seems redundant with another epiclesis occurring later. The new prayers were approved on April 27, 1968. Three Eucharistic Prayers for use with children and two for Masses of reconciliation were authorized in 1974. Requests from Belgium and the Netherlands for more Eucharistic Prayers met a cold reception in Rome, although many priests had already taken such matters into their own hands.

A major development, also heralded in the Low Countries, was the theological development of a new way of describing what the Church experiences in the Eucharist. Trent had said that this was most aptly *(aptissime)* called "transubstantiation." But in the course of time, "substance" had come to mean for modern people a chemical, as in "substance abuse." It was shown that the term no longer conveyed what was intended when it was first used in the late twelfth century

31. (Nashville: Abingdon Press, 1992).

32. Cipriano Vagaggini, *The Canon of the Mass and Liturgical Reform* (London: Geoffrey Chapman, 1967; Italian ed. 1966).

or even in the sixteenth.[33] Theologians began to speak of "transsignification" as a more adequate way to communicate this reality to the modern mind. In this approach, meaning constituted the being of an object, just as strips of colored cloth sewn together become something entirely different—a flag.

Edward Schillebeeckx argued that in the Eucharist "the real, ontological meaning of the bread, that is, the bread itself, is thus radically changed—it is no longer orientated towards man as bread. . . . A new object comes into being . . . the sacrament of Christ's body and blood."[34] While encouraging theological research, Paul VI issued a cautious encyclical, *Mysterium Fidei,* in 1965, insisting that transubstantiation involved an ontological change. The bread and wine "take on this new significance and this new finality . . . simply because they contain a new 'reality' which we may justly term ontological."[35] Schillebeeckx seemed to be trying to meet these terms while communicating in a way that makes more sense to moderns than do Scholastic formularies based on Aristotle. Much less has been written in recent years about the Mass as sacrifice and much more as memorial meal. Yet the current meanings of these terms (which, after all, may be the same) are far from resolution.

How much these theological debates have helped the average worshiper is uncertain. Catholics were being bombarded by further changes in familiar practices. Not only is Communion received standing, in the hand, but under both kinds (Constitution, no. 55). Furthermore, frequently the ministers of Communion are lay people, including women. One thing is certain: far more people are receiving Communion. One rarely sees many non-communicants at Mass; almost everyone present receives sacramental Communion. One survey found that in most parishes studied about 90 to 95 percent of those present communed.[36] The bad news was that for many respondents, the sense that they were doing something together, even at the

33. Piet Schoonenberg, "Transubstantiation: How Far Is This Doctrine Historically Determined?" in *The Debate on the Sacraments,* Concilium 24 (New York: Paulist Press, 1967) 78–91.

34. *The Eucharist* (New York: Sheed and Ward, 1968) 116.

35. *Mysterium Fidei: On the Holy Eucharist* (Washington: National Catholic Welfare Council, 1965), par. 46, p. 14.

36. Kathleen Hughes, "Speaking in the Future Tense," in *The Awakening Church* (Collegeville, Minn.: The Liturgical Press, 1992) 132.

coffee hour, was more important than the fact of actually feeding on the Body of Christ. The hunger for community may outweigh the ritual forms by which it is signified.

A further disquieting fact is the increasing shortage of priests. Measures have been taken for the growing number of priestless parishes. So-called Sunday "Communion services, in which bread, consecrated by an absent priest, is given in Communion, have proliferated. It is something like using a catering service instead of enjoying home-cooked food. Unless something changes in the existing discipline of ordination, this situation is likely to get worse. Historically, two methods have been used to deal with similar situations: the conservative approach is to ordain more presbyters; the liberal, to allow lay celebrants. The latter developed on the American frontier among Protestants; today it happens (unofficially) in frontier situations among Roman Catholics in Brazil and the Yukon or even among Catholic feminists in metropolitan areas.[37]

RHYTHMS OF THE LIFE CYCLE

Unlike the Missal, the Ritual has been published only as separate volumes. There is, after all, no need for the ritual wedding book at a funeral. But that may tell us something significant about the attempt to make the Ritual and its sacraments relevant to the vastly different circumstances of life's passages and journeys. The Constitution had mandated that the rite for infant baptism was to be revised to show that it is actually meant for infants (no. 67). Each rite, then, is distinguished and defined by its recipient.

But there are, nonetheless, some common factors. Generally the rites are simplified: the blowing and the giving of salt are no longer mandated at baptism. All the rites have introduced some form of Liturgy of the Word, even if brief. The rites all have a variety of options to adapt them to the persons, place, and time. And a brief (emergency) rite is provided in each instance for use when necessary. There is no question that the rites have been reformed and, in several instances, quite drastically so.

In Christian initiation there is a tendency to envision the whole process as unitive, although this has not yet been accomplished with infants as in the Eastern Rites. It was new for Catholics to have a rite

---

37. Leonardo Boff, *Ecclesiogenesis: The Base Communities Reinvent the Church* (Maryknoll: Orbis Books, 1986) 61–75.

expressly designed for infants; the 1614 rite was really an adult rite adapted for children. The rite for infants was finally published in 1969, effective on September 8. Within a decade infant baptism itself was being seriously questioned by some European theologians as meaningless in a secularized culture, and a few Americans echoed these sentiments, although in a different sociological context. Rome issued an Instruction in 1980 defending the baptism of infants of Christian parents, a defense unneeded since Trent.[38]

Much more exciting was the new Rite for the Christian Initiation of Adults. Balthasar Fischer of Trier took the lead in producing a whole new process that resembled greatly that of the *Apostolic Tradition* of the third century. The rite was finally published on Epiphany, 1972. Important aspects involve the restoration of the catechumenate as a reality, not just as a brief formality. The candidate proceeds through several stages or steps: acceptance into the order of catechumens, election or enrollment of names, and celebration of the sacraments of initiation. Each of these involves prior periods of evangelization, catechumenate, purification, and enlightenment. All are succeeded by a period of post-baptismal catechesis.

What has happened is that once again the process of conversion is ritualized in a communal way.[39] Apparently the RCIA, as it is known, has been little utilized in Europe but has become an important aspect of parish life in North America. This widespread use is due partly to the energetic role of Aidan Kavanagh, a former student of Fischer's, who became an evangelist for the new rite.[40] The new rite has helped to renew the American Church, since, of necessity, the rite has involved many lay people as catechists. Their faith is strengthened in strengthening that of others. The whole process comes to a grand climax at the Easter Vigil as new Christians are baptized, confirmed (usually by a priest), and given first Communion on the morning of the Resurrection. It is a highly dramatic occasion.

If the RCIA gives important answers to the making of Christians, the isolated rite of confirmation raises only questions. In 1994 the American bishops were still debating the age of confirmation and

38. Sacred Congregation for the Doctrine of the Faith, *Instruction on Infant Baptism* (Vatican City: Vatican Polyglot Press, 1980).

39. *The Rites of the Catholic Church*, vol. 1 (Collegeville, Minn.: The Liturgical Press, 1990) 15–356.

40. *The Shape of Baptism* (New York: Pueblo Publishing Company, 1978).

finally allowed a latitude reaching from seven to eighteen years. Beyond that is the question of what confirmation does that baptism has not already done. The new Rite of Confirmation was published in August 1971. The question was raised, "What is the chief act, anointing or laying on of hands?" Chrism prevailed and the form was changed to: "Be sealed with the gift of the Holy Spirit." This is a change in the Western tradition, moving, as on so many other occasions, in an Eastern direction.

The new marriage rites proved less controversial, since many of the changes were inevitable, especially those affirming the equality of the spouses. The rites appeared in February 1969. Adaptability was a necessity; forms had to be provided for marriage during a Mass or outside Mass and for marriage of a Catholic and an unbaptized person.

Funerals were even more complicated, partly because of the great differences in funeral customs in various lands. The whole purpose of the revision was to express the paschal nature of Christian death. In view of different customs, various possibilities are presented of stations at the home, the church, and the cemetery, with various combinations possible. Texts are provided for the burial of a child and other pastoral situations, such as a suicide.

In the development of the funeral rites, experimentation was done in the United States and Europe. The rite was published in Latin in 1969. Years of experience on the pastoral level led to an American revision finished in 1985.

Few Catholics would have recognized the term "reconciliation" as the sacrament of confession before the 1970s. Revision was a slow process, and the rites were not published until December 2, 1973, when most of the other new rites had already become quite familiar. Theological battles had ensued over the formula of absolution and over general absolution, delaying completion of the rites. An effort was made to express the necessity of a sense of reconciliation of individuals to the community as well as to God. Three rites were provided: reconciliation of individuals, reconciliation of a group with communal preparation for individual confession and absolution, and communal preparation and absolution.

Subsequently, restrictions were increasingly placed on communal absolution. What seemed to be the wave of the future has apparently dried up. On the other hand, the number of individuals coming to confession has dropped drastically. The environment has changed too. Instead of salvation by claustrophobia in a small confessional, reconciliation rooms have become common, where priest and penitent talk face to face and unhurried spiritual counseling can occur.

The most drastic change of all occurred with extreme unction, now known as anointing of the sick. The new name indicates a whole new (and very ancient) orientation directed to healing of the body and soul. The new rites were approved in November 1972. The sacramental formula was changed, as well as the context: "Through this holy anointing may the Lord in his love and mercy help you with the grace of the Holy Spirit. May the Lord who frees you from sin save you and raise you up." The sacrament may be repeated when necessary. A new continuous rite of penance, anointing, and Viaticum for those in grave danger is provided. The whole is to emphasize God's grace rather than human sinfulness. Anointing remains an act of the ordained priest, although lay persons have become active in bringing Communion to the sick.[41]

CHURCH MUSIC

It is difficult to trace a single theme in church music. Indeed, despite valiant efforts, there has been more discord than harmony. Out of this ferment definite patterns are hard to trace.

In the early years of the reform, the idea of a singing congregation was exciting. Already in 1958, The Liturgical Press, under the direction of Father William Heidt, had published *Our Parish Prays and Sings*, followed in 1959 by *Book of Sacred Song*. Pioneers in the years immediately after the Council were Dennis Fitzpatrick and the Friends of the English Liturgy (F.E.L.), who began publishing in the 1960s with such items as *Hymnal for Young Christians* (1966). Not to be outdone, the World Library of Sacred Music produced the *People's Mass Book* in 1964. Soon they were joined by other hymnals: *The Catholic Hymnal* (1966) and *The Book of Catholic Worship* (1966), among others. The genre has continued to multiply.

In the shuffle the Gregorian effort virtually disappeared except for a few monasteries. It would now seem elitist, and perhaps the "mud level" has prevailed. The Liturgical Conference published the proceedings of a symposium, appropriately entitled *Crisis for Church Music?*[42] giving positions entitled right, left, and far left. Those who

41. John J. Ziegler, *Let Them Anoint the Sick* (Collegeville, Minn.: The Liturgical Press, 1987).
42. (Washington: Liturgical Conference, 1967).

had been trained to see music as the performance of professionals were very much threatened by what they saw as the deterioration of musical standards. Those who looked to music as participatory saw their day at hand. Liturgical music of the few was to be replaced by musical liturgy of the many.

Guidance was needed, and in 1967 the Congregation of Rites issued the Instruction on Music in the Sacred Liturgy *(Musicam sacram)*. This argued that "the Church does not exclude any type of sacred music from liturgical services as long as the music matches the spirit of the service."[43] Congregational singing was encouraged, choirs were to be developed, singing of the responsorial psalm particularly stressed, and a variety of instruments were permissible.

In the United States, the Bishops' Committee on the Liturgy issued *Music in Catholic Worship* 1972. It contained what soon became a slogan: "Good celebrations foster and nourish faith. Poor celebrations weaken and destroy faith."[44] Music was to be seen as a pastoral element, particularly in singing the acclamations, processional songs, responsorial psalm, and the ordinary chants. Ten years later, instead of a revision, *Liturgical Music Today*[45] was published. This treated matters omitted previously.

In the early years of the reform it was soon discovered that the pipe organ was not the only instrument that could be used in worship. For a time the guitar seemed to be the instrument of choice, especially among younger Catholics. A whole variety of other instruments were enlisted.

New service music in the vernacular began to be composed, such as that by David Isele and Howard Hughes in a neo-classic, contemporary style. In the 1960s and 1970s, the settings of the psalms done by Joseph Gelineau had great popularity as a means of congregational singing of the psalms without forcing them into metrical paraphrases. This method utilized a cantor or choir to sing the verses, alternating with a congregational refrain. Cantors and song leaders became a permanent fixture in many parishes.

Most important and most problematic was congregational hymnody. Here much borrowing went on, and for a time it was hard to go to Mass without hearing "A Mighty Fortress," despite the fact that one was never quite clear whether the "ancient foe" to whom Luther

43. *DOL*, no. 9, p. 1295.
44. (Washington: Bishops' Committee on the Liturgy, 1972) 1.
45. (Washington: United States Catholic Conference, 1982).

referred was the devil or Pope Leo X! Eventually the compliment was returned as newer Protestant hymnals served up generous helpings from the St. Louis Jesuits and others.

Unlike Protestant services, hymns do not seem to have an integral place in the Mass but get plunked down somewhat *ad libitum.* One gets the impression that hymns are not really considered worship or else they would be regulated by Rome. They seem to be more singing *at* the liturgy than singing the liturgy. As a consequence, a wide variety of hymnals are in use in the United States, depending on the taste (or lack thereof) of the parish. Canadian Catholics have a standard hymnal, but American Catholics rejected that possibility for a hymnic free-enterprise system, in contrast to mainline Protestant congregations, which feel obliged to use an official denominational hymnal. In hymnody, Catholic parishes experience more freedom than their Protestant neighbors.

At one time, "They Will Know We Are Christians by Our Love" was almost inescapable at Mass. Today that is forgotten, although the folk-music genre seems to be a permanent option. A hymnal is a very political document, and recent ones seem to contain something for everyone.

Continually efforts have been made to introduce liturgical dance into worship. These are often stymied because liturgical dance is often seen as a highly professional art that excludes most people. Rome put out a rather negative statement on this subject, "La Danza nella Liturgia," largely asserting that dance was not an "integral part of the official worship of the Latin Church."[46] A minimum of gesture has been successfully introduced, especially the exchange of the sign of peace.

PREACHING

It is difficult to describe the changes in preaching in a systematic way. One frequently hears of Catholics choosing to attend Mass at such and such a parish because "I get so much out of Father So-and-so's preaching." The audience of television evangelists (or televised worship) is said to be 30 percent Catholic. Preaching is an important part of the consciousness of Roman Catholics today and is no longer regarded as a brief interruption of their devotions during Mass.

In the years after Vatican II, Protestant professors of homiletics found their books selling briskly among Catholic seminarians, and

46. *Notitiae* 11 (1975) 202–205.

this is still true for some. But a whole literature on Roman Catholic homiletics has now developed. Homiletics is a major discipline in seminaries, and at least one foundation has been established to promote and improve preaching in Roman Catholic parishes. Lay people have also learned to preach, and in several seminaries sisters now teach homiletics.

Much of the improvement has come about as a result of the three-year Sunday Mass Lectionary. A far "richer fare" of Scripture is read than at any time since the early Church. The Liturgy of the Word is now an important part of every Mass. For the preacher, there is an abundance of scriptural commentaries, mostly ecumenical. In many communities clergy discuss the texts with their peers in other traditions each week in a spontaneous form of grassroots ecumenism. A busy pastor now has a jump start in doing exegesis and collecting ideas from both printed and human sources.

The net result has been a move to a much more exegetical style of preaching in which a text is explored and then applied. As a rule, sermons tend to be based on the gospel, occasionally on the second reading, and rarely on the Old Testament reading. Far fewer sermons on the Old Testament reading seem to be preached than in other traditions. In some parishes a committee of clergy and laity prepares the homily.

In 1982 the Bishops' Committee on Priestly Life and Ministry published *Fulfilled in Your Hearing: The Homily in the Sunday Assembly.* This booklet stresses the importance of the homily as "a part of the liturgy itself." Regarding its relation to Scripture, the document states: "The homily is not so much *on* the Scriptures as *from* and *through* them."[47] Practical details are provided on "homiletic method," including the use of a homily preparation group.

The advent of a sizable number of black Catholics has also given a boost to preaching. Black preaching styles may be limited to a particular cultural setting, but they constantly demonstrate the power of the spoken word.

PUBLIC PRAYER

The news on public prayer is less encouraging. The revision of the Breviary proved to be a wearisome task. It was renamed the Liturgy of the Hours and was not published until 1971. By that time many clergy

47. (Washington: United States Catholic Conference, 1982) 20.

and not a few religious had become accustomed to devising their own means of daily prayer, and the Liturgy of the Hours may affect only a minority. No survey seems to exist of those using the official texts and might be too embarrassing to take.

Certainly many reforms were made: the psalms are distributed over a four-week period, the emphasis is on Morning and Evening Prayer; only one of the Little Hours is read; the Office of Readings, a liturgical anomaly, can be at any convenient time; and Compline fits its time at night. Each Hour has a Scripture lesson, each opens with a hymn, and problematic portions of the psalms are excluded. A major effort to reform the Breviary for the use of clergy and religious was certainly made.

But some have questioned whether this was enough. The new Liturgy of the Hours is monastic in concept and in most details. "Such an office, more a contemplative prayer than a popular devotional service, may be eminently suitable for the private prayer of clergy and religious. But this skirts the real issue, which is whether the Liturgy of the Hours should be a prayerbook for the clergy, or something more."[48]

Unfortunately, that "something more" has yet to appear. The Bible services that the Constitution on the Liturgy and the [First] Instruction mentioned never happened. In some parishes a Sunday Vesper service has gained some popularity, and Benediction has been reinstituted in others. The whole daily Hours are prayed together in a few parishes, especially during Advent and Lent. But as far as providing a viable alternative to the Mass as public prayer, especially on a daily basis, no provision seems to have been made successfully. In this sense, the revised Liturgy of the Hours is the chief failure of the revised books. But we must not be too harsh; the revisers were not really concerned about producing services for other than religious professionals. And one failure out of so many successes is certainly an enviable record.

48. Robert Taft, *The Liturgy of the Hours in East and West* (Collegeville, Minn.: The Liturgical Press, 1986) 316.

Chapter Seven

The Journey Beyond
the Second Vatican Council

The end of publication of the major revised liturgical books after the Second Vatican Council marked the beginning of an ambiguous journey in liturgical history. It also marked a period of cultural turmoil in which the world moved from relief that the cold war had ended to apprehension of what a world on high alert for terrorism might experience.

Many of the reforms initiated at Vatican II continued to thrive and grow. But bit by bit some of those reforms began to be challenged or even reversed. Latin Masses were again allowed under certain circumstances, after they had almost disappeared except among radical fringe groups. Images that had been banished from churches began to traipse back in the doors. Reforms that seemed to be irrevocable were challenged even to the point of a high Vatican official praising the location of the altar against the wall. People who had devoted their entire ministries to liturgical reform were abruptly dismissed. At the same time, other new features of parish life such as the Rite of Christian Initiation of Adults continued to grow in outreach and depth. And numerous polls showed that the laity approved of the post-Vatican II reforms by majorities usually exceeding two to one.

Apparently nothing is irrevocable today any more than when Pius V reformed the Mass irrevocably in 1570. But it does seem unlikely that the enthusiasm for public participation largely facilitated by the use of the vernacular will slacken. Nor does it seem that the laity will willingly recede into a passive role at Mass. But the lesson is clear: the path of liturgical reform is a zigzag process, not a straight line. Clearly there are divisions among those who think and care deeply about the liturgy, and these have increasingly come into sharp conflict in recent years. A number of books dispute any benefits from post-Vatican II reforms, for example, *Losing the Sacred* (David Torevelli, 2000) and *The Recovery of the Sacred* (James Hitchcock, 1974). We shall survey briefly the conflicts over liturgy and the ambiguous process of liturgical reform since 1984.

BUILT OF LIVING STONES

Many of the architectural trends already noticed in Chapter Six continued in the following years. The strange development is that they came to be both challenged and affirmed. Much encouragement for new possibilities came from the *Environment and Art Letter* published by Liturgy Training Publications in Chicago. The same publisher put out a series of ten provocative booklets, significantly entitled *Meeting House Essays*. In Number 5, *Renewing the City of God*, Michael E. Sanctis states that "of the forms resulting from modern experimentation in Catholic architecture, those that have proven most popular are the following: 1) the hall church, 2) the fan-shaped church, and 3) the modified long church."[1] Observation would indicate that by the early twenty-first century the fan-shaped plan, with altar, pulpit, and presider's chair in the middle of the long side, had become the most popular in new Catholic churches. A good example is St. Robert's in Grand Rapids, Michigan. Almost inevitably, such buildings are contemporary in design; period styles do not readily adapt to new floor plans. The attraction of the fan shape is that all the liturgical centers for Mass are visible and accessible to everyone present.

The last two decades have experienced a major recovery of the importance of the sacrament of baptism; efforts have been made to make it an act of the entire community and one having the highest sign value. Evidence of this shift in priorities is apparent in many experiments on a local level,[2] none of them imposed by either Rome or the American bishops, but simply the consequence of grassroots decisions. The results have been varied and not always satisfactory. Fonts have been placed in locations such as where the high altar once stood (St. Clement's, Chicago), near or in the sanctuary, or most frequently,

1. (Chicago: Liturgy Training Publications, 1993) 15.
2. Johan M. J. van Parys, "A Place for Baptism: New Trends in Baptismal Architecture since the Second Vatican Council" (Ph.D. diss., University of Notre Dame, 1998).

just inside the main door. Fonts have often become baptismal pools so as to accommodate the complete immersion of an adult (Sts. Peter and Paul, Hamburg, New York) or an adult standing so that he or she may be deluged with water (St. Pius X, Granger, Indiana). Sometimes there are two pools—a small one for the immersion of infants and a larger one for adults (St. Elizabeth Seton, Carmel, Indiana). At stake is the signification of baptism as a meaningful act of beginning life as a Christian, not just a ceremony of Christian cuteness. These changes have come about from experienced need on the parish level.

However, there have been some contrary currents, some of them from aesthetic reasons, others from liturgical or devotional concerns. On the popular level, Thomas Day articulated both of these concerns in his witty *Where Have You Gone, Michelangelo?*[3] Traditionalists became more vocal in insisting that much that was precious had been lost in the post-Vatican renovations and rebuildings. Maybe all those images discarded from churches were not all that bad. Some of them began to reappear either out of nostalgia or from genuine attachment. By then most were completely foreign to a younger generation of Catholics, who were accustomed only to sparse churches that focused on liturgy, not on devotions.

A more organized assault on the recent developments appeared in various quarters at the same time that major cathedrals were being renovated by Richard Vosko, Robert Rambusch, and others. The Archdiocese of Los Angeles was also building a great new cathedral (2002), quite simple in images and definitely contemporary in form.

At the University of Notre Dame a new periodical appeared from the School of Architecture. It was called *Sacred Architecture* and advocated a return to historic styles, with little regard to modern liturgical changes. In 2001 the Liturgical Institute at the University of St. Mary of the Lake/Mundelein Seminary, Mundelein, Illinois, sponsored a conference on church architecture for the year 2010. It initiated a competition for a church designed in a classical style. *Environment and Art in Catholic Worship*, which had been regarded by many as a significant, if not the most significant, American document on liturgical reform, was suddenly being disparaged and its authority questioned. The result was that in 2000 a new document appeared, this time fully approved by the American bishops. *Built of Living Stones*[4] was the result

3. (New York: Crossroad, 1993).
4. (Washington: United States Catholic Conference, 2000).

of four years of work on a document originally entitled *Domus Dei*. The new document lacks the inspired words of *Environment and Art* but details in much more specific and legalistic fashion the needs of Catholic liturgical space. All is fully documented, offering security instead of imagination. Obviously, we have entered into a different era than that which produced *Environment and Art*.

LITURGICAL EVENTS AND PERSONS

Liturgical reform had definitely turned a new corner by the time the last of the major liturgical books, the Ceremonial of Bishops, was approved on September 14, 1984. (The ICEL translation did not appear until five years later.) The book was seen as a move to a much more juridical and legalistic approach than the previous books. The books that had preceded seemed much more adventuresome by comparison. Emissaries from Rome received a rather cool reception when the book was presented at a West Coast conference.

Increasingly there were signs that a new era was beginning. Although it did not appear until 1996, a major article by M. Francis Mannion, then a priest of the Salt Lake City diocese, stated what was to become a strong minority position: the need to "recatholicize the reform." In his discussion of options then current, Mannion succeeded in placing this option somewhere near midstream of "five liturgical movements." These range all the way from a return to the Tridentine Mass as the only route to orthodoxy at one extreme to radical surgery on the existing rites in favor of drastic inculturation at the other extreme. Mannion does not reject the official reform outright. "What distinguishes the recatholicizing agenda," he says, "is that it regards the principal challenge of ongoing liturgical reform as *spiritual* rather than *structural*."[5] He speaks of "a recovery of the sacred and the numinous in liturgical expression that will act as a corrective to the sterility and rationalism of much modern liturgical experience." This, he hopes, would rescue "present-day liturgical practice from its excessively pragmatic, didactic and functional conceptions." Far from rejecting the revised books, he seeks greater depth in their use but is vague on specifics.

Mannion denies the insidious anti-Protestant sound of "recatholicizing," although the late Mark Searle once remarked that what

5. "Agendas for Liturgical Reform," *America* 175, no. 17 (November 30, 1996) 16.

Vatican II really said is that it is "okay" to be Protestant when it comes to worship. Much of the liturgical history of the last half of the twentieth century can be described as a dialogue between Catholic and Protestant liturgical practices and concepts. The terms "pragmatic, didactic, and functional," which Mannion condemns, seem to be characteristics of the culture of the time. But they might also describe the needs for which Gregorian chant was first invented.

In order to carry out this "recatholicizing," several institutions came into being. The Society for Catholic Liturgy was organized in 1995. In response to this, a more liberal group named the Catholic Academy of Liturgy was formed at the annual meeting of the North American Academy of Liturgy in 2002.

The Society for Catholic Liturgy began a publication called *Antiphon: A Journal for Liturgical Renewal* in 1998. Its articles take a consistently conservative approach, while the journal *Worship*, published by The Liturgical Press, is much more liberal, generally favoring the official reforms and ICEL, although not uncritical at times.

The new millennium brought the opening of the Liturgical Institute at the University of Saint Mary of the Lake/Mundelein Seminary in Mundelein, Illinois. This was established in 2001 in direct competition with the long-established Ph.D. and M.A. programs in liturgy at the University of Notre Dame and the M.A. programs in liturgy at Catholic Theological Union in Chicago, both nearby. Since the early 1970s the Notre Dame program has been fully ecumenical both in faculty and student body. Some of the doctoral students and faculty in liturgy at Drew and Graduate Theological Union have been Catholics, as well as all the faculty and most of the students in liturgy at The Catholic University of America.

Clearly liturgy has again become a battleground among Catholics, and efforts at finding "common ground" have done little to reduce the casualties. Catholics now have their own "worship wars." Those who have given many years of devoted work to the official agenda were among the wounded. Gabe Huck was relieved of his work in making Liturgy Training Publications a major publisher for liturgical renewal, and John R. Page left after years of heading up the work of ICEL. The Bishops' Committee on the Liturgy received a new chairman in 2002, the conservative archbishop of Chicago, Cardinal Francis George, O.M.I. Clearly the pendulum was now swinging in a different direction.

No doubt many of the changes on the American scene reflected a similar shift to the right in Rome. Petitions from the American bishops to adopt the ecumenical marriage rite or the Revised Common Lectionary were rebuffed by Rome. Ecumenical work on liturgical renewal went from being put on hold to the line going dead. One leading ecumenist declared in 2002 that "the entire ecumenical liturgical conversation and dialogue is over—finished, dead, done."[6] A flap had occurred earlier over the biblical translation allowed in the readings at Mass. To the disappointment of many, the New Revised Standard Version translation was forbidden in the United States but not in Canada, probably over fears that it had made mild concessions to feminist critiques of gratuitous sexist language in earlier versions.

The real conflict was over a growing conviction on the part of many liturgical scholars that the chief liturgical issue was inculturation. This term, which Anscar Chupungco attributed to a Protestant missionary, G. L. Barney,[7] was picked up, eventually appearing even in papal documents. Chupungco himself defined inculturation as "the process of inserting the texts and rites of the liturgy into the framework of the local culture."[8] A somewhat broader definition appears in Aylward Shorter as "the creative and dynamic relationship between the Christian message and a culture or cultures."[9]

All this provided much stimulus for further exploration. Chupungco described three stages: "Dynamic Equivalence," "Creative Assimilation," and "Organic Progression." He picked up with relish one of the more radical passages from *Comme le prévoit* of 1969: "Texts translated from another language are clearly not sufficient for the celebration of a fully renewed liturgy. The creation of new texts will be necessary."[10]

Much ferment continued. In 1969 the bishops of Zaire began planning a distinctively African Mass. After long delays, the Vatican approved in 1988 the Roman Missal for the Dioceses of Zaire. This allowed for the inclusion of congregational liturgical dance, reverence of ancestors, and placing the penitential rite and sign of peace at the

6. Quoted from Horace T. Allen, "Liturgist Says Ecumenical Dialogue Is Dead," *National Catholic Reporter*, vol. 38, no. 29 (May 24, 2002) 7.

7. Anscar Chupungco, *Liturgical Inculturation: Sacramentals, Religiosity, and Catechesis* (Collegeville, Minn.: The Liturgical Press, 1992) 25.

8. Ibid., 30.

9. Aylward Shorter, *Toward a Theology of Inculturation* (London: Orbis Books, 1989) 11.

10. *Documents on the Liturgy 1963–1979: Conciliar, Papal, and Curial Texts* (Collegeville, Minn.: The Liturgical Press, 1982) no. 43, p. 291.

conclusion of the Liturgy of the Word. Clearly the long delay indicated that the Vatican was nervous about the more radical implications of inculturation. The larger issue was centralization of liturgical control versus local control and openness to "legitimate variations and adaptations" that the Constitution on the Liturgy had advocated (nos. 37–40). It was a question of authority—whose authority?

Rome made its position crystal clear in the Fourth Instruction on the Roman Liturgy and Inculturation *(Varietates legitimae)*,[11] issued by the Congregation for Divine Worship and Discipline of the Sacraments on January 25, 1994, nearly thirty years after the previous instruction. It insists, as does the Constitution, that "the process of inculturation should maintain the *substantial unity* of the Roman Rite," but whereas the Constitution envisions that "the competent territorial ecclesiastical authorities" should take the initiative, that seems to be preempted by the Congregation. In effect, "episcopal oversight of liturgical inculturation is reduced to the level of 'making proposals' that can be summarily vetoed as 'undesirable' or 'unnecessary' by a Roman dicastery."[12] Far from promoting exploration and experimentation, the Fourth Instruction gives faint hope for "the creation of new texts." There is more than a strong hint of return to the tight control that the old Congregation of Sacred Rites exercised for so many centuries.

If any doubts remained about the direction things were heading, they were resolved by the Fifth Instruction on the Use of Vernacular Languages in the Publication of the Books of the Roman Liturgy *(Liturgiam authenticam),* which the same Congregation issued on March 28, 2001. *Liturgiam authenticam* tightens the process of translation into the vernacular, effectively changing much of the process. Control passes to national or regional conferences of bishops rather than such joint enterprises as ICEL in the English-speaking world. The Instruction insists on fidelity to the Latin originals. No softening of exclusive language is to be allowed; inclusive language is not to be substituted.[13] Phrases such as "Son of Man" or the masculine terms for members of the Trinity are to be kept, while the Church itself is to be treated to feminine pronouns. In other words, efforts at linguistic

11. Text in *Liturgiam Authenticam:* Fifth Instruction on Vernacular Translation of the Roman Liturgy (Washington: United States Conference of Catholic Bishops, 2001) 213.
12. Nathan Mitchell, "The Amen Corner," *Worship* 68 (1994) 373.
13. *Liturgiam Authenticam,* 63–64.

justice are to be ignored. The whole document appears to discourage ecumenical cooperation on liturgical translation, and the rebuff to inclusive language raises a massive barrier to any further joint work.

The journey *beyond* Vatican II, it seemed to many, was turning into a journey *from* Vatican II, although both sides on every issue faithfully quoted from the Constitution on the Liturgy. Inculturation was such an explosive issue that Rome was making it certain that nothing got out of its control. Still, various pressure groups called for more local control, more recognition of the presence of women, and respect for various minorities. Perhaps the real issue was not liturgical incultura-tion but liturgical centralization, a systemic problem.

RHYTHMS OF TIME AND DEVOTIONS

No major tinkering with the liturgical calendar occurred in the last two decades of the twentieth century. All the churches seem to have accepted the consumer culture in making convenience a priority. Hence Saturday afternoon celebrations continued to flourish, even though the reference to the weekly day of resurrection seemed to be impoverished. An eloquent praise of the significance of Sunday came on Pentecost, 1988, in the apostolic letter of Pope John Paul II, *Dies Domini* ("The Day of the Lord"). It describes the Sunday Eucharist as "the paradigm for other Eucharistic celebrations" and insists that nothing else "is as vital or as community-forming as the Sunday cele-bration of the Lord's Day and his Eucharist."[14] Sunday is day of the Resurrection, day of the Church, and day of the Eucharist. Thus each Sunday is Easter, and Christian faith should have its focus on the joy of the Resurrection, not the gloom of the Crucifixion.

This impressive document had been preceded ten years earlier by *Paschale solemnitatis* ("On Preparing and Celebrating the Paschal Feasts"), published by the Congregation for Divine Worship as a circu-lar letter. No new departures are announced here, but strong encour-agement is provided so that during Lent and Easter "the great mystery of our redemption be celebrated in the best possible way."[15] Divided into sections on Lent, Holy Week, the Easter Triduum in general and in detail, and Easter Time, it leads one through two seasons of the year with great pastoral sensitivity. Appropriately, the Easter

14. *Liturgy Documents: A Parish Resource* (Chicago: Liturgy Training Publica-tions, 1999) 2:24.
15. *Liturgy Documents*, 2:60.

Vigil receives the most attention, with concern expressed that the whole community experience "the riches of the prayers and rites." A continuing practical problem remains in the tendency of pastors to schedule the Easter Vigil in daylight hours for convenience. Yearly scoldings appear in various official publications to remind them that the rich symbol of light and dark demands a time after nightfall. Symbols ought to take precedence over convenience.

A few changes have happened in devotional life. Gradually Benediction of the Blessed Sacrament began to reappear in some parishes in the 1980s. In some churches the Stations of the Cross crept out of hiding in chapels and were reinstalled in the nave again. Other images reappeared in some churches, although rarely in such abundance as before the Council. Obviously, some felt that the cleansed churches were too sterile and wanted more warmth and color. But less conservative parishes tended to resist these moves with buildings that shouted liturgy and only whispered devotions.

At long last, other spiritual traditions within Catholicism were beginning to be recognized. In 1990 the United States Catholic Conference (USCC) published *Plenty Good Room*, with a very positive emphasis on African-American spirituality. It described this as contemplative, holistic, joyful, and communitarian. *Plenty Good Room* concludes that "African-Americans must pray so as to continue exploring and searching the established traditions of the Church and the powerful gifts of the African-American culture." Repeatedly the document makes apparent the community of these gifts with other Christians.

THE MASS
Attendance at Mass remained high and almost all present communed. The most ominous sign was not crowded churches but absent priests. The long-term consequences of the pedophile scandals of 2002 will probably be further decreases in vocations to the priesthood, a calamity that could affect parishes for another forty years. The American bishops issued in 1993 service materials in *Sunday Celebrations in the Absence of a Priest* (SCAP) for the thousands of parishes where there is no resident priest. This is obviously an emergency situation; bread previously consecrated by an absent priest is distributed in the context of a Liturgy of the Word or Morning or Evening Prayer. But the great thanksgiving of the Eucharistic Prayer remains unheard.

All this has increased pressures for more ordinations drawn from the vast pool of married men or women. In a few instances married clergy from other Churches have been (re)ordained; about eighty Episcopalians and one United Methodist now serve as Catholic priests. Half a million Eastern Rite Catholics in the United States are served by priests most of whom are married. So this possibility has no theological impediments; only the disciplinary problems and habits of a thousand years of Western celibacy remain.

The other possibility is the ordination of women. Rome has steadfastly refused this option, claiming that there is no authority for such a drastic action. Scholars, meanwhile, have searched diligently for ancient sources and found, at least, clear indication of ancient rites for the ordination or blessing of women deaconesses.[16] On this basis, some Orthodox Churches have reclaimed this as part of the tradition. The position of Rome, though, remains that the subject is not even to be discussed. Such prohibition, of course, has incited far more discussion and organizing among those who disagree.

A somewhat happier development was the concession in 1994 that women and girls could serve as acolytes. Many parishes had not waited for such permission, but it has been a welcome change, even though they are not formally installed as boys or men may be. Many priests began service at Mass as altar boys, so this may not be an insignificant change.

Receiving Communion remains divided between those who cling to Communion in the mouth (mostly older Catholics) and the majority who prefer Communion in the hand. Efforts to restore Communion from the chalice have not been widely successful; only a minority at most Masses seem comfortable with drinking from the chalice. Whatever we believe, we certainly have faith in germs, though most of us have never seen them! What once was a hot-button theological issue in the Reformation now seems a matter of hygiene rather than theology. Instructions given in 2002 for the possibility of intinction (Body and Blood simultaneously) may resolve some of this.

Kneeling to receive Communion has almost universally been replaced by a standing posture, though not forbidden. Once again, convenience has prevailed, though most Anglicans, Methodists, and Lutherans still kneel for Communion. There was a division between parishes and within parishes about kneeling after the *Sanctus* in the

16. Paul F. Bradshaw, *Ordination Rites of the Ancient Churches of East and West* (New York: Pueblo Publishing Company, 1990), Byzantine, pp. 137–139; East Syrian, 162–163; Georgian, 168–169.

Eucharistic Prayer. Liturgists generally preferred standing throughout as an objective act of respect; the American bishops decreed uniformity (April 25, 2002), with all kneeling as a subjective act of humility.[17]

In addition to the four original Eucharistic Prayers and the subsequent addition of three such prayers for children and two for Masses of reconciliation, another, widely known as "the Swiss" prayer, was approved for universal use. ICEL made efforts at composing others for English-speaking Catholics, but these never received approval.

Some changes did come about in a third edition of the Roman Missal, published in April 2002 but not yet definitively translated. This replaces the editions of 1970 and 1975. The General Instruction involves a number of changes, mostly minor, such as that the priest is not to stray from the sanctuary in giving the sign of peace. New Mass texts have been included for votive Masses of the Blessed Virgin Mary, for various needs, for Masses when most of the congregation are children, and for newly canonized saints. American emendations appeared in May 2002.

An alarm was sounded by a *New York Times*/CBS News poll of April 1994,[18] in which most respondents seemed wide of the mark of official Catholic doctrine on the Eucharist. While older Catholics generally gave traditional answers, the majority of those under fifty indicated that they saw the Eucharist as a service in which the bread and wine were simply memorials of Christ rather than his Body and Blood. In 2001 the American bishops tried to remedy this situation through a publication of the Committee on Doctrine setting forth official Catholic teaching.[19] It is clear how important an ongoing teaching ministry remains.

Theologians have continued to wrestle with the problems of describing and interpreting what the Church experiences in the Eucharist. One of the landmark discussions was the last book of Edward Kilmartin, S.J. (1923–1994), *The Eucharist in the West*, in which he claims that "the modern average Catholic theology of Eucharistic sacrifice is, in general, a weak synthesis without a future."[20] Too much

17. "Confirmation of USCCB Adaptations to the *Institutio Generalis Missalis Romani," Committee on the Liturgy Newsletter* 38 (May 2002) 69–72.

18. *New York Times*, June 1, 1994, A1 and B8.

19. *The Real Presence of Jesus Christ in the Eucharist* (Washington: United States Catholic Conference, 2001).

20. Edited by Robert J. Daly, S.J. (Collegeville, Minn.: The Liturgical Press, 1998) 365.

focus has been placed on the act of consecration and the role of the priest; too little emphasis has been placed on the act of Communion by the entire Church as essential. In Communion the whole Church realizes its union with Christ and with one another. Through this action the Church discovers itself as an eschatological community. The medieval Scholastics left a legacy that neglected the role of the Holy Spirit in sanctifying the bread and wine and the community as "the communicants communicate spiritually with the Lord whom they encounter sacramentally in the consecrated gifts."[21] Kilmartin looked to theologians of the third millennium to continue the quest to a better understanding of what the community receives in the Eucharist.

RHYTHMS OF THE LIFE CYCLE

Without doubt one of the great successes in liturgical reform in the United States has been the Rite of Christian Initiation of Adults (RCIA). Partly because of the shortage of priests, this has necessitated the use of many lay persons in instructing converts. It is difficult to teach the faith to others without one's own faith being challenged and changed. Thus many lay catechists have seen their own faith deepened by passing the faith on to others. Yet report has it that there are dioceses in which the RCIA has had little impact, and it is virtually unknown in much of Europe.

An abundance of resources has been made available by publishers, including the journal *Catechumenate*, published by Liturgy Training Publications. Conferences have been designed to train catechists, and the whole process has been kept visible by making the various stages a part of the public worship of the entire community, from the initial Rite of Acceptance into the Order of Catechumens, through the Rite of Election or Enrollment of Names, until the final Celebration of the Sacraments of Initiation. Thus the entire parish has a role in meeting and praying for the candidates for baptism. It is general practice for the local pastor to confirm RCIA candidates, so that the entire act of initiation occurs on one occasion, usually at Easter.

We have already mentioned the architectural implications of the renewed interest in baptism. Immersion of infants or of adults certainly gives the fullest sign of God's promise of forgiveness both present and future. Many parishes have wrestled with making baptisms a public act of the whole parish. The Easter Vigil provides opportunity for this

21. Ibid., 382.

in a paschal context. But the best location of the font or pool remains debatable. Some would argue that it belongs in full view of all the people (the actual church); others prefer the symbolism of placing it at the entrance (the building). Neither location is without problems. Much depends on the shape of the building and the number of entrances that fire laws dictate.

Rome issued in 1990 a revised *Order for Celebrating Matrimony*. Work on American adaptations of the *Order for Celebrating Marriage* were completed in 1998. But final translation and approval of these changes have not yet occurred (2002). A leading pastoral problem is the high number of mixed marriage between people of other Churches or other religions. *An Ecumenical Liturgy: A Christian Celebration of Marriage* was published in 1987 under the auspices of the ecumenical Consultation on Common Texts. A revised edition appeared in 1995 under the title *A Christian Celebration of Marriage.*[22] It has long been hoped that this material would be approved by Rome and solve a problem involving many, if not most, marriages in the United States.

Funeral rites are also based on the customs of various lands and groups. Years of experience with the rite of 1969 led to an American revision finished in 1985. Years of delay ensued in which considerable tension arose when Rome gave approval to a version in which English rhetoric had replaced American. This text was approved in 1987 and published for American use in 1989 as the *Order of Christian Funerals.*[23] It shows the value of pastoral experience in liturgical revision and increased flexibility. For American Hispanics, the *Ritual de Exequias Cristianas* was approved in 1999 and published in 2002 by The Liturgical Press.

In the case of reconciliation, there are few Saturday afternoon queues as in former times! Probably greater depth is achieved in fewer but more extended meetings face to face in reconciliation rooms. The alternative of communal services of reconciliation seems to have been indefinitely postponed.

Ministry to the sick has always been a major concern of Christians. Whether in private circumstances such as a sick room or in the public gathering of a community, forms of prayer and anointing have been a constant force for hope and healing. The shortage of priests has made it more necessary to rely on lay persons to visit the sick and to bring

22. (Minneapolis: Augsburg Fortress Press, 1995).
23. (Chicago: Liturgy Training Publications, 1989).

Communion. On the other hand, public services of healing seem to be growing in popularity, either in the context of Mass or outside it. Just as there are frequent calls for allowing lay confessors and lay anointers of the sick, these ministries remain restricted to priests. The Eucharist is not alone in being a priestly monopoly, for all these three sacraments require the proper minister, now in short supply. Future reforms may allow lay people to reclaim some of these ministries they once filled.

CHURCH MUSIC

Music has entered a phase of loud dissonance. Depending upon whom one hears or reads, the conditions have improved greatly or are deteriorating weekly.

On the positive side, there seems to be a gradual acceptance of hymn singing as a normal part of parish worship. The semi-serious book of Thomas Day, *Why Catholics Can't Sing*,[24] argues paradoxically that things have never been better and never been worse. The reason seems to be that most Catholics, unlike their Protestant neighbors, do not have a living experience of hymn singing at Mass. Day argues that four and a half centuries of it have made it seem only natural to Protestants. Many attend church partly as their sole opportunity in our society to sing in concert with others. For Catholics, developing such a musical spirituality will take time. So there still are Sunday Masses at which the congregation is mute as far as singing is involved, whether hymnody, psalmody, or service music.

That is not to say that tremendous efforts have not been made to enhance congregational song. *Worship III*[25] is probably the most widely used hymnal, together with its somewhat more lowbrow cousins, *Gather*[26] and *Gather Comprehensive*.[27] Oregon Catholic Press, The Liturgical Press, and J. S. Paluch Company provide missalettes with collections of hymns. *Lead Me Guide Me*[28] reaches out to African Americans. These hymn collections are our most ecumenical documents. Catholics must now sing "Amazing Grace" as often as anyone. Eighteenth-century hymn writers, such as Isaac Watts and Charles Wesley, are

---

24. (New York: Crossroad, 1990).
25. (Chicago: G.I.A. Publications, 1986).
26. Second edition (Chicago: G.I.A. Publications, 1994).
27. (Chicago: G.I.A. Publications, 1994).
28. (Chicago: G.I.A. Publications, 1994).

well represented in these hymnals; the more subjective nineteenth-century hymn writers, such as Fanny Crosby, are noticeably absent. To the classics have been added an increasing number of modern Catholic hymn writers, such as Michael Joncas, Bernadette Farrell, Dan Schutte, Harry Hagan, Genevieve Glen, Suzanne Toolan, and others. Not many of the new hymns seem to be on Marian topics.

Abundant new service music has been written, particularly the works of Richard Proulx and Marty Haugen. Haugen, a Lutheran who works in a United Church of Christ congregation, seems to have caught the imagination of many a Catholic music director with tunes that are simple but fit the liturgical texts admirably. So the effort to prove that Catholics *can* sing is well underway. Still, it is a slow process, and if one sings energetically at Mass, one often gets compliments afterwards, as if such behavior were exceptional.

Instrumental music has found a greater openness to other instruments than the pipe organ. The *New York Times* frequently runs articles about the decline of popular interest in classical music (despite the fact that Lincoln Center is thriving), and classical-music radio stations are being replaced by popular, easy-listening programming. An openness is gradually emerging to new possibilities besides pre-Stravinsky music. Some find this profoundly disturbing, a loss of nerve; others rejoice in contact with our culture, even pop culture.

These conflicting viewpoints came out in dramatic fashion in two unofficial statements in recent decades. Under the leadership of the late Theophane Hytrek and Archbishop Rembert Weakland of Milwaukee, a series of symposia were held, culminating in 1992 in publication of *The Milwaukee Symposia for Church Composers: A Ten-Year Report*. This statement surveyed a decade of experience in a document initially drafted by Father Edward Foley. It stresses cultural inclusiveness and "consciously avoiding the ethnocentrism that judges the music of one particular culture and era as superior and the model for all other Christian ritual music."[29] This indicates openness to other possibilities than simply European antecedents. Music is frankly referred to throughout as "ritual music."

A statement of a more conservative nature came from a 1992 conference at a Utah ski resort, the "Snowbird Statement on Catholic Liturgical Music," published in 1995. This calls for "new attention to the theology and practice of beauty in Catholic worship," in opposition to

29. (Chicago: Liturgy Training Publications, n.d.) par. 86.

music that is "pragmatic, ideological, or, political." In its search for music that would avoid the "utilitarian functionalism" of much recent ritual music, it advocates that we "should consult pre-existing forms to a greater extent than has generally been the case in recent decades."[30] It speaks wistfully of a "Catholic ethos" in church music and mentions Gregorian chant in English or Latin as one possibility.

Thus music as well as architecture has been politicized as an object of controversy. Those who wish to "recatholicize" the liturgy seem to wish to turn back the clock; those who wish to recognize the present may seem impatient to adapt to culture. Somewhere between probably lie most worshiping Catholics, who are content with the familiar but do not mind trying something new occasionally.

PREACHING

Good preaching at Mass is no longer a rare and endangered species. One can expect to hear homilies based on careful Bible study of the readings. Indeed, Catholics have learned to be critical about preaching and often base their decision on where to go to Mass on the quality of the preaching. This introduces a subjective factor into parish attendance, but it means that Masses with a good preacher and good music will attract a loyalty based on high expectations of being fed spiritually.

Many factors have contributed to enhance preaching. The seminaries all require courses in homiletics; Lectionary-based commentaries by top biblical scholars are widely available; and the biblical literacy of the faithful is being stimulated by Bible study classes. The American Academy of Homiletics has had full participation by Catholic preachers. There is much ecumenical sharing in this area. Protestants may be more inclined to think that anything less than a twenty-minute sermon is inadequate; Catholics doubt that many souls are saved after the first ten minutes of a homily!

With all the demands on a priest's time, it is a struggle to find time for Bible study and sermon preparation. The use of lay preachers at Mass is a sensitive area, since ideally the priest is minister of both word and sacrament. However, lay people sometimes give meditations that are often well received. As we have seen in so many areas already, an abundance of priests would resolve many problems; a shortage simply compounds them.

30. *Pastoral Music* 20:3 (February–March 1996) 15.

It is probably no surprise that there have been no major breakthroughs in the last two decades in finding popular forms for public prayer other than the daily Mass. In most parishes the Mass remains the only option for daily public prayer. In a few parishes there may be daily prayer services, especially during Lent. But the busy calendar of parish activities tends to put a higher priority on softball leagues, scouting, and other activities that a consumer society expects. With non-resident priests, even the daily Mass is in jeopardy.

Who knows but that the absence of clergy may lead in the future to an upswelling of lay-led meetings for prayer? Nineteenth-century prayer meetings empowered women to play a leading role in many of the social reforms of that century. Spiritual movements are impossible to predict, but the time may be ripe for public meetings for prayer to become a major part of Roman Catholic worship.

Chapter Eight

The Future of Roman Catholic Worship

The future of Roman Catholic worship will be long, but this chapter will be brief. It will give us a chance to trace some trajectories that now seem still in process, and we shall add a bit of speculation in some other directions. Prophecy is dangerous business; some of us now wince at the prophecies we made about worship over thirty years ago during the age of the now long-forgotten media expert, Marshall McLuhan.

The task is a bit simpler because some excellent studies have already been done, notably Anscar Chupungco's *Liturgies of the Future*,[1] which is particularly concerned about inculturation, and the seven-volume series *Alternative Futures for Worship*,[2] which brings together some of the most distinguished liturgical scholars of our time. At the same time, we are chastened by the prophecies of the 1940s and how far they fell short of the advances of the 1960s. Perhaps this chapter is more our own word with considerable wishful thinking.

Often the way forward in recent years has gone through the past. Historical scholarship has changed much of the present in worship. History is a very subversive discipline. However, history is not always what it used to be. New discoveries continue. What if, as some scholars now suggest, the *Apostolic Tradition*, on which so many recent reforms are based, turns out to be a compilation of sources from several periods, and not even Roman at that? Yet we must always start from the current state of our knowledge of history. The first lesson of history is that history is messy; everything is more complicated than it at first

1. (New York: Paulist Press, 1989).
2. (Collegeville, Minn.: The Liturgical Press, 1987).

seems. Frequently we have to choose between historical possibilities. The more we learn about liturgical history, the less homogeneous it appears to be and the more choices we are offered as we look into the future.

CHURCH ARCHITECTURE

It is always difficult to predict architectural trends, although it seems likely that some present trends will continue, especially the emphasis on baptism and the importance of signifying the making of a Christian through the full sign value of immersion. This will also indicate a location of the baptistery where the whole community can assist in the baptism and welcome into the community. Few churches will go as far as St. Benedict the African in Chicago, where the baptismal pool is twenty-four feet in diameter, as deep as three and a half feet, and contains close to ten thousand gallons of water.[3] But that church does say clearly that baptism is important as the entrance into the Christian community. St. Benedict's is not the only new church where the baptismal pool appears as important as the altar.

Another matter depends upon a variety of future variables but may be central to the future of liturgy. That is the question of scale. How large an assembly can recognize itself as a community without becoming an impersonal mélange? The shortage of priests indicates an ever-increasing scale for Catholic assemblies. But is this the desired future when the scale of a gathering often dictates the dynamics of its life together? At what size does a sense of community evaporate and simply become a public performance? The degree of participation usually slackens the larger the gathering becomes. We come to church to meet our God, but what happens first is that we meet our neighbor. But can we identify with thousands as easily as we do with hundreds? The larger the scale, the more inclined worship is to become a performance, passively observed. This may indicate the building of more but smaller churches as a goal to be sought if a sufficient number of priests were available.

UNFINISHED BUSINESS

Several items remain of immediate concern in the present and for long-range exploration in the future.

3. Regina Kuehn, *A Place for Baptism* (Chicago: Liturgy Training Publications, 1992) 46.

Surely the greatest of these is the question of the liturgical act itself. Romano Guardini raised this question forcefully decades ago: "The central problem . . . [is] the problem of the cult act, or, to be more precise, the liturgical act."[4] Guardini wondered if modern humans could overcome the individualism that isolates them from one another to become part of a corporate whole that celebrates the liturgy and achieve a "solidarity of existence." He did not sound terribly optimistic about that possibility, and it still seems problematic today. He even suggested that humans in our age are "no longer capable of a liturgical act." Yet his life, and that of many others, was spent in pursuit of that possibility. The ceremonies following September 11, 2001, show some indication that corporate grief can still take visible form. In many newly evangelized parts of the world, communal life has not yet been diluted by individualism and sign-acts still function to unite people in corporate expression.

A second major concern is the nature of ordained ministry. We have said nothing directly about ordination, although the implications have often been apparent. We can hope that in the future a truce will be declared in the Vatican's current war on women. At stake is the nature of ordained ministry as representative of the whole Body of Christ or just a part of it. Some have even doubted the validity of modern Roman Catholic ordinations on the basis of the defect of single-genderedness. The implications for justice within the Church are enormous and vitiate its ability to address the world on issues of justice.

The resolution of this question will determine much of the future of Roman Catholic worship. Once again the scale of assemblies comes into focus. As the number of ordained men who are celibate becomes ever fewer, the alternatives under the present system all seem equally depressing: fewer Eucharists, ever larger assemblies, or a move to non-sacramental worship. Some say that a clergy person can only know and effectively relate to seven hundred people at the most, maybe considerably fewer. It becomes even worse when the pastor is a commuter. The scale of celebrations becomes increasingly depersonalized with growth in size. Much of the quality of celebrations is at stake.

A third concern is the nature of truly inclusive worship in terms of roles, actions, and words. This applies not just in terms of women but of all those marginalized in worship. How much does worship recognize

4. "A Letter from Romano Guardini," *Herder Correspondence* 1 (1964) 24.

the full human worth of all present? Does it profess inclusivity but bar those who think as children? Are children even mentioned in the Mass? Is hospitality denied by buildings that have stairs that a wheelchair cannot negotiate? Our worship often makes self-contradictory statements that embarrass us once they are recognized: we profess inclusivity and often exclude many. The pursuit of justice within the liturgy is a never-ending process of observation, analysis, reflection, and reform.

Closely related is a fourth item: recognizing the value of different cultures. These are not merely between nations but within a single country, a single city. Ethnic parishes were once a mute witness to this; our differences now are a bit more subtle but just as real. North American culture, especially, is a salad bowl of different ingredients. This is not to deny equally pressing differences between various parts of the globe. Any resolution would seem to demand a relaxing of the efforts at complete liturgical centralization on the part of the Congregation for Divine Worship.

RHYTHMS OF TIME AND DEVOTIONS

Despite all the good resolutions of past reforms, fresh crops of saints harvested in each century confounded the priorities of the liturgical year. It is hoped that the reform of our times will prevent such future congestion, but that remains to be seen. At least, a firm grasp on the centrality of the dominical cycle seems to have been achieved, and a careful sorting out of priorities is vital.

Various writers have lamented the absence of devotions for most contemporary Roman Catholics, although nostalgia may distort some of the realities of the past. There does seem to be emerging a biblical piety as God's Word becomes more important in the lives of the devout. Biblical study groups have made their advent in recent decades. Perhaps these can form the basis for Bible services as the Constitution on the Sacred Liturgy hinted. Devotions, after all, have changed over the centuries, and if the love of Scripture is where spirituality seems directed at the present, more public ways of celebrating the love for God's Word may develop. Here the base communities of Latin America have already pointed the way to biblical study and action.

THE MASS

Here, as everywhere else, the most pressing problem seems to be that of inculturation. For many centuries Latin was defended as a necessary sign of the unity of the Church. Now the same argument is being used to ward off adaptations of the Roman rite whatever the language. There seems to be a problem of confusing unity with uniformity. Yet diversity is not inimical to unity but may actually be a way to express it. In some cultures it may be natural to carry the sacred vessels on the top of the head or to squat before a table barely one foot high. The unity in obedience to the Lord's command "Do this" still remains firm. The Zaire Missal was an important development, but it still remains unique.[5]

Perhaps in the future some less conservative administration in Rome will see possibilities in a communion of churches in which various local uses are held together by a unity of purpose rather than uniformity in identical wording. Essentially this is what prevailed for centuries before Trent. England alone had several different liturgical texts in the Middle Ages. Uniformity is still a relative innovation in liturgical history; the technology that made it possible has been with us for only five and a half centuries, and the legislation that made it mandatory for just over four centuries.

Much will change, we hope, when more priests become available. The situation in Brazil, where there is now only one priest for every five thousand lay Catholics, is intolerable. It is one reason why that nation, with the world's largest Roman Catholic population, is projected to have a majority of Protestants by 2010 if present trends continue. Even if it were possible for everyone to attend Mass, the quality of celebration would suffer greatly because it would be so large and impersonal. Again, the question of scale is crucial.

Minor details might shift. There are advantages in placing the penitential rite as a response to the Liturgy of the Word, as was done in Zaire. Only then can one really reflect on what the readings and the homily have to say about our failures before God. Also, one could argue that the sign of peace belongs in the same location as an enacted rite of reconciliation and preparation for the eucharistic rite. That is also its oldest location. Hymnody could be better integrated into the Order of Mass as well. Some changes in the Sunday Lectionary are desirable, too, especially to do justice to the Old Testament as narrative and to recognize the presence of women in salvation history.

5. See the video recording *The Dancing Church*, prod. Thomas Kane (New York: Paulist Press, 1991).

A further issue is the desirability of daily Mass. Does this, as some authors suggest, tend to trivialize the Eucharist? Would the presence of a viable daily service make the Eucharist more significant as the weekly gathering of the entire community? Then the Mass could appear as a distinctive festal celebration for the Lord's Day. The present Order of Mass makes each day festive without much discrimination. Perhaps a different order should be produced for daily use, with significant differences for the Lord's Day and other feasts. But a functioning daily alternative to the Mass itself seems highly desirable.

RHYTHMS OF THE LIFE CYCLE

Great changes have come about in all the sacraments of the Ritual, but some fine-tuning is still a possibility, and in some cases a major overhauling is needed. Is it too much to hope that the unity of initiation may be restored for infants as it has been recovered for adults? The Eastern Churches have always kept it intact, as did the West until the twelfth century. Then it fell apart for reasons extraneous to initiation. It is absurd to baptize infants and then immediately "excommunicate" them. Infants were given Communion (through wine) at their baptism until the twelfth century, when the laity ceased to receive the wine. If the rites were reunited, the Eucharist as the only part of baptism that is repeated would be in its proper context—something God prepares us for, not something we prepare for.

In such a context it would be possible again to reserve baptisms for the paschal season. No one seems to worry anymore about adults dying in the course of a long catechumenate; infants need not be rushed any longer to the font. In the context of the Resurrection, baptisms call the whole community to the source of their faith.

Perhaps in the process confirmation will stop being a theological football. The best evidence seems to be that it was probably originally a dismissal from part of the baptismal process.[6] On the other hand, the more we know of human development and how strictly life is governed by stages of growth, the more one can argue for making much more of the annual renewal of baptismal vows at the Easter Vigil (or the Baptism of the Lord, Pentecost, or All Saints' Day).

Much progress has been made in the marriage rites. More needs to be done on a cultural level so that weddings testify to the equality of

6. Aidan Kavanagh, *Confirmation: Origin and Reform* (New York: Pueblo Publishing Company, 1988).

the spouses rather than make the bride a star for a day and a shadow for a lifetime. Approval of the ecumenical rite will make many things more gracious on a pastoral level. "Wedding ministers" may develop with responsibility for teaching the meaning of the rite as well as presiding at it. The serious problem of remarriage of divorced persons will have to be dealt with on a more satisfactory basis. It seems to be natural law that when couples survive to a considerable age, for about half of them love for each other does not. The Orthodox have dealt with remarriage in a somewhat satisfactory way, although on different theological premises by making the priest, not the couple, the minister of the sacrament.

The new Order of Christian Funerals (1989) is pastorally apt but will need to evolve as burial customs change in each culture. It seems inevitable that lay presiders will be necessary. Many are now serving as "ministers of consolation" and have the most immediate contact with the bereaved.

Despite changes in the rite and canon law, individual confession seems to be in serious decline. Perhaps a reinvestigation of the current third rite with general absolution would be useful. Some have suggested an order of confessors that would include lay people with training in theology and counseling. Many of the confessors in the early Irish Church were lay men and women. General services of reconciliation could become a more prominent part of the penitential seasons of the Christian year. But they could also be important reminders of communal sin, as when a nation goes to war or neglects its homeless.

A strong case can be made for anointing of the sick by specially designated lay persons. Some, especially those with medical and nursing skills, might bring more pastoral knowledge than those ordained. Again, the argument can be made that anointing of the sick with oil blessed by the bishop was practiced by the laity in many areas of the world in the early Church.

CHURCH MUSIC

In music and the other arts, it is important to be open to new possibilities. Whether the music of Philip Glass or John Corigliano will appear in church services may be unlikely but may also be desirable. Whoever comes after them the Church should be able to claim whenever possible. The tradition of the best musicians being paid by and working for the Church may have died with Bach, but it has had various resuscitations from time to time and needs a real resurrection. If it is not good music, it will not last; but if it is, we should not miss out on it.

Metrical hymnody and folk song seem to be the most successful forms of congregational song for our time. It is to be hoped that hymnody will become a more integral part of the Mass. Such words and music can reflect the special character of any season or occasion. They can help the congregation "own" the service and also function to mark transitions in the order. In time, Catholics will sing, and worship without congregational song will seem an anomaly.

It is exciting to live in an age when electronics make it possible to hear sounds that have never before entered the human ear. There is no reason why new sounds cannot be used for the glorification of God. Each instrument developed in history was a new technology once, and most of them were eventually put to praising God. The possibilities before us are more varied than at any time in the history of technology. But it will take trained imaginations to enlist them for worship.

PREACHING

Major shifts are underway in preaching, especially a shift from sender-oriented to receiver-oriented communication. Still, a real democratization of preaching is only vaguely glimpsed. Too often it seems to be a message handed down from on high, the "pulpit six feet above contradiction." Whether group preparation of homilies is the answer remains to be seen; at present it shows signs of promise. Black congregations can teach us all much about faith confirmation through the whole community responding vocally to what it likes (and occasionally dislikes) in preaching. But how faith-sharing can be enhanced still remains a major concern. Obviously, the preacher is not the only person present with faith to share, as Quakers so clearly demonstrate.

The question must also be raised whether a ten-minute homily can seriously handle a difficult biblical text or explore complicated human problems. The great sermons of the past moved at a more leisurely pace. Brevity has its advantages, to be sure, but it can also encourage superficiality. Trying to explicate, for example, the Transfiguration or the Ascension, in a few words may be more confusing than helpful. Wrestling with God's Word can take time and should not be rushed.

PUBLIC PRAYER

For many reasons there seems to be a need for alternatives to daily Mass, not the least of them being the shortage of priests. Liturgists have expressed much interest in the ancient cathedral Office as the alternative to the monastic hegemony of daily public prayer. The cathedral Office, which simply means the form of morning and evening prayer practiced in large downtown churches in early centuries, was directed to the spirituality of ordinary people. Like most popular religiosity, it was highly repetitive; favorite psalms, hymns, and prayers recurred frequently. It also reflected the time of day; people are different before the day's work and after it. And there were action and gestures, such as the lighting of lamps in the evening and incense.[7]

Above all, the cathedral Office could be led by lay people and attended by lay people. It did not involve the athletic discipline of edification and contemplation found so congenial to monastics. Basically the cathedral Office was "Lord, get me through this day" and "Thank you, Lord, for helping me today!" The contents were praise (psalms and hymns) and prayer (largely intercession and petition). It provided a means of praying together that the Church in the West has lost for a millennium. But many things lost for a thousand years have been found again and put to good use in our time. Daily public prayer may become another one.

In any case, Roman Catholic worship will continue to evolve. Even though the texts were largely frozen from Trent until Vatican II, we have tried to show in this book that all else continued to develop. Let us hope that the texts will not be frozen this time. But in any case, all else will certainly continue to evolve as the Spirit teaches believers new ways to praise God. After all, it is the same restless Spirit that has continued through two millennia to give Christians new ways to express that which is "too deep for words." The same Spirit will not leave us speechless but will go on interceding for us (Rom 8:26) throughout all time.

7. Paul Bradshaw, *Two Ways of Praying* (Nashville: Abingdon Press, 1995).

Glossary

apostolic constitution: a papal document intended to resolve an important issue or controversy.

base communities: a modern term for small groups of lay Christians who meet for worship, study, and action, often in Latin America.

Benediction: a devotional service during which the consecrated Host is displayed and used to bless those present. Hymns, Scripture, and silence accompany the action.

Breviary: the term formally used for the books containing the text of the Liturgy of the Hours or daily Office and used by clergy and members of religious orders.

bull: an important document published by papal offices, known from the seal that formerly confirmed its authenticity.

Caeremoniale Episcoporum: the Ceremonial of Bishops, a book containing detailed instructions as to how bishops should perform the ceremonies for which they are responsible or entitled to receive.

Canon: the Eucharistic Prayer, or great thanksgiving, of the Mass, a term used less now except to refer to the Roman Canon (Eucharistic Prayer I).

Compline: the last prayer service of the daily Office before the night's rest.

concelebration: the practice of two or more priests saying the Canon or parts of it together instead of in separate Masses, now common but forbidden in the West before Vatican II.

Congregations, Sacred: the departments of the Catholic Church in Rome, originally established as fourteen in number in 1588.

Corpus Christi: a feast on the Thursday after Trinity Sunday commemorating the institution of the Lord's Supper.

Curia: the Congregations, tribunals, offices, and commissions that assist the pope in the government and administration of the Church.

Daily Office: the services said in the course of each day, sometimes known as the Liturgy of the Hours, Choir Office, Divine Office, or *Opus Dei.*

dicastery: an office of the Roman Curia.

editio typica: the official Latin version of service books as approved by the Vatican, now used as the basis for translations.

elevation: the lifting of the bread and chalice during the Eucharistic Prayer, formerly necessary for the congregation to see them.

encyclical: a pastoral letter, now usually applied to those written by the pope for guidance of bishops, priests, and laity. Individual bishops and conferences of bishops also write them.

epiclesis: a prayer invoking the Holy Spirit in the Canon of the Mass with the intent of consecrating the gifts and asking for benefits for the communicants.

Exposition: a devotion focused on adoration of the consecrated Host, often placed in a monstrance.

Gradual: a proper part of the Mass sung between the epistle and gospel, varying according to the date; also the book of chants for Mass.

historicization: the tendency to make liturgy a commemoration of the past events of salvation history as narrated in Scripture instead of a focus on the imminent return of Christ.

Holy Office: the Roman Congregation that handles matters of faith and morals, now known as the Congregation for the Doctrine of the Faith.

Jansenism: a religious movement of the seventeenth and eighteenth centuries centering on strict observance of morality.

maniple: a vestigial towel worn by clergy before 1967 on the left arm but now obsolete.

Martyrology: a liturgical book containing the dates of commemoration of saints and martyrs with brief accounts of their lives and deaths.

metrical paraphrase: a translation and adaptation of a psalm in recurring meter so as to be sung to a metrical scheme.

Milanese (Ambrosian) Rite: a non-Roman Western rite used in the province of Milan for the Mass and other services.

Missal: the book of prayers and other materials necessary for the priest to say Mass.

monstrance: an instrument to display the consecrated Host for adoration and used in Exposition and Benediction of the Blessed Sacrament.

Modernism: a variety of theological positions originating late in the nineteenth century that sought to apply modern historical-critical methods to biblical study and theology, condemned by Pius X in 1907 but mostly unexceptional today.

motu proprio: "by his own accord"; a papal document written in an informal manner at the pope's own initiative.

novena: a devotion celebrated over the course of nine days, often preceding a feast.

paschal mystery: the mystery of Christ's death and resurrection used in the context of the worshiping community's celebration of these events.

penitential psalms: Psalms 6, 32, 38, 51, 102, 130, and 143, sometimes said on a daily basis.

Pontifical: the book of services performed normally only by a bishop, such as confirmation, ordination, and various blessings.

Preface: the opening portion of the Eucharistic Prayer from the dialog to the *Sanctus,* varying according to occasion.

Proper: those items in the Mass that change according to the occasion: antiphons, prayers, and readings.

pyx: a container in which to reserve the consecrated bread, formerly often in the shape of a dove.

Ritual: the book used by a priest (hence *sacerdotale, manuale,* or *pastorale*) for baptism, marriage, anointing of the sick, burial, and various blessings.

roodscreen: a wooden partition between the chancel and nave, named for the rood (cross) that surmounted it in medieval churches.

rubrics: the instructions on how to carry out a service, often printed in red ink.

sanctoral cycle: having to do with the commemoration of the saints, often on the anniversary of their death.

sanctuary: the space about the main altar.

scapular: a vestigal apron worn as part of the monastic habit.

Scholasticism: the intellectual tradition of the twelfth and thirteenth centuries for organizing knowledge, especially in philosophy and theology.

Sequence: hymns sung between the epistle and gospel according to the occasion but limited to four texts after 1570.

tabernacle: an enclosure for the reserved Sacrament with a lock, situated on the main altar until Vatican II.

temporal cycle: those portions of the Church year centered on events in the life of Christ, such as days determined by the Christmas and Easter seasons.

Thomism: the philosophical and theological schools based on the work of St. Thomas Aquinas (c. 1225–1274).

Ultramontanism: the view favoring centralized authority in opposition to national, regional, or diocesan control.

Vespers: the daily prayer at the end of the working day or at sunset, often known as Evening Prayer.

Select Bibliography

Abbott, Walter M., ed., *The Documents of Vatican II*. New York: Guild Press, 1966.

Austin, Gerard. *Anointing with the Spirit*. New York: Pueblo Publishing Company, 1985.

Botte, Bernard. *From Silence to Participation*. Washington: The Pastoral Press, 1988.

Brilioth, Yngve. *A Brief History of Preaching*. Philadelphia: Fortress Press, 1965.

Bugnini, Annibale. *The Reform of the Liturgy, 1948–1975*. Collegeville, Minn.: The Liturgical Press, 1990.

Cabié, Robert. *The Eucharist*. Vol. 2 of *The Church at Prayer*. Collegeville, Minn.: The Liturgical Press, 1986.

_____ and others. *The Sacraments*. Vol. 3 of *The Church at Prayer*. Collegeville, Minn.: The Liturgical Press, 1988.

Cattaneo, Enrico. *Il culto cristiano in Occidente*. 2nd ed. Rome: C.L.V.-Edizioni liturgiche, 1984.

Crichton, J. D., ed. *English Catholic Worship*. London: Geoffrey Chapman, 1979.

_____. *Lights in the Darkness*. Collegeville, Minn.: The Liturgical Press, 1996.

Dallen, James. *The Reconciling Community*. New York: Pueblo Publishing Company, 1986.

Dalmais, Irénée Henri, and others. *Principles of the Liturgy*. Vol. 1 of *The Church at Prayer*. Collegeville, Minn.: The Liturgical Press, 1987.

Documents on the Liturgy 1963–1979: Conciliar, Papal, and Curial Texts. Translation and compilation by the International Commission on English in the Liturgy. Collegeville, Minn.: The Liturgical Press, 1982.

Empereur, James. *Prophetic Anointing*. Wilmington, Del.: Michael Glazier, 1982.

Fellerer, Karl G. *The History of Catholic Church Music*. Baltimore: Helicon Press, 1961.

Finn, Peter C. and James M. Schellman, eds. *Shaping English Liturgy*. Washington: The Pastoral Press, 1990.

Flannery, Austin, ed. *Vatican Council II: The Conciliar and Post Conciliar Documents*. Rev. ed. Collegeville, Minn.: The Liturgical Press, 1992.

Gusmer, Charles W. *And You Visited Me: Sacramental Ministry to the Sick and Dying*. New York: Pueblo Publishing Company, 1984.

Hayburn, Robert F. *Papal Legislation on Sacred Music*. Collegeville, Minn.: The Liturgical Press, 1979.

Hughes, Kathleen, ed. *Voices of the Early Liturgical Movement*. Chicago: Liturgy Training Publications, 1990.

Jungmann, Joseph A. *The Mass of the Roman Rite*. 2 vols. New York: Benziger Brothers, 1950.

Kavanagh, Aidan. *The Shape of Baptism*. New York: Pueblo Publishing Company, 1978.

Klauser, Theodor. *A Short History of the Western Liturgy*. 2nd ed. New York: Oxford University Press, 1979.

Koenker, Ernest B. *The Liturgical Renaissance in the Roman Catholic Church*. Chicago: University of Chicago Press, 1954.

Lang, Bernhard. *Sacred Games: A History of Christian Worship*. New Haven: Yale University Press, 1997.

Leaver, Robin A., and Joyce Ann Zimmerman, eds. *Liturgy and Music: Lifetime Learning*. Collegeville, Minn.: The Liturgical Press, 1998.

The Liturgy Documents: A Pastoral Resource. 2 vols. Chicago: Liturgy Training Publications, 1991, 1999.

Martimort, Aime Georges, ed. *The Liturgy and Time*. Vol. 4 of *The Church at Prayer*. Collegeville, Minn.: The Liturgical Press, 1986.

Megivern, James J., ed. *Worship and Liturgy*. Wilmington, N.C.: McGrath Publishing Company, 1978.

Peckler, Keith. *The Unread Vision: The Liturgical Movement in the United States of America: 1926–1955*. Collegeville, Minn.: The Liturgical Press, 1998.

Rutherford, Richard, and Tony Barr. *The Death of a Christian: The Order of Christian Funerals.* Collegeville, Minn.: The Liturgical Press, 1990.

Searle, Mark, and Kenneth W. Stevenson. *Documents of the Marriage Liturgy.* Collegeville, Minn.: The Liturgical Press, 1992.

Seasoltz, Kevin. *The New Liturgy: Documentation, 1903–1965.* New York: Herder and Herder, 1966.

Stevenson, Kenneth W. *To Join Together: The Rite of Marriage.* New York: Pueblo Publishing Company, 1987.

Taft, Robert. *The Liturgy of the Hours in East and West.* Collegeville, Minn.: The Liturgical Press, 1986.

Tuzik, Robert L., ed. *Leaders of the Liturgical Movement.* Chicago: Liturgy Training Publications, 1990.

Vogel, Cyrille. *Medieval Liturgy: An Introduction to the Sources.* Washington: The Pastoral Press, 1986.

Westermeyer, Paul. *Te Deum: The Church and Music.* Minneapolis: Fortress Press, 1998.

White, James F. *Protestant Worship: Traditions in Transition.* Louisville: Westminster/John Knox Press, 1989.

Wilson-Dickson, Andrew. *The Story of Christian Music.* Oxford: Lion Publishing, 1992.

Zimmermann, Joyce Ann. *Pray Without Ceasing: Prayer for Morning and Evening.* Collegeville, Minn.: The Liturgical Press, 1993.

Index of Persons

Index of Subjects

CPSIA information can be obtained at www.ICGtesting.com
Printed in the USA
BVOW03s0953260514

354425BV00001B/13/P